M.K. NAMBYAR

A CONSTITUTIONAL VISIONARY

M.K. NAMBYAR

A CONSTITUTIONAL VISIONARY

K.K. VENUGOPAL

with

SUHRITH PARTHASARATHY & SUHASINI SEN

EBURY
PRESS

An imprint of Penguin Random House

EBURY PRESS

Ebury Press is an imprint of the Penguin Random House group of companies
whose addresses can be found at global.penguinrandomhouse.com

Published by Penguin Random House India Pvt. Ltd
4th Floor, Capital Tower 1, MG Road,
Gurugram 122 002, Haryana, India

First published in Ebury Press by Penguin Random House India 2024

Copyright © K.K. Venugopal 2024

ISBN 9780670099801

Typeset in EB Garamond by MAP Systems, Bengaluru, India
Printed at Thomson Press India Ltd, New Delhi

www.penguin.co.in

Contents

Preface   vii

Introduction   xi

1. Transcending the *Tharuvaad*:
   M.K. Nambyar's Formative Years   1

2. Touch of Fate: From the Mofussil to the
   Madras High Court   17

3. Taking the High Road: From Kanara to Kilpauk   37

4. The First Constitutional Case: *A.K. Gopalan*   51

5. The Aftermath of *A.K. Gopalan* and
   Life in the Madras High Court   66

6. Piercing the Dark Shadows of Preventive Detention:
   S. Krishnan v. The State of Madras   77

7. The Right to Property and Parliamentary Powers
   to Abridge the Fundamental Rights:
   The First, Fourth and Seventeenth
   Constitutional Amendments   88

8. *I.C. Golak Nath v. The State of Punjab:* Laying
   the Foundations of the Basic Structure   113

9. The March of the Law: Nambyar, the Constitutional
   'Colossus'   126

Epilogue   147

Acknowledgements   153

Appendix   155

Notes   211

Preface

I had an inheritance from my father,
It was the moon and the sun.
And though I roam all over the world,
The spending of it's never done.

—Ernest Hemingway,
For Whom the Bell Tolls

I had always been keen to bring out a biography of my father, Sh. M.K. Nambyar. Over the span of nearly twenty years, I had contacted three separate writers to draft his biography based on the material I had in my possession as well as on the basis of any independent material that could be unearthed. The difficulty was that my father was born in 1898. My eldest sibling was born in 1925, and I in 1931, therefore, both the memories and the material dated back many, many decades, and recounting or unearthing them proved challenging. Not only that, in those days, i.e. several generations back, the father rarely showed intimacy to the children, though there was no question that there was mutual love and affection. When I look at the children of today, I am amazed at the change in attitude towards one's parents. My sons will not hesitate to put their arms around my shoulders and my grandchildren often hug their parents without hesitation. But back then, it was a different world. In fact, I was forty-four years old when my father first sat down to have a drink with me and my elder brother, which was a rare instance of informality in our relationship. I am saying all this to show that my father would not dream of chatting with me about his problems or speaking to me or the other children about the various events in his life. Therefore, for these and other reasons, I was told that there was a dearth of sufficient material for a full-length book, and so none of my efforts to bring out my father's biography could bear fruit.

I made one more attempt when I began to write my own memoirs. I decided that I would make my best effort to lay out his life as best as I could remember in the pages of my own autobiography. But I knew that my father was so fundamental to the trajectory of my own life that I could not have written about myself without first publishing his biography.

My earliest memories of my father as a lawyer were probably when the family lived in Mangalore (present-day Mangaluru), where he was a government pleader and public prosecutor. He had an office in one wing of our house, and I remember that there used to be a steady stream of police officers and other government officials who would come to brief him in regard to the criminal cases he was prosecuting. At that time, though being a public prosecutor and government pleader was quite prestigious, he would prepare his cases himself without the assistance of juniors. All that changed rather dramatically once we shifted to Madras (present-day Chennai) and particularly after the A.K. Gopalan case. His daily list would be very long, and he had a number of juniors who would be running behind him from courtroon to courtroom in the Madras High Court so that no matter was missed. My father, if I had to sum him up in one sentence, was a very proper person. He had an unwavering moral compass, and whether it be in law or in life, he was a gentleman.

One of my last and most poignant memories of him, which has left a lifelong impression upon me, was when I had just built my own chambers, on Harrington Road in Madras, on a plot he had given me, next to his house. He had come to the house-warming puja despite his serious illness. Though the office was on the adjacent plot, he was then unable to walk the few dozen yards to it. He had to come in his car and without getting out, he handed me a letter in his own handwriting. This was on 4 December 1975. He passed away on 18 December 1975. Out of all the things he could have written to me, in the sunset of his life, this was his most fervent wish and speaks volumes about the kind of person he was. I have tried my best to live up to his expectations.

The letter is reproduced below.

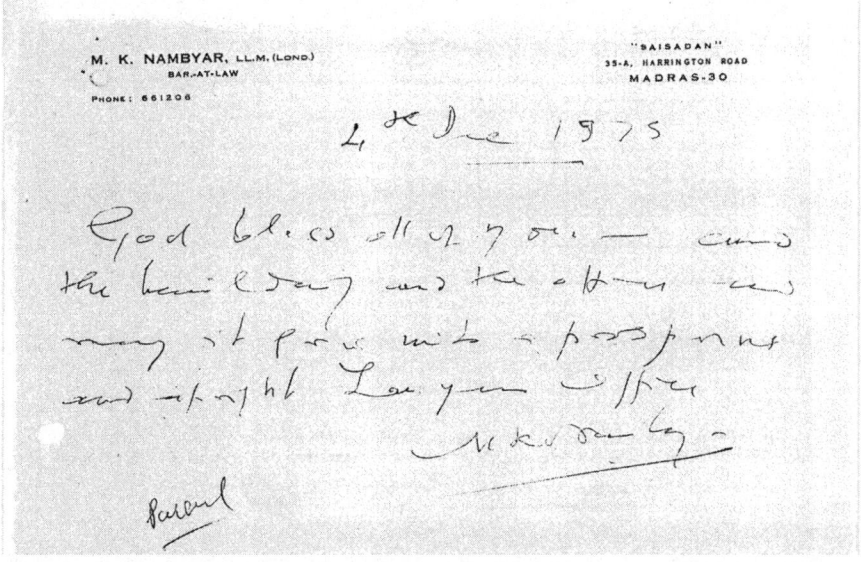

'*4th Dec 1975*

God bless all of you—and the building and the office—and may it grow into a prosperous and upright lawyer's office.'

I firmly believe, speaking not just as a son, that the story of M.K. Nambyar's life is one that must be told. Under the new Constitution, my father was perhaps modern India's earliest pre-eminent jurist, and the telling of his life story would both befit his stature as well as benefit members of the legal profession. Though my father was born nearly 125 years ago, it is a remarkable feat that the cases he argued and the interpretations of the Constitution that he propounded are still quoted in the Supreme Court of India. It is a matter of great happiness to me that with some renewed efforts and research, the biography of my father, M.K. Nambyar, is now finally published. I hope those who read it will enjoy his life story.

K.K. Venugopal

Introduction

'I sit in the frail bark of my body and steer with all my might,' wrote M.K. Nambyar in one of his latter-day reminiscences about his life as a lawyer. 'But I find I am neither the master of my vessel nor the captain of its decisive direction. For the momentum of its movements has often been gathered from the impact of the unknown.'

Nambyar was paraphrasing William Henley's classic poem 'Invictus', and, in modifying the words to suit his own voyage through life, he revealed the characteristic humility that was his trademark. Though his success was achieved through a combination of intellect and the sheer dint of hard work, it was indeed in some ways, an element of the unknown that shaped many of the events of M.K. Nambyar's life and later gave him his first big break as a constitutional lawyer.

The year was 1950, and the case was that of *A.K. Gopalan v. The State of Madras*, the first constitutional case in India. It was a time of both tumult and excitement. The Indian State was barely three years old, and the country had just adopted its Constitution, laying the foundations for its republic. The Supreme Court, itself a creature of the Constitution, had begun to function only on 28 January of that year.

The *Gopalan* case involved a constitutional challenge in the Supreme Court of India to preventive detention laws. Having till then practised mostly in *mofussil* courts[1] at Mangalore, and later the High Court of Madras, M.K. Nambyar was virtually unknown in Delhi and certainly not known as a constitutional lawyer. Yet, as destiny would have it, it was he who led the arguments, which day after day were widely reported in every single newspaper in the country as this was a novelty for the nascent population of the new republic of India. Nambyar's mastery of the principles embedded within the text of the Constitution was so complete that he argued the *Gopalan* case with only the Constitution of India in one hand and without even the benefit of any previous judgments of the Indian courts available for citation, as this was the first constitutional case in post-Independence India.

Though Nambyar partially lost the case, the legal erudition that he displayed before the new Supreme Court was enough to guarantee him a brief in virtually every major constitutional case that was to arise in the Supreme Court for the next two decades or so till his death in 1975.

Constitutional cases are significant markers of key political developments in a nation's history, and therefore Nambyar's life is significant not only as a guide to members of the legal profession, but also because its trajectory traces some of the major legal developments in post-Independence India. For example, Nambyar's interpretations of the Constitution had a significant bearing on several issues of seminal importance—the contours of the Right to Life and Personal Liberty, the Right to Property and the State's ability to redistribute wealth, the Right to Religion and the management of religious institutions, and of course, the doctrine that underpins the very basis of democratic India—the basic structure.

It should come as a surprise to the reader, therefore, that a man who would go on to become one of India's towering giants of constitutional law came from a family that had very little concern with the legal profession except as an instrumentality to protect its interests. How did the ideas of constitutionalism—equality, freedom of expression and a principled application of the rule of law—take root in the heart of a man whose initial years were marked by the benefits of great social inequality? Not only that, how did a man whose life began with a rather humble practice in the mofussil courts in Mangalore go on eventually to handle many of the most important cases that came before the Supreme Court of India and the high courts, through the decades till he passed away on 18 December 1975.

This book is an attempt to answer some of these questions and preserve in perpetuity the life and impact of one of the great constitutional lawyers of modern India.

1

Transcending the *Tharuvaad:* M.K. Nambyar's Formative Years

Man knows himself only inasmuch as he knows the world;
he knows the world only within himself and he is aware of
himself only within the world. Each new object truly
recognized, opens up a new organ within ourselves.

—Goethe

There exists a particular school of philosophical thought which holds the view that man is but the product of his environment. The opposing view is best expressed by Mahatma Gandhi who once said that man is but the product of his thoughts—what he thinks, he becomes, and thus, the power to control and shape one's destiny is purely intellectual and is in the hands of each human being. The truth, as most people would probably attest to, appears to be somewhere in between these two views. That an individual is greatly impacted by the circumstances into which he or she is born is certain, that what he or she makes of those circumstances is a matter of personal ability, equally so. M.K. Nambyar's story, the circumstances in which he found himself and what he ultimately chose to do with them, begins in what we now recognize as the South Indian state of Kerala.

Kerala, in its modern form, was created on 1 November 1956 by the integration of certain portions of Travancore–Cochin with Kasaragod and Malabar. The state with its unique geography— mountains on one side and the sea on the other—created a peculiar social milieu, an agrarian society reliant upon a lush natural environment, yet not an insular one, being heavily influenced by the presence of the sea and the trade and commerce that it naturally brought. The poet Mahakavi Vallathol penned an ode to Mother Kerala intended to explain its unique geography and said:

> While you sleep
> With your head on the lap
> Of the 'Sahyadri' clad in green
> And your feet pillowed
> On the crystal ocean sand,
> Kumari at one end
> God of Gokarna at the other
> Watch over you, Mother![1]

The Malabar region, with which this book is concerned, was initially administered by the commissioners and supervisors of the Bombay Presidency, but in 1800, the district was transferred to the Madras Presidency. The history of this particular region is deeply fascinating, for the area represented a confluence of castes, religions and cultures—of Hindus, Mappilas (Muslims) and some Christians as well. And of course, ever present within the Hindu community, in all its rigidity and inhumanity, was the caste system. The caste system dominated social life in Kerala and was the primary dictator of social behaviour till at least the middle of the twentieth century. One writer has even remarked that 'Kerala is one of the most caste-ridden parts of India'.[2] The caste system had been prevalent for centuries, and many a foreign traveller passing through Kerala documented its irrational and inhumane practices. The caste hierarchy was as follows: the Nambudris (i.e., the Brahmins) on top, the Nairs or Nambyars immediately below (who also enjoyed a significant level of wealth, power and societal influence) and below them a number of lower castes, particularly the Tiyyas and Izzuvas (toddy tappers) who were numerically the most significant, though socially weak.[3]

At the time the Dalits or oppressed classes, who were considered and called 'untouchables' were not even included in the four varnas (or the four castes) that prevailed in India—namely the Brahmins or the priestly class, Kshatriyas or warriors, Vaishyas or trading class and the Shudras who were supposed to belong to the working class. The Dalits—or Harijans as they were called by Gandhiji—were outcastes and were subjected to the most outrageous treatment. They were reduced to scavenging of night soil or cleaning the hides of cows or being consigned to the worst kinds of employment. The caste system was enforced with such rigidity that if a member of the oppressed classes touched an upper caste person by mistake, the latter became polluted and then had to bathe and perform pujas or ceremonies to cleanse themselves. Dalits could not be found walking in the fields or in the same lane as the upper castes, and had to move away from the road after removing their upper garment with their head bowed and their hands folded. The atrocities inflicted by the upper castes on the oppressed castes were indescribable. They could not even be found on the road leading to the entry of the temple. This tragic state of affairs was to continue for several years.

The Nairs or Nambyars (for they were essentially the same caste) were landed and extremely wealthy, and their own history and how they came to acquire this wealth is a fascinating one.

In 1553, Portuguese soldier and poet Luis de Camoens Voltaire penned the following words to describe the Nairs:

Polias the labouring lower clans are named;
By the proud Nayres *the noble rank is claimed;*
The toils of culture and art they scorn,
The warrior's plumes their haughty brows adorn;
The shining faulchion brandish'd in the right,
Their left arm wields the target in the fight;
Of danger scornful, ever armed they stand
Around the king, a stern barbarian band.[4]

There are multiple theories as to the origin of the Nairs. One theory postulates that after the legendary hero Parshurama reclaimed Kerala from the sea, he brought the Nambudris and gave them ownership of the land, and along with the Nambudris, he brought the Nairs, a servant class who would serve and protect the Nambudri lords. Another theory holds that the Nairs were descended from the Nagas—the snake-worshipping warrior class of South India—a fearsome clan whose function was to act as protectors of the land. Yet another view prevalent among anthropologists is that the Nairs were originally descendants of the Newars of Nepal.

In a fascinating account penned by Phillip Baldeus in the 1700s, the Nairs were described as follows:

> . . . And upon this occasion we ought not to pass by the Nairos. These are the Gentlemen of Malabar, descended for the most part either from Royal Families, or Brahmans, and are for that reason exceedingly haughty, proud and bold: if they meet any of the common people in the street, they cry out, Po, Po, i.e. Give way, Give way . . .
>
> . . . They are all bred to the War, even from the seventh year of Age, when they begin to anoint their Limbs with certain Ointments to render the Nerves pliable, which makes them very active and nimble, and the best Wrestlers in the World. They are not only well acquainted with the use of Bows and Arrows, but also with Musquets and great Cannon; for I have seen them give a Salvo with the same order and dexterity as our best disciplined Troops

in Europe; and they are of late years arrived to that Perfection, that they make their own Gun-barrels, Gun-powder and Matches . . .

The Power of the Kings of Malabar is generally esteemed by the number of the Nairos under their Jurisdiction. If any of their Kings should be murdered, they would sacrifice all to revenge his Death. As they are naturally fierce and addicted to all manner of Lust and Pride, so they are declared Enemies of the Christians . . .[5]

Whichever be the view, what is certain is that the Nairs or Nambyars, though a caste lower than the Nambudris, were themselves very much an upper caste, whose chief identity at least originally was as a warrior group occupied with protecting the Brahmins. History is replete with praise of Nair martial prowess, and it is well known that all young male Nairs would receive rigorous training for several hours per week in martial arts in traditional *kalaris* or gymnasiums.[6] The prohibition against intermingling, so rigidly enforced against the lower castes, did not prevail between Nambudris and Nairs, and in time, most probably as a reward for their services, the Nairs too became the owners of vast tracts of land and the wielders of immense social power.[7] For example, as Barbosa noted in the sixteenth century, when Nairs walked down the roads, they would shout to the lower castes to get out of their way, and if the latter did not, they could be killed. This was because even the mere sight of a lower caste person was enough for the upper caste to consider himself polluted.[8] Another historian, Ralph Fitch,[9] who visited Malabar around the sixteenth century, described the Nair soldiers thus: 'They have their heads very full of hair and bound up with a string and are good archers with a long bow and arrow which is their best weapon.' Though the Nairs would eventually lose their weaponry, the tuft of hair, which was bound up and fell to the side of the head, continued for many years.

Meloth Krishnan Nambyar was born into the complexities of the Kerala Hindu caste system at the end of the nineteenth century—on 1 January 1898—in Chemnad village (in present-day Kasaragod district), in what was a traditional Nair joint-family set-up, known as the *tharuvaad*. The social organization of the Nambyars centred on the tharuvaad. As the historian L.A. Krishna Iyer notes,

> The constitution of a family or tarawad of people living together, is very complex . . . There are instances of Nayar tarawads with about 200 members belonging to different branches, and separated from one another by generations of descent, and yet all are able to trace their descent from a common ancestor . . . The oldest male is, by legal right, appointed as the karanavan or managing head over the whole of the groups of members living in one tarawad . . . The undivided family lives under the same roof.[10]

Nambyar belonged to the Meloth tharuvaad, and since Nairs follow the matrilineal system, he took his mother's maiden name of Meloth. He was born, however, in the joint-family home of his father, who belonged to Echikkanom—a powerful and wealthy tharuvaad, owning vast tracts of land stretching across the entirety of the southern portion of Bekal taluk. Its eldest male member was Kelu Nair (referred to as Valiyor or senior chief) who was the *karnavar* or nominal head of the tharuvaad and the second eldest was A.C. Raman Nair (referred to as Cheriyor or junior chief)—M.K. Nambyar's father. Nambyar was born, therefore, into a family of extreme wealth and influence and in his childhood, knew none of the sufferings of the lower castes, save what he must have witnessed around him. The traditional architectural design of tharuvaad houses was a large single-storey building, with rooms built around a quadrangle—the word for this was *nalakettu, naal* being the Malayalam word for four. It is said that the houses were single-storeyed, as it was socially impermissible for any home, however wealthy its inhabitants, to be taller than the temple of the village. A testament to the Echikkanom wealth was that the family home was not a nalakettu but an *ettukettu—ettu* meaning eight—and was a structure with two quadrangles.

Nambyar's stepbrother, K. Madhavan, who passed away in 2016 at the age of 100, described the family in great detail in his autobiography[11] thus:

The family house was an *ettukettu*, a structure with two quadrangles situated on the slope of a hill, about three miles east of Kanhangad town. It overlooked vast stretches of paddy fields which had a tributary of the Nileshwaram river flowing right through the middle. There was a pond on the western side of the hill and close to the pond was a *maalika* or multi-storeyed house. A little higher stood a *madhom* that was meant to house visiting Brahmins and a long *agrashala* or the dining hall. If one climbed still higher, there was the Palakkaal *padippura* or gatehouse and a bungalow close by to accommodate important guests. To its south was a large pond with a bathhouse adjacent to it and a huge *pathaayappura* or barn house that doubled up as living quarters as well. The *karnavar* of the tharuvaadu occupied the *Kizhakke maalika* on the eastern side and the second eldest member lived in the *Vadakke maalika* on the northern side.[12]

The location was relatively inaccessible, yet this in no way hampered Echikkanom's tremendous financial and social power. At the height of its glory, the tharuvaad had seven elephants, and when Nambyar was a boy, the number of residents of the tharuvaad to be fed, clothed and looked after, with all the amenities befitting their status, came to about 200 men, women and children. But then the karnavars (family heads) could afford it. All the cultivable lands belonged to the tharuvaad with not less than sixteen barns (farmhouses) interspersed all over, where tenants brought their levies in kind. The two brothers Kelu Nair and A.C. Raman Nair looked after the administration and running of the tharuvaad, and apart from this, Raman Nair, Nambyar's father, also found time to oversee agricultural operations on his own in about 100 acres of paddy cultivation, besides devoting his entire morning to running an eye clinic at the family outhouse. Through the course of his own life, Raman Nair had acquired knowledge of indigenous medicine from palm-leaf Sanskrit treatises to treat eye ailments. Poor people from far and wide, high caste and untouchables alike, came to the Echikkanom house to have Cheriyor treat their problems. He treated them all for free, and inpatients were cared for till they were cured. This tradition was passed down to M.K. Nambyar as well, who, whenever he would visit his home in later years, would treat the villagers for minor ailments.

Raman Nair's first wife, Chirutheyi Amma, belonged to the equally influential Meloth tharuvaad. Their marriage, though, was to last only fifteen years. Nambyar, the fifth of six children born to them, was barely four years old when his mother died of asthmatic complications. But Raman Nair married again, not once, not twice, but thrice—his second and third wives also died early. Each of his marriages was into well-known and reputed tharuvaads—Konath, Mavila and Kozhumal. Raman Nair had twelve children in all from these marriages.

Thus, M.K. Nambyar was the fifth son of the first wife of the second son of the Echikkanom house—not destined to be the leader of the clan, but in no way insignificant. One might think that Nambyar's upbringing and education were fuelled by the immense wealth of the Echikkanom tharuvaad, but this was not so. The Nairs followed the matrilineal system, which meant the sons of the men of the house had no claim to the wealth of the tharuvaad for their upbringing and education. It was the children of the daughters who inherited the wealth. But Nambyar was fortunate in that his father, Raman Nair, was a wealthy person in his own right. As the junior partner to the nominal head of the Echikkanom house, he possessed the resources to provide for his sons. He had more than 100 acres of paddy fields and extensive plots of pepper vines and aromatic plants—all of which was self-earned and would go to his children.

It was the beginning of the twentieth century, and though centuries of colonial rule had wrought significant changes in India, certain traditions still prevailed. For example, Nambyar wore his hair tied to one side, in the traditional Nair way, as did all male members of the family and his elementary education began at home, when he was five, following the celebration of a traditional *ezhuthoottu* ceremony. Each day, an *ezhuthassan* (a teacher) would come to the Echikkanom house, and the children of the family would sit together to take their lessons. According to journalist T.V. Krishnan, the ezhuthassan catered primarily to the tharuvaads, but a few outsiders would join in too. These usually comprised children from those classes of people who were indispensable to the functioning of a landlord's family—such as the *maniyani* (mason), *mannan, kaniyan, pullon* and *malayan* (all of whom were engaged in traditional occupations). As always, social hierarchy was so deeply entrenched that the boys, and sometimes girls, from these outside families, would have to sit at a distance from the Nair children when they took their lessons.

Growing up, Nambyar, therefore, had no dearth of company: the house was full of children from the various members of the joint family. But his mother's early death meant that although he was associated with the Meloth house, he spent much of his childhood—virtually the entirety of his formative years—in his father's home in Echikkanom. Though early deaths were a common phenomenon in those days, since medicine had not yet advanced, it is inconceivable that his mother's death did not have an impact on the young Nambyar. Not only did it reduce his contact with the Meloth house, it deprived him of a maternal presence during the most vulnerable stage of his life. This void, however, came to be filled to some extent by Raman Nair's fourth wife Unnanga Amma (K. Madhavan's mother), who took a special liking to the boy, and in her later years recollected that 'Kittan' (as Nambyar was affectionately called) carried a quiet and unassuming presence in the tharuvaad house, traits which, by all accounts, he carried through the entirety of his life.

The enforcement of caste separation continued through Nambyar's childhood, and so too the luxury and privilege that came with it. When Nambyar outgrew home schooling and moved up into primary school, about a mile away from the Echikkanom house, A.C. Raman Nair would dispatch a manservant who would take the young boy to school and ferry him on his shoulders across streams. Accompanying them was another servant who would carry a chair for the boy to sit in the classroom, as a Nair boy could not sit on the same bench as a lower-caste boy. What a young Nambyar made of these traditions, one would not know, but it is safe to say that the practices had prevailed for so long that they were not questioned and were most likely accepted as the natural order of things, at least to the mind of a little boy. In any event, change was in the air, and a year later with English becoming essential to those who wanted to join the ranks of the government, Nambyar was moved to the local Christian missionary school. He was chaperoned to and from this school by a servant but sat separately.[13]

Therefore, Nambyar and his brothers and sisters initially lived an extremely sheltered life, protected by the imposing boundaries of the tharuvaad lands and the even more unbreachable circumference of their caste. Yet, outside the tharuvaad, fierce battles were brewing, and the very system of land tenure that had so benefited Nambyar's family was at the very heart of it. The system of land tenure—i.e., the *jenmi* system—had existed in Kerala for centuries. When the English East India Company arrived, they made inquiries about the pre-existing land relations in the Malabar and retained a good portion of the traditional system with the aim of 'minimising the administrative expenses through the utilisation of the traditional institutions of the society'.[14] Under the jenmi system, all the land in a district was recognized as private land owned by one or the other of the jenmis or landlords. Most of the landlords were Nambudris and Nairs, with a few Tiyyas and even some Mappilas. *Jenmam* was the full proprietary right in the land, subject to payment of revenue to the government. The fruits of the land were shared between the landlords, the government and the tiller (the lower caste who was given subsistence wages by the landlord in exchange for his labour). This system was successful till about the middle of the nineteenth century when an increase in the prices of agricultural products brought with it social tension. Historians suggest that the triggering point for the social unrest was the landlords' habit of ejecting their tenants for obtaining higher amounts of rent. It is significant to note that the number of evictions, which was about 355 in the middle of the nineteenth century, had by the year 1880 risen to about 8000.[15]

This agrarian discontent resulted in frequent outbreaks of violence, often termed by historians as 'Mapilla outbreaks', wherein some tenants would attack the landowning Nambudris or Nayyars (Nairs) and then wait to be shot dead by the government law enforcement agencies. Sad though the plight of the tiller was, it was a testament to their extreme social weakness that though they formed the vast majority of the population, their discontent did not result in any meaningful change for many years. Just a few years before Nambyar's birth, the Malabar Compensation for Tenants Improvement Act, 1887, was passed, which was supposed to provide evicted tenants with the market value of the improvements made by them on the land. In practice, however, all that was taken into account was the cost of the improvements themselves, such as by planting trees, etc., and not the market value of the improvements. Needless to say, reforms of this nature did little to quell the tensions, and the tenant movement continued to fester and grow, merging ultimately into the nationalist movement, where it gained its real strength.

Thus, M.K. Nambyar, born in the year 1898, grew up in the midst of tremendous social churn. It is likely that the Echikkanom house too faced some measure of tenant unrest. It is not known as to whether the heads of the house feared for their safety during the Mappila outbreaks or not, but being one of the wealthiest and most powerful houses, it is unlikely that they emerged from this period unscathed. What is known is that the Echikkanom clan was by no means saintly: Nambyar's stepbrother K. Madhavan recollects an incident that he says left a deep scar on him:

Once my *Valiachan* went to the *pathaayapurra* at Pilicode. On his return to the *tharuvadu* three or four days later, he found that the box in which he kept money for sundry expenses was missing. When a thorough search failed to yield results, an astrologer was summoned. His calculations pointed an accusing finger at Panakool Kelu, the man in charge of the cattle of the *tharuvadu*.

But Kelu did not admit his guilt. He was immediately tied to a coconut tree and then the torture session began. Finally, unable to endure the pain any longer, he confessed to having sunk the box in a river. He was then asked to retrieve it. As the river was deep, a few others joined him in the search but to no avail. Kelu was tied to a coconut tree again and this time the gravy of pickles was poured into his eyes. That poor man screamed in agony but it had no effect on the landlord or his managers. In the end, only when Kelu fell down unconscious did the torture come to an end . . . A month later, *Valiachan* discovered the box inside a locked cupboard. It was then that he remembered keeping it there himself . . .

Madhavan says that in his childhood he witnessed countless such incidents and though Kelu survived and lived to a ripe old age, many others died. Given that Madhavan was about seventeen years younger than Nambyar and lived at a time when reform was already underway, it is almost certain that Nambyar too must have borne witness to these and other horrors. It is, therefore, very likely that the Echikkanom house too faced some of the inevitable tenant backlash in those years.

Looking, therefore, at the lives of M.K. Nambyar and K. Madhavan—both from the same family, born a few decades apart—we find that one would go on to choose the conventional life of a barrister and espouse his liberal ideas in the courts, while the other would fling himself into the nationalist movement, embracing the Gandhian struggle. Though their methods were different, at the root, their ideas were similar—both were aware of the deep inequities in society, yet, their inherent personalities coupled with the period of time in which they were born led them to make very different choices. Nambyar was no social revolutionary: the quiet boy who Unnanga Amma remembered adopted a more calculated and understated approach to his life. Yet, beneath the unassuming exterior, it is evident that considerable intelligence brewed, an intelligence which could not countenance the life of the tharuvaad, and perhaps could not countenance the social practices followed there.

It was fortunate for Nambyar that at the time he was growing up, as a consequence of colonialism—for all its negativities—the Nairs were beginning to realize the value of a formal English education. Though the Nambudris were initially regarded as the most influential members of Kerala society, historians suggest that by the third quarter of the nineteenth century, it was the Nairs who had become . . .

> . . . the best educated and most advanced of all the Hindu communities of the Malabar region . . . At the end of the 19th Century the majority of the graduates, undergraduates and matriculates, as well as officials of the government, were Nairs. The nature of the *taravad* organisation of the Nairs made the junior members of the *taravad* free to go up for education as well as to take up government jobs without bothering about the management of the joint property of their matriarchal families, which was duly attended by the *karanavars* or heads of the *taravads*.[16]

British rule had run its course for the first 100 years, and the early decades of the twentieth century saw facilities starting to emerge, rare and far between though, towards collegiate education for at least the eldest of the young sons and nephews of the karanavar. The work of the Christian missionaries had already laid the foundation for English education. The leading Nair tharuvaads of the region were the first to seize the emerging opportunities. A doctor, engineer or a lawyer in the family was no longer an unattainable dream but a goal right within reach for many a landowning house. The Meloth house was no exception. Nor for that matter, the Kodoth or Echikkanom houses.

Nambyar was a younger son of the tharuvaad and an academically gifted one at that. His eldest brother Kunhi Raman Nambyar was brought up to look after his mother's inheritance after her time. Only Kunhambu Nambyar, younger than Kunhi Raman Nambyar, studied up to intermediate, which in those days was on par with the pre-degree of later years. That was sufficient for him to get a good government job in the agricultural department in far-off

Kumbakonam at a starting salary of Rs 20 per month. Kunhambu recognized Nambyar's academic talent and took a special interest in the boy. It was Kunhambu who impressed upon their father, A.C. Raman Nair, that Krishnan Nambyar be enrolled in St Aloysius High School at Mangalore, along with the other similarly inclined boys of the tharuvaad. At the instance of A.C. Raman Nair, a house was specially rented out for the Echikkanom boys and an entourage of servants was retained to meet their everyday needs.

If Krishnan Nambyar's early years were spent in the confines of his Echikkanom house, surrounded by the traditions and customs of a Nair family, his years in high school and later at St Aloysius College pursuing an intermediate degree were spent in a far more cosmopolitan environment. It was an environment that Nambyar took full advantage of, and with every passing year, he found himself less in sync with the traditional ways. It was clear to Nambyar that he had to move beyond his upbringing and he threw himself into his studies with dedication. At the age of sixteen, he passed his SSLC (Secondary School Leaving Certificate) with distinction, which was no mean feat, and with further encouragement from his brother Kunhambu, Nambyar enrolled in the Government Arts College, Kumbakonam, in early 1917.

Nambyar, despite being from a family of landlords, was not unaffected by some aspects of the caste system, though, of course, there could be no comparison whatsoever to the treatment meted out to the Dalits or oppressed classes. Nambyar once narrated a story of having gone with four of his friends for tea and eats at a vegetarian restaurant while studying at the Government Arts College. Three of his friends who were Brahmins were accommodated in the dining hall, while he and his non-Brahmin friend had to sit on a platform that had been built on the veranda of the restaurant. He didn't take this amiss because one had necessarily to adapt oneself to this discriminatory treatment. The few non-vegetarian restaurants in the town were all called military hotels where no Brahmin would dream of entering.

Though his thoughts in those days were undoubtedly veering towards modernity, his appearance had not yet kept pace for he still bore the traditional side tuft of hair worn by all Nair men. This must have embarrassed him, or perhaps he simply desired to remake himself after a different image. So, with permission from the elders of his house, he cut his hair short, removing the traditional tuft and flung himself into academic life. After obtaining his BA in 1920, he obtained a degree in law from the prestigious Madras Law College, as was the trend that was being followed by several young Nair men of the time.

Having found his calling in the legal profession, he joined the chambers of the legendary Sir C.P. Ramaswamy Iyer as an apprentice. When Nambyar joined the chambers of Sir CP, the latter was the advocate-general and the doyen of the Madras Bar. A very handsome figure with a turban, he was well known throughout the country for his stature as a brilliant lawyer. It was no wonder that the Queen Regent of Travancore invited him to be the Dewan of Travancore (which may be roughly compared to the chief minister of a state). Sir CP had brought in tremendous reforms during his stewardship of the state, with one of his most outstanding contributions being the passage of the Temple Entry Proclamation of 1936.

The proclamation was a watershed moment in the caste upheavals that had beset South India for several years, a caste system that had endured despite all the progress of the independence struggle and the unifying missions carried on by Mahatma Gandhi and the efforts of B.R. Ambedkar and others. With the passing of the Temple Entry Proclamation, Sir CP threw open the doors of all temples in the princely state of Travancore for the unrestricted entry of Dalits and oppressed classes who could worship gods in the physical structures housing them, which hitherto had been inaccessible to the so-called untouchables. It is a terrible tragedy that even as late as 1936 such a thing was unheard of and unthinkable, and even today, temple priests in many parts of India try their best to prevent Dalits from worshipping though it has, of course, since been made a serious penal offence by the legislature of independent India.

It is no wonder, therefore, that Nambyar saw Sir CP as a guru. As previously mentioned, the time when Nambyar worked in his chambers, Sir CP was serving as advocate-general of the state of Madras, having been appointed to the post in 1920 by the Governor of Madras, Lord Willingdon. Work in the office of the advocate-general was of an unmatched vintage, and it had an impact on Nambyar's approach to constitutionalism.

When Nambyar returned to South Canara after his time with Sir CP, there were celebrations in the village, as neither the Echikkanom side nor the Meloth side had ever produced a lawyer. Nambyar was faced with the choice of either practising at the local Munsiff and Magistrate's Court or going to Mangalore, which was the administrative centre of the Malabar district. Astrological predictions favoured Mangalore, and therefore, in 1924, at the age of twenty-six, Nambyar formally entered the Mangalore District and Sessions Court Bar.

2

Touch of Fate: From the Mofussil to the Madras High Court

> To the average American, India is a remote land where tigers
> and cholera and the 'Bandar-log' thrive, and where English
> is spoken only by Kipling and the army . . . a glance at this
> journal before us will teach this average American that
> he has much to learn about India.
>
> —Praise for the *Mangalore Magazine*[1]

Astrological predictions aside, the mofussil town of Mangalore was a natural choice for a young lawyer from Kanhangad in the early 1920s. The roots of the English legal system had been sown in the Madras Presidency in 1802, about a century before Nambyar's birth, and saw the establishment of a district court in Mangalore in 1806, with its jurisdiction covering what was then the regions of Kanara and Sonda. As was the unquestionable norm in those days, a British judge trained in common law presided and assumed charge over all the civil and criminal cases in the district, as well as the Registration Court and the Local Commissioner's Courts. Additionally, the district judge was provided with the services of a government pleader. A few years later, in 1816, the powers of a district magistrate (i.e., the criminal court) were transferred from the district judge to a separate post of district collector, and criminal courts were established in all district headquarters under a given district judge.

Mangalore, therefore, was in many ways eminently suitable for the phase of life that Nambyar was entering. Not only was it geographically close to his home town, its status as a district headquarters with both a civil and criminal court ensured a steady stream of criminal and civil cases, including numerous disputes between landlords and tenants.

Still, Mangalore could hardly be described as a hotbed of litigation and was in many respects a one-horse town in the early 1920s. Yet, one must not gather from this the impression that Mangalore was in any way devoid of social activity. The reforms that the British made to the legal system were accompanied by reforms in other areas as well, particularly agrarian, and their imposition of high land revenue assessment in the absence of an adequate market for farm produce. The British referred to the uprisings by the farmers as 'koots', and the struggle reached the level of an armed uprising in 1837 in Mangalore, nearly twenty years before India's first war of independence in 1857. Though the uprising was quelled, the seeds of the freedom struggle were sown deep, and the area continued to be an extremely important southern centre during the nationalist movement, producing leaders such as the great K. Sadashiva Rao, M. Umesh Rao and many others. In 1919, when the Rowlatt Act was passed, authorizing the use of several emergency powers against the leaders of the freedom struggle, Mahatma Gandhi declared his first satyagraha and visited Mangalore in 1920, just a few years before Nambyar would arrive. Gandhiji travelled with none other than Shaukat Ali, who had spearheaded the Khilafat movement, and the purpose of the duo's visit was to further the agenda of Hindu–Muslim unity. To reach Mangalore, the pair had to travel through Kasaragod district, where they received a poetic greeting:

. . . Revered brothers! Like a child rushes to its mother when something distressing happens to it, India, aggrieved and dishonoured, India looks up to you for help and guidance at this crisis . . . In your intimate brotherliness we see an ideal of living example of Hindu–Muslim unity and the sight fills us with joy and enthusiasm. We envisage in that fraternity the hope of a glorious future for our land . . .[2]

From there, Gandhiji and Shaukat Ali were taken to Mangalore, where they were warmly greeted and garlanded as they proceeded through the town. Finally, on the eve of 19 August 1920, Gandhiji gave his address at the Central Maidan, where he extolled the virtues of peaceful non-cooperation:

We cannot possibly combine violence with a spiritual weapon like non-co-operation. We do not offer spotless sacrifice if we take the lives of others in offering our own. Absolute freedom from violence is therefore a condition precedent to non-co-operation. But I have faith in my country to know that when it has assimilated the principle of the doctrine to the fullest extent, it will respond to it.[3]

This was a crucial point in the history of the Malabar region, when 'Congress, Khilafat and local concerns of agrarian inequities came together'[4] till the Mappila rebellion of 1921 broke the alliance between Congress and Khilafat. The Mappila rebellion was another important inflection point in the region. As caste and other social tensions continued to build throughout the traditional tharuvaad systems and all across South Malabar, the rebellion turned communal as it was felt, and probably correctly, that the prevailing feudal system of which Nambyar's family (though of North Malabar) had been a direct beneficiary was deriving further support from the colonial rulers.[5] The rebellion, which at its height covered nearly 5200 sq. km of South Malabar, was stamped out within a few months, but the seeds of discontent were not entirely washed away.

It was into this social foment that Nambyar arrived in Mangalore in 1924. For Nambyar, this was his second phase in Mangalore, having studied earlier for his intermediate degree at St Aloysius School and College. One cannot understate the impact that St Aloysius College must have had on Nambyar, and indeed on the social fabric of Mangalore. Established by the Jesuits, who first came to Mangalore in 1878, the school was the prime organ through which Christian missionary thought was disseminated in the region. The college published a highly regarded magazine, *The Mangalore Magazine,* whose purpose in its own words was 'not directly religious and controversial, but there being no other organ in Mangalore to defend our altars and our homes, we do not think it is alien to its purpose to devote a few of our pages to a defence of all that is most dear to us . . .'[6]

Mangalore was thus in the sway of several simultaneous social forces—Christian missionaries, colonial rule, Hindu–Muslim dynamics and agrarian unrest. Perhaps the influence of his Jesuit education created a certain reticence on the part of Nambyar to fling himself wholeheartedly into the Independence movement, which was in those days building towards a crescendo. It could also be that he was still in some regard beholden to the tharuvaad system, from which he had gained so much, and they in turn were beholden to the British Raj. Nambyar had always been a quiet and reserved person and therefore, it would have been extremely uncharacteristic of him to agitate for independence. But whatever the reason, even several years later, he saw it fit to send all his sons to St Aloysius School and College as soon as they came of age.

On the personal front, Nambyar was now of age to be married as the conservative social mores of the times dictated. Since Nambyar now held the respectable tag of being a junior of Sir CP, combined with his birth into a prestigious and powerful tharuvaad, it was time to find a suitable match, and his father, Raman Nair, was on the job. Marriage was not a matter of personal choice for most Nair youngsters in the early twentieth century, but rather a practical decision taken by the head of the family where prestige, economics, caste and the overall advantages and disadvantages to the clan were closely considered. The historian Dilip Menon, making a reference to the Echikkanom tharuvaad in his work on the history of communism of the Malabar, wrote:

> Since the property of matrilineal tharavadus passed through the women, a strategic marriage could bring with it the property in dispute. Madhavan recollects that many of the conflicts over land between his own powerful household Ecchikanam and the neighbouring Kodom were settled by such methods.[7]

Even before Nambyar returned home from Madras, Raman Nair had set the ball rolling in finding a bride. Ultimately, after discussing with several of the other elders from the family, a bride, Kalyani, was decided upon for Nambyar. She came from an influential Nair family in Cherukunnu, some 50 km south of Kanhangad. Kalyani was the niece of Kunjappa Nambiar, the chieftain of the Kottayan Katankot house. The two tharuvaads had previous marital connections forged between them to build upon. Raman Nair's niece from the Echikkanom tharuvaad was married to K.K. Nambiar, an up-and-coming civil engineer who later became the chief engineer of Madras State. Kalyani was the younger sister of K.K. Nambiar and hence the exchange. Prevalent social customs did not preclude 'exchange' marriages which, as an extension of 'arranged' marriages, had the advantage of brothers and sisters of one family getting married to sisters and brothers of another family, provided the horoscopes matched and the educational and material clout of the prospective pairs were fairly similar.

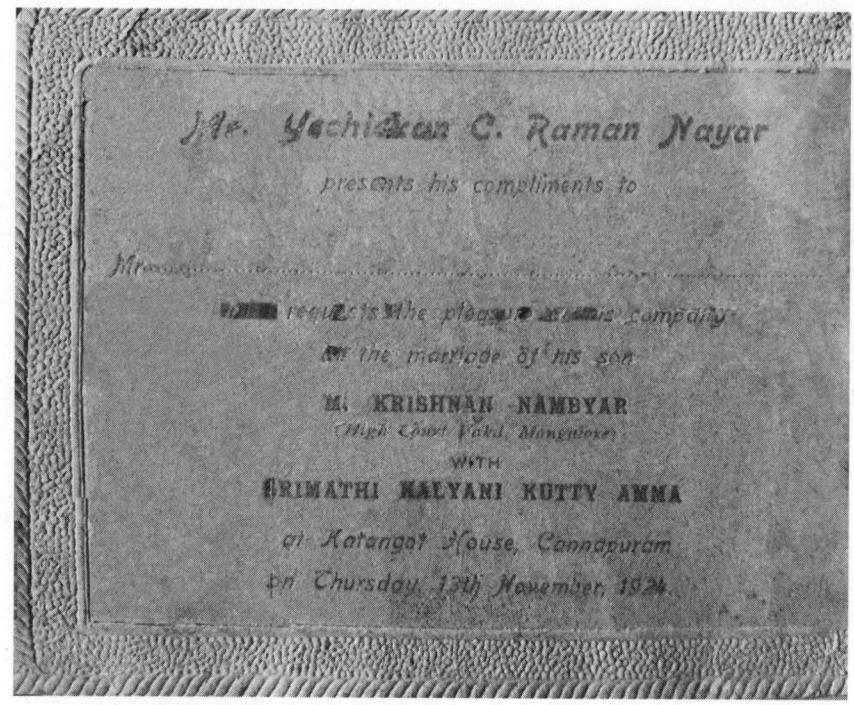

Wedding invitation of M.K. Nambyar and Kalyani Amma

The couple got married on 13 November 1924 at Katankot house, i.e. Kalyani's tharuvaad, and within days of the marriage, the pair travelled to Mangalore to begin a new life. Nambyar began his practice as a young lawyer, and took on rent the premises belonging to a Christian family by the name of Lobo. The house was one of four inside a gated compound and was the place where he began his work as a lawyer. Nambyar was, by all accounts, an extremely hard-working person, as well as being intelligent. Additionally, the most noticeable trait that he possessed was of being extremely persuasive in oral argument. Word soon started to spread of the young orator, and cases began to come to Nambyar.

As was the norm in those days, Kalyani was expected to take care of the house so that Nambyar didn't have to worry about anything but his professional life. Yet, the girl was just fourteen years old when she was married to Krishnan Nambyar and had scant exposure to the world outside her own tharuvaad. In Cherukunnu village, the question of sending a girl child to a faraway town for better education was unthinkable and, indeed, Kalyani did not even know English when she first accompanied her husband to Mangalore, let alone the first thing about running a house. M.K. Nambyar was clearly conscious of the disadvantage his wife would be at without the knowledge of English, and therefore, he arranged for an English tutor. Gradually, through patient study, Kalyani came to speak the language fluently. The tutor, an Anglo-Indian lady, would come to the house every afternoon in a crisp saree with a long-sleeved blouse and spend her time with Kalyani, taking her through the motions of learning a new language. Nambyar also made sure that Kalyani had assistance in learning the various other skills needed to run the house: how to sew, how to greet guests, manage the food preparation, etc. Clearly a highly intelligent girl, Kalyani focused her intellect on the administration of the home and before long, started running affairs in much the same way as an admiral runs a ship.

Kalyani adjusted to life in Mangalore well and soon made friends with the wives of Nambyar's professional acquaintances and relatives, even playing badminton every evening at the Mahila Sabha. Nambyar, an avid bridge player, would drop Kalyani to the Ladies Club for badminton and head off for an evening of bridge at the Officers' Club in Mangalore. Nambyar and Kalyani forged a bond that stayed strong until his death. Kalyani and Nambyar had seven children, and in the years to come, their home was full of children and later, grandchildren, all of whom brought a significant amount of joy and purpose to their lives. Their first child, Nalini, was born on the first year anniversary of her parents' wedding, i.e. 13 November 1925, followed by a son, K.C. Mohan, who was born in 1927. A third child, Ramkumar, was born in 1931. While Nambyar was not particularly religious—though he would sit for the morning puja every day—his wife Kalyani was exactly the opposite, and ensured that no ritual or prayer was missed out. Among her hobbies, the one that had the strongest hold on her mind was the pursuit of astrology. She would spend hours poring over astrology books and trying to discern what the future portended for her and her family. This passion was shared at a later age with her son Ramkumar, and the two would frequently discuss various planetary movements and their impact on the family members. Whether she believed it or not, whenever she felt that one of her children was going to do something she did not approve of, she would be heard cautioning them that their planetary outlook was not favourable, and therefore, they should refrain from whatever mischief they had planned!

And so, during this period, both Nambyar's success as well as his family grew. He and Kalyani, who at that point had three children, would go on to have four more and it was clear that the Lobo house would no longer be suitable for them. On the opposite side of the street was another house that belonged to a doctor who was interested in making a sale. Nambyar bought it and renovated it, even constructing an impressive and imposing porch with a driveway for cars. He also built a small extension room that became his office chamber, with a separate entrance. The office saw a steady stream of clients. Nambyar worked alone and kept long hours; in those days, he did not feel the need to hire any junior associates.

Nambyar had clearly always been academically gifted, but in these years, his aptitude for the legal profession became truly evident. Between 1924 and 1930, he was able to rapidly expand his practice and earn himself a name as an advocate of considerable repute. Yet, it was clear that this practice in the mofussil did not fulfil his ambitions, and after some years, he began to consider his next steps. Under ordinary circumstances, one could expect that a successful lawyer practising in the district courts of South India would have their sights set on the Madras High Court. However, for some reason, Nambyar could not yet see that far. He was, by all accounts, a cautious, quiet and reserved man, and the future that he envisioned for himself at that stage was far more local: to be a district munsif, the equivalent of today's civil judge—the junior-most rung of trial judges on the civil side. If successful, Nambyar envisioned a long career in the judiciary, and, given his intellectual ability, he was confident of his chances of success in the interview and perhaps an elevation to the higher judiciary at a later stage.

In his methodical way, Nambyar studied and then wrote the written test for this purpose and passed it, but to his utter shock, he failed in the interview. This was a tremendous blow to Nambyar psychologically, especially given that he was a hard worker who till that point in his life was accustomed to seeing the fruits of his labour pay off. Why a person of Nambyar's calibre should not have been selected is perplexing, and that he was not found qualified in the much more subjective assessment of the interview stage is perhaps telling of the manner in which appointments to such posts were made in those days. Interestingly, this also affected Nambyar's plans for his future, as he had clearly envisioned becoming district munsif as being the next logical step upward in his progression in the legal profession. Nambyar's former junior, the late M.N. Krishnamani— himself a senior advocate—said of this period in Nambyar's life:

> He was upset, his life's ambition being completely shattered. He could not eat or sleep for a few days. He never knew how a great future for him was in-built in that failure . . . if he had only not failed, (he) would have retired a district judge, unknown beyond a few Districts in Karnataka. The failure made him a great constitutionalist and made his name immortal.[8]

And so it was. Fate struck, and an unexpected series of events unfolded thereafter that would prove to be a turning point in his professional life.

In 1912, a dispute, which had been simmering for some years, erupted between the feudal houses of Kodoth and Echikkanom. In a parcel of land in Madikai village that otherwise belonged to the Echikkanom house, a Thiyya (Ezhava caste) household called Cherukui Pura had a janmam[9] claim over their residence, which was a thatched structure. Thiyyas were historically lower castes often engaged in tilling the lands but who nonetheless had, over time, acquired some small amount of social influence themselves, in part owing to their very sizeable numbers.[10] What sparked the dispute was a mere triviality—the Thiyya family had grown tired of the inconveniences of their thatched residence and wanted to build a tiled house in place of the existing thatched structure.

Since the land was not their own, and the rigidities of the caste system still existed, it was customary that, in order to build their new house, they would need the consent of the Nair tharuvaad. But Echikkanom sensed an opportunity. Using the influence of an estranged member of the Thiyya family, Echikkanom managed to purchase the janmam rights over the parcel of land, and virtually overnight, the existing owners of the house became tenants of the Echikkanom house. Next on Echikkanom's agenda was to evict the occupants. But this proved far harder than expected. The Thiyya family was defiant, and when elephants and a whole labour force were sent to drive the family out, the womenfolk of the family prostrated in front of their house. But the Echikkanom house was undeterred. They pressed on and forcibly evicted the Thiyyas from their house.

The Thiyyas, though, hit back. They approached the karanavar of the Kodoth tharuvaad for protection and transferred the remaining janmam rights that the other brothers owned to the Kodoth house. Echikkanom thought this a betrayal by Kodoth, howsoever unethical their own actions might have been. In response, Raman Nair made use of a closely guarded secret relating to a substantial number of properties that the Kodoth had amassed. He knew that the entirety of Beloor village, which originally belonged to one Konginiyan (a Tulu Brahmin), had come into the possession of the Kodoth on a lease for a monetary consideration of Rs 3000. Almost everyone had forgotten about the absentee landlord of Beloor village. But not only did Raman Nair track Konginiyan down, he also invited Konginiyan to Echikkanom, where he was made a guest of honour for weeks on end, at the end of which Konginiyan transferred the entirety of the janmam rights over 1000 acres of land at Beloor village to Echikkanom. In one fell swoop, Echikkanom had made Kodoth its tenants.

This naturally led to a long battle in the courts, with Kodoth filing a civil suit before a subordinate judge in South Canara in 1921. Echikkanom, though, was successful both before the subordinate judge and on appeal before the Madras High Court, which decreed in its favour in 1929. But Kodoth was keen to fight till the bitter end, even if it meant taking the case all the way to the Privy Council in London. To this end, Kodoth briefed the best of English lawyers, throwing all their financial resources into the case. George Simon of the Simon Commission fame appeared for Kodoth. By now it had become more than a mere battle over a parcel of land; egos were at stake and Echikkanom thought it could ill-afford to lose the case.

The Echikkanom chief, Kelu Nair, had an idea. Preparing for a case of this kind in those days took over two years and arguments often longer. Why not, he thought, depute Nambyar, the sole lawyer in the tharuvaad, to go to England to assist the barristers before the Privy Council while simultaneously studying for his bar-at-law? During the colonial period, the Judicial Committee of the Privy Council was the court of final appeal for the United Kingdom's overseas territories and Crown dependencies. It also served those Commonwealth countries that retained the appeal to Her Majesty in Council. As far as India was concerned, the Privy Council acted as an appellate body and was empowered to hear appeals from the Indian high courts. The Privy Council was the final court for the British Empire. Nambyar, thus, left for England, leaving his wife Kalyani, who at that time was pregnant with the couple's fourth child. On her husband's departure, Kalyani shifted to her own village of Cherukunnu, where she raised her three children and would deliver the fourth. This meant stopping their education, as the village did not have access to proper schooling, but it had to be done.

Kelu Nair thought that his plan would be a double blow to Kodoth. Not only would it likely lose the case, but Echikkanom would return with its flag flying high, with a barrister in hand.

Kelu Nair's plan worked. Nambyar ably assisted P.V. Subba Rao, a leading counsel, and the Privy Council dismissed Kodoth's appeal.

While in England, Nambyar obtained a master's degree in constitutional and administrative law from the London School of Economics and was called to the Bar from Lincoln's Inn. Not only that, Nambyar performed extremely well in his master's and stood first in constitutional and administrative law. It was now time for Barrister Nambyar to make a successful return. Naturally, he expected a hero's welcome. He had sent by sea mail the various documents relating to the case, including the Privy Council's judgment, to his cousin Koran Nair, who had by now succeeded Kelu Nair as the chief of the Echikkanom house. For some strange reason, Koran Nair was not empathetic to his cousin, who was seeking higher education.

Nambyar also forwarded details of his pending bills and travel expenses to enable him to sail back to India. The expenditure for his stay and education had till then been borne by the Echikkanom house, as he had been sent as per the wishes of Kelu Nair, the karanavar. But he waited for more than a month, with no reply. Reminders were sent, and still there was no response for another two months. To his shock, Nambyar discovered that his family had abandoned him. Ultimately, his brother-in-law, K.K. Nambyar, chief engineer, Highways of the Madras State, helped fund Nambyar's return ticket and clear his pending bills. Later, he learnt that a rumour had been spread that he had married an English woman, an anathema to a traditional Indian family. The rumour naturally was false. Kalyani, his wife, was at home, waiting eagerly for his return, with their new-born fourth child, Venugopal.

Nambyar could never forget the tharuvaad's ingratitude. One evening reminiscing over the family's past, he told a close relative: 'He [Koran Nair] was the meanest and foulest personality ever to be born in our family.'

Regardless of the personal blow, Nambyar's trip to England had been a professional success. When he returned from England, he came with a stack of books, some of which contained citations to him for having stood first in constitutional and administrative law.

He also returned with a little gramophone that could be wound up and played—an article of delight for his children who used to play it regularly. Nambyar's academic feat itself was tremendous. The racial atmosphere in England, especially towards Indians who were very much still inhabitants of a colony, was anything but friendly; it is testament to Nambyar's calibre that he was yet able to make a mark. After all, it was only the peculiar circumstances of his family's legal troubles that had helped him become a barrister. This status propelled him immediately to the higher echelons of legal service in Mangalore.

Nambyar and Kalyani had three more children: two boys—Gopinath and Shivashankar—and their last child, a girl—Malini. Having taken the trouble to give his wife a form of education that she had not otherwise been provided with, Nambyar was extremely particular that each one of his children should receive the best possible education which he could give them, irrespective of whether they were girls or boys. Nalini, the eldest daughter, obtained her BA degree, even though she had been delayed for two years by her time in the village, when Nambyar had gone to England. As a result, she completed her degree around the age of twenty-two or twenty-three, which was considered to be well past the age at which a girl could respectably be married. This caused Nambyar and Kalyani some stress, though they ultimately were to secure her a very favourable match: a young doctor, Vasudevan.

Their house in Mangalore was frequented virtually the whole year round with relatives from the smaller villages who came to Mangalore to seek medical treatment, which in those days was still hard to come by in the countryside. This nearly constant presence of guests coupled with seven children no doubt kept Kalyani on her toes, though she was never known to complain. The house, though luxurious for its times, was still devoid of running water, and water had to be drawn from a large well on the property, and food in large quantities had always to be kept ready.

This period of his life saw Nambyar building up a very respectable legal practice, which saw clients expressing their gratitude to him through means that would today seem unconventional, at least in the big cities. The relationship between client and lawyer was different in the mofussil than what it was in the high courts and the Supreme Court. Clients would naturally pay fees to Nambyar but they also believed that they should bring some gifts in addition. One client who lived in the rural areas brought wild hare which he had shot, or a leg of venison, as there were no strict rules prohibiting hunting in those days. He had trained prize-winning cockerels, and as a gesture of deep gratitude, he gave his prized cockerel to Nambyar. When it was slaughtered and cleaned, they found stitches all over its body befitting a professional warrior that had been in many cockfights. The leg of the deer would have small pellets embedded in it. Another client, who owned the Taj Mahal Hotel, would send huge vats of delicious biryani and bundles of sugarcane with their leaves sticking out like flags. There would also be large baskets of fruits from grateful clients.

In the mid-1930s, Nambyar had acquired a 75-acre plot of barren land between Bekal and Kanhangad, adjacent to the national highway. Named Ramagiri, this was where he built his holiday home. Nambyar planted hundreds of cashew, coconut and mango trees. While the cashew and mango trees flourished, he had less success with the coconut trees, which were infested with a beetle that would eat away at its roots and continued to do so even after truckloads of salt from Mangalore were put at the base of the trees.

Every summer, Nambyar and his family would spend about a month in Ramagiri during the court vacations, and it was one of his favourite places. He had a passion for cars and would travel by road rather than train from Mangalore to Kanhangad for the summer vacations. He had purchased a Hillman Minx car, which he would drive all the way to Kanhangad from Mangalore. That journey required the crossing of two rivers that had no bridges in those days. The car had to be driven carefully on to a platform made of wood fixed between two boats and then ferried to the opposite riverbank.

Ramagiri was where Nambyar would unwind with his wife and children. The food was good and in the early morning, the tender toddy fresh from the trees would be given to the children as well. Nambyar had learnt from his father the basics of native medicine, and villagers from the surrounding areas would make a beeline in the evening to the Ramagiri house where he would give them basic medicines for their ailments. In return, he would receive a leg of venison or freshly caught fish. Nambyar would often go hunting, and one day he came back with a huge python about 12 to 15 ft long, which he had shot. Whoever hunted deer or wild boar in that area would bring a part of the meat to him as well.

It was expected of him that he would host a big dinner for all his relatives and friends living in the surrounding areas. A goat would be slaughtered and cashew *feni* would be served. There were also *theyyams* whose ritualistic, frenzied dancing around a fire was said to cause the gods to descend from the heavens and enter their bodies. The theyyams would make various predictions while they danced, prophesying wealth or destructions for the various houses in the village. They would then fall on to the fire, to be dragged out by the villagers. Strangely, they would be unhurt, though their skirts, made either of bamboo or coconut fronds, would be burnt. All this was an essential part of the holiday in Ramagiri.

While the Mangalore house as well as the Ramagiri bungalow were frequented by family, friends and others, there were also those members of the family who did not share such a warm relationship with Nambyar and his family. On Nambyar's return from England and in the years that followed, Koran Nair's ire and vendetta turned more vicious when Nambyar, on assuming practice at Mangalore initiated court proceedings for the partition of the Echikkanom tharuvaad properties at the behest of the rest of the family. He had no personal axe to grind, no material gains at stake. Nambyar was only a son of Echikkanom. Beneficiaries by right were the nephews, nieces and their mothers. When all of them made common cause and insisted upon the division, Nambyar as the lawyer-son of the family did not want to refuse. Even otherwise, none could have prevented the disintegration of the joint family assets, and with it, the system itself, for it had outlived its purpose. Matters reached a head when the division was effected and the schedules drawn between the two major contenders—A.C. Koran Nair and A.C. Koman Nair, brothers both and direct nephews of Echikkanom Cheriyor (Raman Nair, M.K. Nambyar's father). The schedule which Koran Nair was served from the court was not to his liking, and for this he blamed Nambyar, even threatening to physically annihilate him. Nambyar took this threat seriously enough for him to stay away from Koran Nair. Whenever he had the occasion to visit his village, he'd stay at the 'Ramagiri' bungalow, some distance away from the tharuvaad house. Ramagiri was about 10 km before Kanhangad town and Echikkanom house was another 10 km beyond. During his frequent stays at Ramagiri, Nambyar never once stepped into his ancestral home because of the antagonism shown to him by the new karanavar, Koran Nair.

In 1938, there was a vacancy for the post of government pleader and public prosecutor of the Mangalore Bar. V.P. Krishnan Nambiar, a renowned advocate of Tellicherry, recounts that the then chief minister of the Madras Presidency, C. Rajagopalachari, had introduced a rule for selecting law officers that they should be selected by an elected panel of three persons. This panel was to be voted into office by members of the local bar who were to be the electorate for that purpose. According to V.P. Krishnan Nambiar, the system was proving to be rather unsatisfactory as it allowed electoral politics to flourish at the cost of merit. The collector of South Canara was a man of high integrity and calibre and convinced the government that it was for them to select their law officers. Ultimately, M.K. Nambyar was appointed, with the law minister of Madras, the collector of South Canara and the chief minister approving his appointment. Shortly before Nambyar was appointed, he and Kalyani were to have their seventh and last child, Malini. Mali, as Nambyar affectionately called her, was very dear to Nambyar's heart. Since she was born in the year that Nambyar was appointed government pleader and public prosecutor, he always said that she was lucky for him.

As government pleader and public prosecutor, respect for M.K. Nambyar rose further in the eyes of the people of Mangalore. The post was an important one, and the government pleader was regarded as a powerful man whose word carried a lot of weight with top government officials of that time. The little office in the house in Mangalore now saw the nearly daily appearance of police officers who would come to brief Nambyar about arguing criminal cases, including several murder trials. As the government pleader and public prosecutor, Nambyar travelled frequently to the Sessions Courts in the various taluks and conducted detailed criminal trials. It is unfortunate that the records of these proceedings are either non-existent or virtually impossible to access, for they would certainly have been a fascinating piece of history. This was the period of World War II when the Defence of India Rules were in force, and therefore, there was strict control over the price of all goods—rice, paddy, and even the movement of paddy from one district to another was controlled. Since black-marketing, especially of food grains, was a major problem, the rules were very strictly followed and nothing could be sold at a price other than that which had been fixed by the British government. The Defence of India Rules were so stringent that even a small article being sold at a higher price would entail imprisonment. The children on their way to school would purchase sweets from a tall Christian running a shop. His name was Nazareth and the children held him in awe. Nazareth, however, was being prosecuted by the commercial tax officer, Krishna Rao, for selling a packet of sewing needles at a very high price, far higher than that fixed by the government. One day, Krishna Rao called upon Nambyar for some work, and somehow or the other, news of this reached Nazareth. The children were surprised to find the tall, fair, otherwise highly dignified Nazareth on his knees before Krishna Rao and Nambyar (who would have been the prosecutor of the case), begging to be forgiven. Krishna Rao strictly admonished him, saying that he would have to go to jail, but Nambyar interceded on his behalf and said, 'Why don't you let him off?' Krishna Rao agreed but warned Nazareth that the next time he would be in jail for six months. All this came as a surprise to the children.

While Nambyar's own career was rapidly evolving, so too was the political situation in India. In the early 1930s, the struggle for freedom was in full swing, and the roots of satyagraha had spread deep throughout the soil of the country, penetrating even into the traditional Nair tharuvaad. Along with the struggle for independence from foreign rule, the people in Kerala were also fighting their own battle for freedom from centuries of oppression and servitude. Being landlords, Nambyar's family had been one of the direct beneficiaries of the labour of the lower castes—benefits that included bearing the costs of nearly all the comforts of Nambyar's early years, his education and the inheritance at his disposal. But Nambyar firmly believed in doing away with these traditional caste bonds, though he performed his role as public prosecutor with an unwavering sense of duty, just as he performed all the responsibilities of his life.

While he was public prosecutor, Nambyar would have several experiences but none as interesting as the Kayyur Riot incident, which forced him to balance his role as public prosecutor, his personal views of the negativities of the caste system and his duty to his family. During the long caste struggles that had become so common at that time in the region, some members of the peasants' union had turned militant. In the infamous Kayyur Riot incident, a constable who strayed into the path of the red-flag demonstration was beaten and killed. One of the accused in this incident was none other than K. Madhavan, Nambyar's stepbrother, whose political inclinations over the course of the previous decade had taken a decided turn towards the communists.

In 1934, together with a number of his associates, Madhavan became a member of the Congress Socialist Party within the larger fold of the Indian National Congress. By 1937, he had plunged into the peasant struggles of the Malabar. As a leader of the peasant union, Madhavan pioneered several campaigns against the eviction of tenants from lands cultivated by them, and against the extortionary practices of the landlords of the Malabar. This struggle naturally saw him come at odds with his own family. Even his own mother thought Madhavan had gone too far astray. The ostracization by the family, though, didn't stop Madhavan from pursuing his fights. As a secretary of the peasant union, Madhavan organized a grassroots struggle in which he brought together a cross-section of farmers, undivided by class, caste or religion.

By the end of the 1930s, his peasant organization had attained substantial strength. But this also meant that there were groups within the organization who indulged in militant clashes with the police. Of these, there were at least two of note. The first occurred in Morazha on 15 September 1940, where a sub-inspector of police and two constables succumbed to mob violence. And the second occurred in March 1941 in Kayyur village, resulting in the death of a police constable. In the Morazha incident, a number of peasant leaders were convicted by the Madras High Court, including K.P.R. Gopalan who was sentenced to death, only to escape the noose thanks to Gandhi and Nehru adding their voice to a 'Save Gopalan' agitation. In the Kayyur incident, Madhavan found himself a wanted man. He was listed as an accused in the First Information Report (FIR) prepared by the police, who were combing through the villages around Malabar to find him.

As public prosecutor, this put Nambyar on the horns of a dilemma. There was therefore one of two choices before him: either Nambyar had to withdraw from the case or Madhavan's name had to be dropped from the FIR. Madhavan was his stepbrother born to a different mother, yet as public prosecutor, Nambyar would have to prosecute the accused persons to the best of his ability. Ultimately, Nambyar felt that he could not prosecute his own flesh and blood. He went to the collector and told him that he would not be able to take up the case. The collector, however, was adamant, and since the case was a prestigious one for the British government, was insistent on Nambyar trying the case. The political advantages of having an Indian barrister prosecuting the accused were far too promising for them to forgo. When Nambyar proved intractable, the collector thought of an alternative—Madhavan's name did not appear along with the sixty or so accused whose names were included in the charge-sheet. Instead, Madhavan was sent into preventive detention at the Salem Central Jail.

Ultimately, Nambyar took up the case with consummate professionalism. But he pointed out to the court that three-quarters of the men belonged to poor and backward classes. Ultimately, however, the court found five of the accused guilty and sentenced four of them—all young peasant sons of Kayyur—to death, while the fifth was spared the gallows only because he was a juvenile at the time when the crime was committed.

By this time, it was clear that Nambyar was cut out for bigger things. The words that his Valiyachan, Kelu Nair, said to him before he set sail for England continued to inspire him. 'Krishnan, our country has a great future,' Kelu Nair had told Nambyar, who had his head bowed before the house chieftain in deference. 'Mangalore is too small a place and you have a great future and a bigger world to conquer.' To access that bigger world, Nambyar realized he had to move to Madras. It was 1947; India was soon to gain independence and there would be a new Constitution on the anvil. These were exciting times for India, and Nambyar wanted to be at the heart of it. As Justice Krishna Iyer of the Supreme Court of India would later say: 'When Nambyar came to Madras, it coincided with the Independence of the country and shortly after the Constitution came and India awoke to a new order, to a new human order, where constitutional civilisation became the essential part of culture.'

3

Taking the High Road: From Kanara to Kilpauk

It had been nearly twenty-five years since Nambyar and Kalyani had moved to Mangalore. During this period, the nationalist fervour raged all around them and many men from prominent Nair tharuvaads had joined the movement. An interesting scene has been described by historian Dilip Menon pertaining to the salt satyagraha:[1]

> The salt satyagraha in the Chirakkal taluk involved mainly those from prominent Nayar tharavadus and served to create a unity of purpose between them. Political activity was carried on amidst considerable restraint from the police who owed their jobs to the influential satyagrahis acting against the law. On 12 April 1930, K. Kelappan led a march of Congress volunteers from Calicut to Payyanur, traversing the villages of the interior to manufacture salt . . . Fortified by the securing of finances, the marchers proceeded from Calicut to Payyanur through unfamiliar terrain, clad in white khadi and singing nationalist songs. They must have been watched by a bemused rural population who saw either strangers or the younger members of locally dominant tharavadus in an unfamiliar role; acknowledging the crowd with none of the arrogance of their elders. The police kept a respectful distance and

in the countryside there was none of the violence that characterised their encounters with satyagrahis in the towns. The chief reason may have been that the participation of village elites in processions elicited pragmatism from constables. Moyyarath Sankaran (1889–1948), writing of a procession he had organised from Badagara to Payyanur, mentions that the constables on duty came up to some of the participants to get their beat registers signed . . .

Nambyar, being the government pleader and public prosecutor at that time, could hardly have participated in any of these activities, yet a man as intelligent as he could scarcely have lacked an opinion on the movement, or on the British Raj. Instances such as these were replete throughout this period, and there must have been several cases similar to the ilk of the Kayyur murder case, which he would have dealt with.

In his twenty-five-year stint in Mangalore, Nambyar had grown significantly in stature, being referred to in most of Kanara as 'Barrister Nambyar', a name that sparked significant respect when it was uttered. As the government pleader and public prosecutor, his expertise as a trial lawyer had greatly developed. Yet, with his chances of entering the judiciary all but gone, Nambyar was surely contemplating his next steps, and given the extent of his English education, particularly his knowledge of constitutional law and administrative law, he would undoubtedly have yearned to be more than a trial lawyer. However, left to himself, despite all his success in Mangalore and the nearby regions, he had not yet taken steps to make the leap to the Madras High Court.

Finally, in 1947, India won independence and the social picture of the country began to rapidly change. There was talk of the new Constitution and a change in the judicial landscape as well. A venerable lawyer by the name of Govinda Menon, who was the crown prosecutor for the Madras Presidency, was elevated to the High Court of Madras (Justice Menon would later go on to become a judge of the Supreme Court of India). Being extremely successful, Govinda Menon's elevation placed him in somewhat of a quandary, for he had a large number of briefs from all over South India, which he would have to ensure were placed in the safe hands of an able lawyer. As he pondered the question of who to entrust his cases to, he consulted with his brother, Narayana Menon, who was a district judge in Mangalore. Narayana Menon had, of course, seen Nambyar argue before him countless times and held Nambyar in extremely high regard—both as a civil as well as a criminal lawyer. He recommended Nambyar to his brother, in the strongest of terms. When Govinda Menon heard the name, he too was satisfied as he had known Nambyar from when the latter would come over to the Madras High Court to argue some cases on appeal, or when Nambyar would send Mangalore briefs over to Govinda Menon to handle at the high court. Given his first-hand knowledge of Nambyar's professional capabilities as well as the glowing recommendation from his brother, Govinda Menon soon wrote to Nambyar and invited him to take over his Madras practice and to keep his nephew and junior, M. Sekhara Menon, as a junior in the chambers. Sekhara Menon knew the practice and the cases, and would be able to guide Nambyar in his transition to the high court. Narayana Menon would be a lifelong friend and mentor to Nambyar, as would his brother Govinda Menon.

Nambyar jumped at the idea and immediately put into motion the wheels to shift to Madras. He resigned immediately from the post of government pleader and public prosecutor, and was succeeded by none other than K.S. Hegde, who went on to become a judge of the Supreme Court of India, and later Speaker of the Lok Sabha.

As soon as his resignation was accepted, Nambyar leapt into his red Hillman Minx MDX 7 and drove all the way from Mangalore on the west coast to Madras on the east coast, a distance of nearly 700 km. Govinda Menon's generosity did not end with handing over the practice and an experienced junior, for he had also left to Nambyar his rented accommodation—a sprawling house on Poonamallee High Road, which even now is regarded as an extremely upmarket part of Chennai (formerly Madras). Here, Nambyar, Kalyani and the seven children began to find their feet in a relatively unknown place, and slowly started to lay down roots in that historical city, which would prove to be the base of the family for generations to come.

At the time of Nambyar's arrival in Madras, the city was already well established as the foremost metropolis of southern India. Though initially, Madras city did not have too much importance despite being the capital of the Madras Presidency, the picture rapidly changed in the 1920s after the introduction of the Montagu–Chelmsford reforms, which created an elected legislature of Indians who would have a say in governance. This in turn provided opportunities to a range of non-governmental actors comprising the most successful legal and bureaucratic families of the time.[2] By the time Nambyar shifted to Madras, the city was very much a modern capital and an important seat of government.

When he arrived in Madras, Nambyar decided he should get a bigger car than the Hillman Minx. The person in charge of allotting the few cars that were allowed to be imported under the Defence of India Rules was a man called Sathe, a secretary in the Government of Madras. Sathe had been the deputy collector in Mangalore and Nambyar knew him well. Nambyar went to see Sathe at his office in Fort St George and managed to persuade him to put down his name in the short list of allottees. Nambyar soon became the proud owner of a Ford Mercury. His brother-in-law, Dr K.C. Nambyar, a double FRCS who was equally fond of cars and had applied for an imported vehicle a few years earlier and was still waiting for his allotment, said jokingly, 'I am going to file a case.'

In Madras, Nambyar now faced the task of familiarizing himself with the dozens of briefs left to him and acclimatizing himself to the new high court practice. While Sekhara Menon was a great asset to Nambyar in the early days, Nambyar had to take on additional juniors to manage the load, for Govinda Menon's other juniors had left for Kerala on his elevation and set up practices of their own. This proved to be fairly easy because it seems that Nambyar's reputation preceded him and many a young lawyer were keen to join his chambers. For Nambyar, this must have been a new and different experience for till that point, he had never had the assistance of junior counsels, being briefed largely by the police and the other government servants in Mangalore. On the home front, the family was doing well. Kalyani and the seven children adjusted well to life in the big city, while Nambyar found his feet in the practice of law. Having returned from England, Nambyar, who was an admirer of what he perceived to be an organized way of life, saw to it (with Kalyani's partnership, of course) that the same aura of quiet discipline pervaded the home. A stickler for tidiness, Nambyar was very particular that he and the family were always dressed to perfection. His shirts for court had to be pristine white, and the children were not allowed to wear clothes with even the smallest rips or tears. When Nambyar was not in court, the children were to be on their best behaviour, which they were not out of fear but simply out of a sense of awe and respect for their father.

By the time Nambyar arrived in Madras, two of his children were already well into higher education, Nalini, the eldest, was twenty-two and had completed her education and even obtained a law degree. Nalini, who had lost two years of study when Nambyar went to England, had stubbornly insisted on completing her studies. Consequently, she was a little beyond what was then considered the marriageable age for girls by the time she was ready to be married. This caused Nambyar and Kalyani a fair amount of stress as they worried that they would not be able to find a suitable match for their daughter. However, their apprehensions turned out to be unfounded, because she married Dr K. Vasudevan, a young and upcoming doctor, and the couple soon travelled to England for Vasudevan to complete his studies. Tragedy struck later when the couple was returning to India from England: Dr Vasudevan unexpectedly passed away of a heart attack on the ship. When Nalini returned, she started law practice and would assist Nambyar in his cases.

Nambyar's next child, K.C. Mohan, who was around twenty at the time of the move to Madras, completed his chemical engineering course in India and thereafter proceeded to England where he obtained from the Imperial College of Technology an MTech and

DIC (Diploma from the Imperial College) qualifications. In fact, it was Kalyani's intervention with Nambyar after Mohan completed his course in India that persuaded Nambyar to send the boy to England. Kalyani felt, and as it turned out rightfully so, that an English degree would propel Mohan to perform much better, career-wise. After he returned from England, Mohan began his professional life at the Bhilai Steel Plant. Mohan was sent to the Soviet Union for training in the design of steel plants, where he rapidly picked up and became proficient in the Russian language. This skill would hold him in good stead some years later, when Nikita Khrushchev came to India and was brought by Prime Minister Jawaharlal Nehru to the Bhilai Steel Plant. Mohan was asked to explain to Khrushchev the technology of the plant, which he did. Mohan's career continued swiftly upwards and thereafter, successively he was the managing director of Metallurgical and Engineering Consultants (India) Limited (MECON)—the steel design company with about 1500 engineers under him—and in early 1980, he became the director of a multinational company in Dubai, the Al-Futtaim group. The top management would not permit him to retire at the usual age; as a result, he continued as group director in Al-Futtaim till the age of seventy-five, after which he finally came back and settled in Chennai at Harrington Road. His wife, Radha Mohan, was the daughter of the famous Sardar K.M. Panniker, who was a diplomat, founding editor of the *Hindustan Times*, historian, novelist and one of the topmost statesmen in India at the time. Radha was with her father while he was ambassador to China, as a result of which she could speak Mandarin fluently.

The five younger children at the time of Nambyar's move to Madras were still in school. Nambyar's third, fourth and fifth sons, Ramkumar, Venugopal and Gopinath had inherited Nambyar's intellect but not his cautious personality. Ramkumar, who trained to be an engineer, chose to bring his choice of profession to his family's notice one evening over dinner, when he informed them that he had joined the Air Force and would be leaving the very next day for his training, which he did. Ramkumar was clearly suited for the armed forces and ultimately went on to become Air Vice-Marshal.

Venugopal, who had joined BSc, failed to complete his degree on account of an illness, and therefore was at a loose end. By this point, Nambyar felt it was time that one of his sons should join the legal profession. With Mohan an engineer, Ramkumar in the Air Force and Gopinath too studying to be an engineer, his sights turned to Venugopal, who thus ended up becoming a lawyer solely at his father's behest. After graduating, he started practising under his father in the Madras High Court for a few years.

Later, Venugopal struck off on his own and garnered an extensive practice initially in motor vehicle cases and then diversified into other areas. He would appear not only in the Madras High Court but also became a regular face in the Supreme Court of India. In 1979, the then Law Minister Shanti Bhushan, during the Janata government, invited Venugopal to be an additional solicitor general. When the Janata government fell, he resigned from the post, built up a lucrative practice and eventually went on to become the Attorney General for India (in 2017), which office he laid down at the age of ninety-one after completing five years and three months in practice. The greatest sorrow of his life was when he lost his wife Shanta at the age of forty, when he was only fifty, a loss that he never got over.

K.K. Gopinath was Nambyar's fourth child, who studied engineering. In college, he declared to his parents that he wanted a motorcycle, a request which they reluctantly acceded to, to ensure that he completed his studies. After completing his studies in India, he proceeded to France for completing a specialized course in automobiles for which he trained with Renault as well as Citroen in Paris. After returning to India, he joined Hindustan Motors and was thereafter general manager at Hindustan Motors, Gujarat, and assisted the company in putting up their factory at Halol. After he retired, he settled down in Madras (Chennai). He played hockey in college, moved on to horse riding and later became an oarsman in which sport he won prizes in the Merchant and Bankers regatta at Chennai. His outstanding trait was that he loved driving all over India; at the drop of a hat he would get into his car and drive all the way to Kolkata and once even to Bhutan. He married Sushila, who was a versatile and highly intelligent person, even obtaining the Chancellor's Gold Medal, i.e. the highest award in the master's category at MS University, Baroda. Thereafter, she studied further and obtained a PhD in ancient history and was also a classical dancer.

The youngest son, K.K. Shivashankar, had a successful career as a manager at Godrej and Co. in Chennai. He married Rohini and both of them seem to have known each other as they had travelled together by ship to the United States where they later got married. In the United States, Sivan obtained a master's degree in business management from Cornell University, and Rohini obtained a master's degree in design and education from Wisconsin University, and thereafter they returned to India. Unfortunately, K.K. Shivashankar passed away at the age of thirty-two following surgery. His death was a terrible blow to the family and especially to his mother, Kalyani Nambyar. His wife, Rohini, embarked upon a career as an interior designer and did extremely well. Her work was in demand in various cities in India including Bombay.

One wonders what Nambyar's feelings would have been when as a moffusil lawyer he was transposed to the capital of the Madras Presidency to build his practice anew in the Madras High Court. Though accomplished, he must certainly have felt a sense, if not of trepidation, then at least of uncertainty as to how he would fare. The Madras High Court was one of the most prestigious in the country, with an impressive legacy of its own, and the bar was brimming with legal stalwarts who were known all over India. Understandably, the history of the Madras High Court was inextricably intertwined with the history of the British rule in India, and the progression of the Madras Bar mirrored closely the political developments of this turbulent yet triumphant time in the country's history.

Established by the Letters Patent granted by Queen Victoria on 26 June 1862, the High Court of Judicature of Madras was part of an endeavour of the colonial government to integrate the British legal system with the customs of the Indian people. The high court was given jurisdiction over the entire Madras Presidency, which in those days was so large that it included present-day Tamil Nadu, the Malabar region of North Kerala, Lakshadweep Islands, coastal Andhra as well as other districts of Andhra, Gajapati district of Odisha and some districts of Karnataka as well. The Madras High Court was initially housed in a building that later became the Collectorate of Madras and about thirty years later, just a few years before Nambyar was born, shifted to its present iconic location. Built by the English architect Henry Irwin, the building is said to be a mix of Hindu, Muslim as well as Christian influences. The building is a most impressive one in red brick with beautiful domes. There were about fifteen court halls all in distant parts of the building connected by round corridors. Famed for its beautiful silver panels, the building is also home to mesmerizing stained-glass windows, which are not merely works of art, but carry their own particular significance. For example, the stained glass behind the chair of the Chief Justice carries the image of an elephant between two owls, with the elephant symbolizing strength and the owls, wisdom. Likewise, the recurring motifs on the outer walls of the high court are swans and snakes, with swans referring to 'Anna Patchi', which has the capacity to separate milk from water, as a judge might separate truth from falsehood. The snake symbolizes the concept of karma in Hinduism, which, of course, has a fundamental relationship to the concept of justice.[3]

In 1947, the Madras High Court, like the rest of India, was still making the transition from its colonial past to a modern future, and in those days, the court would also sit in 'sessions' to try criminal cases where the death sentence or life imprisonment was to be imposed. The judge sitting in sessions would arrive in a procession with the Sheriff of Madras dressed in identical clothes to those which one finds in the pictures of Lord Clive. The sheriff was followed by the commissioner of police and the judge of the high court dressed in scarlet robes and wearing a white wig, which even the Queen's Counsel from England had worn prior to Independence. There would be a retinue of court officials walking behind the judge.

The judge would be seated in the centre of the room on an elevated dais with the sheriff sitting on his right and the commissioner of police on his left. The unfortunate prisoner would be locked in a jail immediately below the sessions court and be brought up via an internal staircase directly opening into the accused box. This system was prevalent only in the city of Madras, and the sessions trial originally followed the jury system, but by the middle of the 1950s or so, the high court sessions was abolished. Thereafter, the cases were tried by a sessions judge as was the case in all the other districts in the Madras Presidency. The solemnity of the sessions also vanished once the district courts began hearing cases where the extreme punishment would be inflicted without any of the pomp of the high court sessions trials as the district judge had to deal with a plethora of other criminal cases.

Of course, it was not just the architecture of the high court building that was impressive, for the Madras High Court was home to several legal stalwarts, both English as well as Indian. In 1947 when India gained independence, there were still a few English lawyers practising in the chartered high courts in India, who soon left for their home country. The most famous among them was Eardley Norton, whose picture still hangs in the portrait gallery of the Madras High Court. Soon after moving to Madras, Nambyar, in V.P. Krishnan Nambiar's words, began to rub shoulders with the giants of the bar. Nambyar, when he made his first appearances among the galaxy of senior advocates, which senior lawyers in India claim is equivalent to the Queen's Counsel in England (having the same rules governing them), would well have felt that he had to tread his way cautiously among these stalwarts.

Thus, it was into this exalted atmosphere that M.K. Nambyar as a mofussil lawyer found himself thrust. How was he going to fare among these people who had established themselves as leading lawyers, who were being briefed by clients from all over the Madras Presidency? But Nambyar had a significant advantage. He had been a public prosecutor conducting very serious criminal trials for at least twenty years of his practice until then. Further, the Madras Presidency included the Malabar districts and Barrister Nambyar was extremely well known in the Malabar districts. He found that he had no dearth of work and was in demand for cases involving the death sentence, since the trial courts could not by themselves impose the death sentence but could only refer the case with their judgment to the high court in what was known as a 'referred trial', where the high court alone could either confirm the death sentence or modify the same.

In this new environment, Nambyar gained prominence with his persuasive advocacy, which was neither loud nor aggressive. Even then, as V.P. Krishnan Nambiar writes, his 'quiet dignity', his 'unostentatious humility' and his 'mellowed wisdom' were obvious. He was a popular choice for the younger lawyers to brief, and was often briefed in criminal cases in the high courts of the neighbouring states as well.

When Nambyar was in England, he had obtained his master's in constitutional law and administrative law from the London School of Economics in 1932 when no one could have anticipated that India would secure independence and the Indian people would give themselves a new Constitution. The academic grounding that he received in these areas reflected in his arguments in the Madras High Court and in the neighbouring high courts even when he was arguing the more run-of-the-mill criminal and civil cases.

An interesting example of this was one of the earliest reported judgments of the Madras High Court that carries Nambyar's name: *A.B. Tonse v. The King* 1949 M W N Cr 45. The case was one of three instances of cheating committed by the accused persons, i.e. Nambyar's clients, who were 'native Indian subjects', in the states of Travancore and Cochin. Nambyar had filed a petition seeking

quashing of the criminal prosecution. At the time when the offences
were alleged to have been committed by Nambyar's clients, Travancore
and Cochin were outside 'British India'. However, such offences
could be tried as Section 4 (1) of the Indian Penal Code applied the
provisions of the code to any offence committed by any native Indian
subject of His Majesty in any place without and beyond British India.
The procedural counterpart of Section 4 was found in Section 188
of the Code of Criminal Procedure, which required sanction of the
political agent before prosecution could be initiated in the Indian
courts. However, between the dates when the offences were allegedly
committed, and the date when the sanction was granted (i.e.,
25 May 1948), the Indian Independence Act, 1947, was passed,
on 15 August 1947. With the passing of the Act, the suzerainty of
the British Crown over India lapsed and Travancore and Cochin
acceded to the new Dominion of India. The question, therefore,
arose as to whether the prosecution initiated against Nambyar's
clients was valid, for at the time when Section 4 and Section 188
applied to the accused persons, no sanction was validly granted. The
case was a difficult one, particularly because with the passing of the
Indian Independence Act, 1947, a consequential amendment to
Section 4 (1) of the Indian Penal Code was made, so that the amended
section read: 'The provisions of this Code apply also to any offence
committed by any British Subject of Indian Domicile in any place
without and beyond the Provinces of India.' Thus, notwithstanding
the fact that no valid sanction had been granted, the amendment to
the Indian Penal Code now made the Code applicable to any British
subject of Indian domicile without and beyond India, and therefore,
to Nambyar's clients as well.

What must be remembered is that Nambyar was at that stage
barely a few months into his move to Madras, and had opposite him
none other than the legendary Public Prosecutor V.L. Ethiraj for
the state. The first Indian ever to be made crown prosecutor by the
British, Ethiraj was nothing short of a legend of the Madras High
Court Bar, with even the great Nugent Grant, one of the most

famous and highly regarded public prosecutors for the Crown, saying
of his advocacy, 'In arguing a criminal appeal, Ethiraj has no equal.'[4]
Ethiraj and Nambyar had studied together in England, where Ethiraj
had specialized in criminal law and Nambyar in constitutional law.
The two would go on to become good friends, and for this reason,
years later, Nambyar sent his youngest daughter Malini to the Ethiraj
College for Women in Chennai for her bachelor's degree. Ethiraj
as public prosecutor had argued a number of very high-profile and
sensational cases, for example, the Kakinada Bomb Blast Case, the
Hyderabad conspiracy cases, and though known for his extremely
pleasant disposition, Ethiraj was an extremely formidable opponent.
Nambyar, though himself an experienced lawyer and former
public prosecutor, was still very new to the Madras Bar, and one
could well have expected him to adopt a cautious or conventional
approach to his arguments for quashing. Yet, in court, Nambyar
was a different person—the self-effacing and cautious attitude that
prevailed in his personal life was shed, and Nambyar applied his own
deep understanding of constitutional principles aggressively and
persuasively to the case.

Nambyar argued that sanction ought to have been validly
given for the prosecution to be sustained, prior to the accession of
Travancore and Cochin to the Dominion of India. More importantly,
he argued that the amendment to Section 4 of the Indian Penal Code
was 'ultra-vires' the Governor-General and also the Legislature of the
Dominion of India to enact laws to be in operation in the acceding
states. This argument, though not accepted by the court, was
essentially a constitutional argument at a time when the Constitution
itself did not exist. Nambyar did not succeed in the case, but this style
of argumentation—of linking issues in criminal and civil law to their
constitutional underpinnings—became characteristic of him, and he
drew on the vast knowledge that he had gained in the subject from
his time in England. Meanwhile, the Supreme Court of India had
issued a direction that all advocates who had practised for more than
ten years could claim the title of Senior Advocate, subject to certain

stipulations, such as giving up the ability to file cases in one's own name, etc. Naturally, Nambyar too had opted for this, as befitted his stature as a barrister.

It was at this stage in Nambyar's career, that V.G. Row, a leading barrister, who was also a leftist, saw Nambyar arguing a death sentence case and propounding very intricate issues of constitutional law for seeking an acquittal for his client. Meanwhile, a prominent communist of Kerala, A.K. Gopalan, had been preventively detained and his case was the very first constitutional case to be listed in the new Supreme Court of India for hearing.

As Justice V.R. Krishna Iyer would later observe, Nambyar exhibited a passionate scholarship: 'I say it is not one of those scholarships like tepid tap water; if you open the tap, it flows,' he said. 'No, not that way. He was committed. There was a commitment about him in the garb of fundamental rights. He fought the case not for the ideology of his client who was a Communist but for the ideology of human rights which found expression in Part III . . . "Man, if born in chains, shall be free, and to the last of my breath I will fight for his freedom." This was the method of Shri Nambyar the lawyer.'[5]

It was this Nambyar that V.G. Row saw, and this Nambyar that he decided to trust. The stage was set for Nambyar to take his next big leap into the world of constitutional advocacy.

4

The First Constitutional Case: *A.K. Gopalan*

The Constitution of India was adopted by the Constituent Assembly on 26 November 1949. It was promulgated on 26 January 1950 and with this, the new Parliament passed the preventive detention laws, by which a person could be detained even before he had committed a crime, on the basis that his past conduct could lead to the inference that he would commit crimes against the State, which required him to be detained in prison. This was a highly authoritarian law, wholly against the noble principles embodied in the Fundamental Rights chapter of the Constitution, but the travesty was that this very chapter included an article that authorized such preventive detention.

There's little question now, that this anomaly of allowing preventive detention through a constitution that was meant to guarantee liberty and equality was a product of India's colonial past. It is clear that the nature of the nationalist movement that had led to freedom in India had also caused the makers of our Constitution to distrust absolute liberty. As Patel would put it, in a view shared by Nehru, the preventive detention law was necessary to save India's democracy from 'disruption, subversion and destruction'. But Nambyar would later write:

> Every system of government that is born of revolution, violent or
> non-violent, bears the indelible impress of the impulses of its being.
> It mirrors the struggles of the past in its provisions to ensure the
> security of the future. It represents the aspirations, achievements
> and ambitions of a people. No constitution is merely a collection
> of clauses or the handiwork of skilled draftsmanship. It is an
> organic growth springing from the forces of the natural vitality,
> and changing in colour and content in the process of time.[1]

In its original form, this new preventive detention law was primarily
used against members of the Communist Party of India (CPI), a group
whose ideology, in and of itself, was regarded by Sardar Patel and
Jawaharlal Nehru as potentially injurious to India's democracy. One
such leader of the CPI was A.K. Gopalan, who had been previously
detained under the Madras Maintenance of Public Order Act, 1947.
Soon after the new Central enactment was enforced, on 27 February
1950, Gopalan was served with a fresh order of detention, even while
he was still in prison. The order claimed that the Governor of Madras
was satisfied that it was necessary to detain Gopalan with a view to
preventing him from acting in any manner prejudicial to the security
of the State and the maintenance of public order.

Despite their relatively similar upbringings—born into the
same caste of Nairs, barely two years apart, in towns in North
Malabar separated by no more than 100 km by road—Gopalan and
Nambyar had little in common, and their lives had, until now, barely
ever intersected. Bereft of complete, formal education, Gopalan
nonetheless began his adult life as a primary school teacher. But even
in this role, he saw an element of social responsibility. 'I taught for
about seven years. The work was pleasing and exhilarating,' he wrote
in his autobiography *In the Cause of the People*. 'Little innocent
children, the knowledge that I was the guardian of all, many holidays,
opportunities for public activities, a chance to earn the love and
regard of the people, a situation in which I could forget the heavy
cares of life and play and live with children—these exhilarated me.'[2]

By 1927 though, still in his mid-twenties, Gopalan had plunged fully into the freedom struggle by joining the Indian National Congress. Three years later, he was so taken up by M.K. Gandhi's famous Dandi march, that unknown to his family, Gopalan left his job and travelled from Calicut to Cannanore to offer satyagraha, only to be arrested the same day. His time in prison imbued in him a commitment to socialism, which would culminate four years later in his joining the newly formed Congress Socialist Party (CSP) in Kerala.

In the years between the formation of the new party and the attainment of Independence, Gopalan performed an increasingly activist role, mobilizing the peasant class, assisting in the formation of workers' unions and often leading struggles against what he termed as 'retrenchment at will'. His general ethos by this time tended to revolt against the very idea of capitalism. 'I starved for want of time to eat food that was available, starved also for want of food to eat,' he wrote in his memoir. 'I worked day and night, starving for one reason or another . . . I could learn well from experience the condition of workers, the capitalist tie-up that emerged against their struggle and the change of colour of the middle classes. I learned how capitalists use workers devoid of class feeling to create a schism in their own ranks.'[3]

Gopalan's membership of the All India Congress Committee (AICC) brought him in contact with a number of communist leaders of lore; these meetings evoked in him 'a revulsion for the policies and the programs of the then leaders of the [Congress Socialist Party].'[4] Soon after Gopalan returned from a trip abroad—which coincided with the advent of the Second World War—where he met Malayalee workers in Ceylon, Singapore, Malaysia and Burma, he attended the Wardha session of the AICC. Here, he said, he was so disillusioned by a politics that was rooted in nationalism as opposed to the class war of Marxism that he decided to quit the CSP altogether and commit himself to communism. This move would soon see him take his struggle underground, where he would remain until 24 March 1941 when he was arrested at Tiruchirappalli.

Six years later, even as India celebrated the declaration of its independence, the government of Madras would release every political prisoner from its cells but Gopalan. 'On August 14, 1947 I was in solitary confinement in the big Cannanore jail,' he wrote in his autobiography.

> There were no other detenue prisoners. I could not sleep at night. Cries of 'jai' issued from all four corners of the jail. The echoes of slogans 'Mahatma Gandhi ki jai' and 'Bharat Mata ki jai' reverberated through the jail. The whole country was waiting for the celebration due after sunrise. How many among them had waited for years for this and fought for it and sacrificed their all in the struggle. I nurtured feeling of joy and sorrow. I was glad that the goal for which I had sacrificed all my youth and for which I was still undergoing imprisonment had been realised. But I was even now a prisoner, I had been imprisoned by Indians—by the Congress government, not by the British. Memories of the Congress from 1927 passed through my mind. I felt proud of the role I had played in the Congress movement in Kerala. A man who was secretary of the Kerala Congress and its president for some time and member of the AICC for a long time was celebrating August 15 in jail![5]

However, even after Independence, when the Congress formed the government, Gopalan continued to find himself consigned to the dungeons. Why did he have to face such larger periods of incarceration, when he hadn't been convicted of any specific offence, when there was no finding through the application of the rule of law of any guilt? This, and more, was at the crux of the first great constitutional case that the Supreme Court of India heard: *A.K. Gopalan v. The State of Madras*. It was, as Gopalan wrote in his autobiography, 'a momentous law-suit,' a case that required an interpretation of Articles 14, 19 and 21 of the Constitution—the holy trinity of the rights to equality, freedom and personal liberty—and Article 22, which created an exception, in certain senses, for cases of 'preventive detention'.[6]

Gopalan's legal cases at the time were handled by Vombatkere Gurunandan Row (better known as V.G. Row), a fellow communist, whose venerable law firm, Row and Reddy, had been specifically established to take up leftist causes. Row's strategy for fighting Gopalan's confinement included, among other measures, the petitioning directly of the newly formed Supreme Court of India under the then freshly minted Constitution. But it came as a matter of surprise when Row engaged the services of Nambyar to argue Gopalan's case in the Supreme Court. At the time, Nambyar had been in Madras for only two years, most of which he'd spent defending criminal cases, using the experience that he had secured as a public prosecutor in Mysore. What's more, unlike Gopalan and Row, Nambyar did not possess any inherently leftist views. But Nambyar was nonetheless a man of principles, a man who believed in the majesty of the rule of law, a man who more than anything else believed in *due process*.

Having seen Nambyar argue these constitutional issues, V.G. Row asked him, 'Would you be prepared to handle A.K. Gopalan's case in the Supreme Court?' Now, here was a lawyer who had been practising in a mofussil, Mangalore (which was the district headquarters), who had never appeared in the Federal Court of India or the Supreme Court of India but was being given an offer to argue what turned out to be the very first constitutional case in the Supreme Court, and a sensational one at that. Nambyar jumped at the offer. Then came hectic days of preparation: the large office room in Poonamallee High Road was strewn with law reports, not merely from India but also from the United States and the Commonwealth countries as well.

The case was argued in the Parliament House's Prince's Chamber, where the Federal Court used to sit. It was here, in these ornate quarters, that Nambyar, a lawyer hitherto unknown in Delhi, would soon make his mark on the nation, his contribution that was, as we can today attest to, indelible in its impact. Soon, it would be Nambyar's tranquil yet imperious voice that would break the court's silence, lifting it from its slumberous start.

Nambyar was fortunate when he was asked to argue the A.K. Gopalan case in having J.B. Dadachanji of JBD and Co. as his solicitor. In the Federal Court, which had existed from 1937 to 1950, there was a system of agents and every reported decision of the Federal Court would show not only the name of the counsel who argued the case but also the name of the agent, since it was essential that an agent be present in every case to ensure that the procedures in every court, the formats of the pleadings and the filing of documents were all done in accordance with the rules.

In 1950, with the Constitution and the Supreme Court of India coming into existence, the agent was replaced by what is termed as 'the advocate on record'. To be an advocate on record, one had to pass a very tough examination and many advocates failed, but no case was argued without the senior counsel being assisted by an advocate on record. JBD and Co. were advocates on record. J.B. Dadachanji, or Jimmy as he was fondly called, had built up a highly respected firm that was in great demand. Nambyar was lucky to have him guide him in his first appearance in the Supreme Court.

When Nambyar and V.G. Row arrived in Delhi before the case started, Jimmy Dadachanji came up to them and said that K.M. Munshi, who was the doyen of the Bar, had sent word that he was going to start the argument as lead counsel. V.G. Row said an emphatic no and added that Nambyar was fully prepared, and this being the first case, he would lead the arguments. The description of Nambyar's arguments is found in many reports. Some lawyers may even have thought that Nambyar would make a fool of himself: how could a lawyer from the mofussil compete with Supreme Court lawyers of great eminence? And so, they waited to hear him speak. Once he began, however, if any of those present had harboured such thoughts, they were swiftly dispelled. As eminent lawyer B. Sen recounted:

> The case I remember best was one that was heard in the very first month of the court—A.K. Gopalan v. Province of Madras. The question of detention without trial was at issue and that involved

interpretation of Articles 14, 19, 21 and 22 of the Constitution. The constitutional questions raised were new, both to the Judges and the lawyers, and when M.K. Nambyar appearing for the detenue, expounded his arguments, day after day, citing case law from all over the globe with comparisons between the Indian, the Irish and American Constitutions, the entire courtroom seemed to be completely spellbound. There were no interruptions nor questions, the all-pervading silence broken only by Nambyar's voice and the rustling pages of the law report.[7]

A.K. Gopalan's continued incarceration post-Independence stemmed from specific provisions that were inserted in the Constitution to permit preventive detention.

Article 22, which was otherwise meant to protect a person against unlawful detention—by making mandatory that anyone arrested ought to be informed of the charges against him, and ought to be granted the right to consult and be defended by a counsel of his choice, among other rights—created an explicit exception in certain cases where the detention was under a law that provided for preventive detention. The concept of detaining persons without due process, Nambyar would later write, was really an offspring of the war. It was, he observed, the uncertain conditions 'at the birth of an independent Republic', which 'impelled the authors of the Constitution to introduce Article 22(4) in the Constitution.' This clause granted the State the power to detain a person for a period longer than three months, provided an 'Advisory Board' comprising persons at least qualified to be a high court judge had opined that there was sufficient cause for such detention. It was this clause that had been invoked to detain Gopalan—he was not only denied many benefits available to undertrial detenus but he was simply kept behind bars with no prospect of a trial anywhere in sight.

The presence of Article 22(4), during times of peace, was certainly unfortunate. But, in Nambyar's argument, it ought not to have been an insurmountable barrier for Gopalan. For he saw the entire chapter of fundamental rights guaranteed by the Constitution as a cohesive whole. To him, Articles 14, 19 and 21, which respectively guaranteed a right to equality, a right to various liberties such as the freedom of speech and freedom of assembly, and a right to life, together vested in an individual a right to what the Americans call due process of law.

The underlying issue in the case was intensely emotive, in the words of journalist Inder Malhotra. 'Politics accentuated the emotions,' he wrote in an essay reproduced in the book *Supreme But Not Infallible*. 'The Communists were not alone in decrying the [Preventive Detention Act]; the Liberals were opposed to it even more vehemently, considering detention without trial repugnant to the very concept of democracy.'[8] Gopalan's petition was, after all, as Chief Justice Hiralal J. Kania would later describe it, 'the first case in which the different articles of the Constitution of India contained in the Chapter on Fundamental Rights have come for discussion before us.' Kania was joined on the bench by his brethren: Justices Saiyad Fazl Ali, Patanjali M. Sastri, Mehr Chand Mahajan, Sudhi Ranjan Das and B.K. Mukherjea. At the bar, Nambyar was opposed by two giants. The State of Madras was represented by its Advocate General K. Rajah Aiyar and the Union of India—which had intervened in the case since the validity of a Union law was in question—was represented by Attorney General Motilal C. Setalvad.

During the several days of arguments, Nambyar, 'in his thorough and exhaustive manner,' as Setalvad describes it in his book *My Life: Law and Other Things*, 'put forward every conceivable argument in support of the petition.' Although numerous critical arguments were raised by him, ultimately, for Nambyar, the contentions concerned two broad threads: the interdependence and nexus between Articles 19 and 21, and the meaning of the word 'law' as used in the latter clause. These arguments were so complex as to draw between the six judges a 'bewildering conflict,'[9] as Setalvad put it.

To appreciate fully the intricacy of Nambyar's argument might require more than an element of knowledge of India's Constitution, but his contention also boasts of elegant simplicity, the kind of which the best legal submissions often tend to contain. To Nambyar, the chapter comprising fundamental rights, i.e. Part III of India's Constitution, constituted a collective whole. Article 19, which guaranteed to India's citizens a wide spectrum of liberties—the freedom of speech, the freedom to assemble peacefully, the freedom to move freely throughout India, among others—and which could be restricted only on reasonable, enumerated grounds, had to be read harmoniously with Article 21, which accorded the State the power to restrict a person's right to life and personal liberty through a procedure established by law. Detention of a person without trial, in Nambyar's argument, not only denied to the captive a right to personal liberty, but it also impinged on his right of locomotion, guaranteed by Article 19(1)(d). Any law that detained a person would therefore have to satisfy the specifically enumerated limitations to this right, contained in Article 19(5). This, Nambyar asserted, was absent in the State's preventive detention law.

In the original draft Constitution, the Constituent Assembly had included a due process clause modelled on the United States Constitution. In the US, both the Fifth and the Fourteenth Amendments to its Constitution contain a due process clause. Broadly, they provide that the State shall not deprive any person of life, liberty or property, without due process of law. As early as 1856, the term 'due process' was interpreted by the US Supreme Court to encompass substantive principles that restrain legislative power. 'The Constitution contains no description of those processes which it was intended to allow or forbid,' the court wrote in *Murray's Lessee v. Hoboken Land & Improvement Co.* 'It does not even declare what principles are to be applied to ascertain whether it be due process. It is manifest that it was not left to the legislative power to enact any process which might be devised. The article is a restraint on the legislative, as well as on the executive and judicial, powers of the government, and cannot be so construed as to leave Congress free to make any process "due process of law," by its mere will.'[10] A few scholars saw these forms of interventions, which seek to check the substantive reasonableness of a law that impedes liberty, as an encroachment by the judiciary into what ought to be the sole domain of the legislature.

But Nambyar, despite the obvious obstacles, in both the text of Article 21 and the debates of the Constituent Assembly, saw things differently. To him, law bore the same connotation as 'law' figuring in the American due process clause. By now steeped in American constitutional law and its traditions, he drew inspiration from the arguments made by the statesman Daniel Webster before the US Supreme Court in 1819, in *Trustees of Dartmouth College v. Woodward*: 'By the law of the land is most clearly intended the general law; a law which hears before it condemns; which proceeds upon inquiry and renders judgment only after trial,' Webster had argued. 'The meaning is that every citizen shall hold life, liberty, property and immunities under the protection of the general rules which govern society. Everything which may pass under the form of an enactment is not, therefore, to be considered the law of the land.'[11]

Nambyar argued that Webster's enunciation was also in keeping with India's dharmic traditions, which some of the judges who decided Gopalan's case time and again harked back to during the hearings. Therefore, Nambyar said the word 'law' used in Article 21 can only mean *jus* and not *lex*, that is, it refers to a *jus naturale*, 'the law above all laws, the moral law, which mankind had accepted as inviolable throughout the world.'[12] Nambyar's argument, wrote the lawyer J.B. Dadachanji, who had practised in the Supreme Court virtually from its inception, comprised 'the most original research', and was a product of a 'creative bent of mind.'[13]

There's little doubt that the Supreme Court understood the gravity of the case before it. The judges 'were deeply conscious of the task before them,' wrote Inder Malhotra. 'They knew they had to interpret the Constitution, especially the precise ambit of fundamental rights and permissible restrictions and limitations on them, to decide whether the impugned law on preventive detention could be upheld or must be thrown out.'[14] The importance of the case naturally lent to the Supreme Court a sense of majesty. The various sets of counsel presented their cases with erudition and elegance, and the six judges were reportedly very thoughtful in their interjections. But, to Malhotra, there would be only one hero: Nambyar. When he opened his arguments, with his slightly nasal voice, with the proposition that there were certain 'immutable principles of justice' which in a democracy that had overcome enormous odds were incapable of being overridden by simple law, in Malhotra's recounting, there was a 'palpable frisson' in the court.

Nambyar would go on to argue with the 'clarity of crystal' that the Preventive Detention Act violated these immutable principles both 'brazenly and flagrantly'. For days on end, he kept enraptured the bench of six judges, who, for large parts, joined with the audience in their appreciation of the neat intricacy in Nambyar's arguments. He elucidated to the bench why in India, unlike in England, Parliament is not sovereign. He pointed out how the sovereignty that Parliament enjoys in England, much as they might claim otherwise, was really a negation of the rule of law. To illustrate the point that law, as a creature of Parliament, can often be arbitrary, Nambyar cited the case of Thomas Wentworth, the 1st Earl of Strafford, who was executed following a summary condemnation to death by special act of Parliament. So too the case when Parliament passed legislation, directing that Richard Roose, who was a cook to John Fisher, the Bishop of Rochester, be boiled to death. 'Acts of Attainder, Bills of Pains and Penalties and Acts of Confiscation cannot be outdone in arbitrariness by any executive order,' Nambyar later wrote, echoing his arguments in Gopalan's case. 'Yet, these too are laws having the same force and sanctity as any ordinary piece of civil or criminal law.'[15] Nambyar's argument was simple enough: the mere fact that a law had the sanction of Parliament cannot be enough to confer on it a sanctity beyond all challenge.

Nambyar's arguments did not end here. He placed a further emphasis on the interweaving, as it were, of several of the fundamental rights. This is a subtle argument that didn't quite capture the imagination of the majority of the Supreme Court judges at the time. But it would later come to represent a thesis that lies at the core of how we today understand the chapter on fundamental rights. Additionally, Nambyar also argued for a general rule of arbitrariness under which a law that is unreasoned, or that is lacking in the basic precepts of natural justice, would have to simply be considered as antithetical to Article 14's guarantee of equality.

These arguments—that an arbitrary State action violated Article 14, that preventive detention laws were as much justiciable under Article 19 as they were under Articles 21 and 22, and that Article 21 stood violated every time the State, in infracting a person's life or personal liberty, acted contrary to due process—would serve to establish a thread that viewed Articles 14, 19 and 21 as a cohesive whole, as a collection of fundamental rights that together guaranteed a rule of law. Or, as Justice Y.V. Chandrachud observed later in the Minerva Mills case, together these articles constituted 'a golden triangle'.

There is little doubt that Nambyar's argument, as we shall see, served as a harbinger for the future development of Indian constitutional law. Although his plea in favour of the majesty of liberty was unfortunately rejected, it was the foundations laid in Gopalan's case, through Nambyar's arguments, that would ultimately cause the Supreme Court more than two decades later to accept the concept of due process, of the necessity for a law that denies a person his or her personal liberty to be founded on an edifice of justness, fairness and reasonableness.

The court itself was heavily impressed by Nambyar's arguments. Indeed, Chief Justice Kania expressly noted the court's indebtedness to Nambyar for helping it interpret the true meaning of Article 21. But despite the persuasiveness of the petitioners' arguments, the court found itself restrained by the debates in the Constituent Assembly, to which both Setalvad and Rajah Aiyar made repeated references. Attorney General Setalvad, a tall, handsome and attractively grey man, in Inder Malhotra's words, was mathematically logical in his presentation. His argument was simple: 'Why would the Constituent Assembly,' he asked, 'substitute the words "procedure established by law" for the expression "due process of law" contained in the original draft Article if its intention was to follow the American pattern?'[16] What followed, in Malhotra's narration, was a fascinating, even thrilling, exchange. Unfazed by Setalvad's counter, Nambyar argued that no properly elected legislature could possibly enact a lawless law. The validity of any law, he argued, ought to depend on its meeting of fundamental precepts of justice. When Justice Das queried Nambyar on whether he was pleading for 'procedural due process'—a standard that operated to ensure that life and liberty could be deprived only upon a fair process being followed—the reply was both precise and cutting: 'That plus more, My Lord!'[17]

Here, the tension in the courtroom, in Malhotra's description, was palpable. Setalvad retorted by arguing that a legislature properly elected was competent to lay down the procedure of law. 'What happens,' Nambyar asked, in response, 'if the legislature lays down death as punishment for a crime and prescribes that it be carried out by beheading the convict?' 'Where is the problem?' asked Setalvad. 'Death is the penalty and decapitation the procedure.'[18]

Nambyar's response was cheeky, to say the least. 'I seek permissions from your lordships,' he said, 'to quote from an authoritative book by a respected author.' There was, wrote Malhotra, 'some fidgeting around the Attorney General's seat.' The Chief Justice appeared to appreciate what might follow. Nambyar was keen on citing a passage from Setalvad's book on civil liberties.

'Is it really necessary?' the Chief Justice asked Nambyar. Before Nambyar could reply, Justice Mahajan intervened: 'You please read,' he told the counsel. 'I want light from whatever source it might be from.'[19] Nambyar would read many passages from Setalvad's book that appeared to run directly counter to the attorney general's arguments in court, but much as the exchange made for enthralling viewing for those present in court, it had no impact on the ultimate judgments.

Days later, the court reassembled to deliver its verdict. 'The law is valid,' declared Chief Justice Kania. 'We have held this by a majority of four to two. We have also held two sections of the Preventive Detention Act to be ultra vires the Constitution, but these are severable.' Justices Fazl Ali and Mahajan dissented on the court's primary conclusion, unshackling themselves from the weight of their experiences as judges in pre-independent India—a burden which each of the other four judges appeared to carry rather heavily.

But Nambyar certainly left his footprints on the sands of time. The view of the majority in the Gopalan case, it's safe to say, has since been consigned to the dustbins of history. That Nambyar's arguments left a lasting impact on the development of the law, in the shaping of the fundamental rights that we today so cherish, is beyond doubt. Credit here, however, goes in no small part to Justice Fazl Ali, whose dissenting judgment captures the core of Nambyar's submissions with great rigour; the opinion was, in many ways, to borrow a phrase used by Chief Justice Charles Evans Hughes of the United States Supreme Court, 'an appeal to the brooding spirit of the law and the intelligence of a future day.'

Nambyar was heavily distressed by the fact that almost at the inception of the Constitution, at what he described as the 'threshold of its life,' Article 21, which represents one of its capital guarantees, became stillborn, 'dead and buried,' with 'little hope of its resurrection'.[20]

But some years later, Article 21 would indeed be resurrected, lifted from its grave by the Supreme Court's decision, first, in what is now commonly known as the *Bank Nationalisation* case, and, later, with even greater verve, in *Maneka Gandhi v. Union of India*, decided on 25 January 1978. While in the former, a nine-judge bench of the court found that Articles 21 and 19 were interrelated, in the latter, the court gave meaning to the phrase 'procedure established by law,' and ruled that any procedure of law that denies a person his life or personal liberty must be just, fair and reasonable.

There could be no better tribute to Nambyar than that which the judgments in *Maneka Gandhi* provided, just short of three years after his death. They vindicated his commitment to the rule of law, to the majesty of the Constitution's core promises, and to his most progressive views on what it means to treat citizens with equal care, respect and dignity.

5

The Aftermath of *A.K. Gopalan* and Life in the Madras High Court

Following his arguments in *A.K. Gopalan*, Nambyar was catapulted from an upcoming senior of the Madras High Court to the national stage. This also impacted positively his practice in the Madras High Court. In due course, Nambyar had to employ a number of juniors/ associates as his practice had expanded exponentially. By this point, Nambyar's practice was so large that he would have to run from one court to another and because the corridors were so long, some of the judges would call upon the juniors who would say he was on his way, and the judges would say they would adjourn the case. He used to have long green notebooks in which he would make notes in green ink with a Parker pen that he loved. Even today, in some of the reports that he had used in his arguments, one will find a tiny green tick in the margin against a sentence he would have quoted during his arguments.

Nambyar, as was befitting his stature, also became more active in the lawyers' associations in the Madras High Court. The lawyers of the Madras High Court had two associations: the Madras

Bar Association and the Advocates Association. The Advocates Association had 2000 to 3000 lawyers at that time and today has about 5000 lawyers. The membership of the Madras Bar Association was restricted to barristers or to lawyers called to the Bar at the Inns of Court in England or to lawyers who had acquired postgraduate degrees, hence the number was limited to about 100 lawyers. The Bar Association had an excellent library of its own and in the main hall where the lawyers sat and studied their cases or gossiped, the portraits of English lawyers as well as of Indian lawyers were displayed on the walls. Nambyar became one of the significant members of the Madras Bar Association which had hoary traditions. The Madras Bar Association would host a large number of visiting jurists from abroad, including Lord Denning and his wife, and invariably, Nambyar would also have to say a few words at the function organized in the Association Hall to honour them.

In 1954, Nambyar built a large house on nearly an acre of land on Harrington Road. He also built an office that was connected to the main building of the house. Next to his own office room sat his juniors. By this time, he had six juniors, leave alone the instructing lawyers who would come to brief him on cases. There was a half swing door separating the two rooms—Nambyar's and the juniors' rooms—and the atmosphere was quiet and focused. By this point, Nambyar had grown accustomed to having younger lawyers assist him, and would entrust briefs to them to prepare fully and then brief him. In those days, the relationship was extremely formal. Though Nambyar was certainly not foul-tempered nor was he known to lose his temper with his juniors, yet the significant respect that he commanded in the profession proved be its own disciplinarian and juniors would never talk or enter Nambyar's room unless called for. Yet, he was fond of his juniors and took care of them as a senior lawyer in the profession would. In his later years, some of the formality disappeared, and some juniors whom he was extremely fond of, for example the late M.N. Krishnamani, senior advocate, would walk into his chamber to have a chat.

Most of M.K. Nambyar's juniors were from Kerala, as someone or the other who was known to Nambyar would have spoken to him to train their wards. When the reorganization of states took place in 1956, all those from Kerala returned to the state and most retired as district judges. Sekhara Menon would go on to become the law secretary of Kerala and retired as such.

Meanwhile, another storm was brewing, for the saga of the detention of A.K. Gopalan did not end in the Supreme Court. The Supreme Court's intransigence in upholding the Preventive Detention Act despite Nambyar's detailed arguments, meant that Gopalan's liberty was in a state of substantial and constant peril. Indeed, even after the Supreme Court's verdict, Gopalan continued to be detained indefinitely in the trenches of Madras jails, under the Preventive Detention Act. Nambyar had his work cut out for him and together with V.G. Row, he continued to challenge the various detention orders passed against Gopalan to the courts. Ultimately, one of those pleas, a Criminal Miscellaneous Petition, number 153 of 1951, found favour with the Madras High Court.

Gopalan argued the case in the first instance in hall number 2 of the Madras High Court, where Justices Satyanarayana Rao and Raghava Rao sat. He argued with great verve and vigour that there existed fresh causes of action beyond the Supreme Court's verdict that ought to really compel his freedom. The validity of the substantive provisions of the Preventive Detention Act may have been upheld by the Supreme Court, but one of its provisions nonetheless mandated that any order of detention must specify the period of such detention, which it did not.

At about 11.40 a.m. on 22 February 1951, the court delivered its verdict. The judges had no hesitation in declaring the detention null and void. The judgment set Gopalan at complete liberty, and despite the heavy presence of police in the court quarters, he was now free to go where he pleased. Needless to say, this was a huge victory for Gopalan, not merely on the legal front but also morally. Waiting outside the court's premises for him was a stream of thousands of people, gathered all around the already crowded confines of Parry's Corner, China Bazar and Broadway, once glorious landmarks of old Madras.

But the real drama was only beginning to unfold.

Soon after the order was pronounced, Gopalan left the court's premises through the gate opening on to China Bazar, with V.G. Row by his side, intending to proceed to Row's offices at the Andhra Insurance Buildings in Thambu Chetty Street, a narrow lane across the road on which the high court stands. They had barely crossed ten yards from the court's gates when two C.I.D. officers, who had followed them closely, walked up to Gopalan and informed him that he was under arrest and that a fresh order of detention had been issued against him. As a subsequent judgment of the court narrates, this arrest was made within five minutes of the court having officially ordered Gopalan's release.

It was quite clear as to what had happened. The earlier proceedings in court and the arguments advanced had made it clear that Gopalan was going to be released. The police were, therefore, armed with a fresh detention order and A.K. Gopalan was arrested. Upon his arrest, however, Gopalan wasn't immediately shown a copy of the detention order. Instead, he was taken in a car to the office of the Commissioner of Police, Egmore, Madras. It was en route this journey, at about 12.30 p.m. that the order of detention was finally shown to him. Thereafter, he was taken to the penitentiary, where, before the Presidency Magistrate, he swore on affidavit that the arrest and detention were not only illegal but smacked of the mala fide intention of flouting the high court's order. On the very next day, even as he was taken away to Cuddalore Jail in a police van, Gopalan, through his counsel, petitioned the high court, seeking his production before the court and an order setting him at liberty through the issuance of a writ of habeas corpus.

Nambyar, with Row by his side, argued vehemently for Gopalan's release. He began by summarizing the crux of his arguments into a strong rhetorical opening—something that had, by then, become customary in his argumentative style. 'The court time is precious, words can't explain,' Nambyar told the bench.

> The court must be wondering why I have come before this court again with the writ of habeas corpus. It is only for the sake of my conscience to make aware that A.K. Gopalan was arrested again. I haven't come before this Hon'ble Court expecting any relief from it. Any order passed by this Hon'ble Court I do not believe will be executed by the government. The ruling government continues to act arbitrarily in the absence of due check kept on it by the judiciary. If the Hon'ble Court accepts my arguments and releases my client, he will be arrested again on some other pretext. This is why I said it would be a waste of time of this Hon'ble Court to hear this case. Even before the ink had dried on the order of release signed by the Hon'ble Judges, my client was arrested right under the very nose of the court.[1]

Arguments thereafter went on for hours on end. At the first instance, Nambyar pointed out that it was an unmistakably clear principle that an order of detention passed under a law relating to preventive detention could be challenged on the ground that there is a lack of bona fides on the part of the authority exercising the statutory power. In this case, he showed the bench that the government had acted on an assumption that the high court would set Gopalan at liberty on technical grounds, and even before the court had formally pronounced its verdict, the government, without so much as examining whether there existed any fresh grounds for detention, ordered Gopalan's subsequent detention. Having made this order, the government proceeded to communicate it to the superintendent of police, Special Branch, C.I.D., who in his turn issued instructions even before the court's judgment had been pronounced, ordering the assistant commissioner to arrest Gopalan. This meant the police had little choice but to arrest Gopalan immediately on his release, should such an event occur on the back of the high court's verdict.

The intentions, therefore, in Nambyar's view were clear: the government was willing to flout the court's order merely to keep Gopalan in its custody.

The judges were furious and sent for the advocate general, who contended, in response, that Gopalan was a dangerous communist and should he have been set at liberty, on the back of the court's earlier judgment, on what were really technical grounds, the State's security and peace would have been under grave threat. The court, however, was hardly inclined to agree with the government and they berated the advocate general saying, 'The detention order must have been kept ready even before the judgment was pronounced. You must therefore have known about this.' Hot words were exchanged, and the newspapers carried headlines about the action of the state government in seeking to subvert the release order of the high court even before the judgment had been delivered, by keeping ready a second detention order.

When wide publicity was given by the newspapers, the Chief Justice of the Madras High Court received a call from the Chief Justice of India who asked, 'What is happening in your high court? Please see that the matter is closed without any further adverse publicity.' The then Chief Justice Rajamannar sent for the concerned parties, i.e. the presiding judge and the advocate general and told them that they had to settle the matter. Therefore, he advised the advocate general to appear the next morning in court as soon as it assembled and to say that he was sorry about what happened. The presiding judge was to reciprocate by saying in his turn that he too was sorry about the exchange of words. The next morning, the advocate general, in accordance with the promise he had made to the Chief Justice of Madras, apologized to the Bench, and the presiding judge nodded in acceptance of the apology and said nothing more. The advocate general was stunned but there was nothing that he could do about it. All that he could do was hide the anguish and humiliation of having to hold himself out as the wrongdoer. M.K. Nambyar, who perhaps was the *causa causans* of all this conflict, could do nothing, though he had tremendous respect for the then advocate general of Madras.

A.K. Gopalan, of course, was released from custody after having made history for the second time. 'It must be observed, as I observed during the course of the arguments, that this court is not concerned with persons or personalities and has to administer justice according to law without consideration of the character of the person who invokes our jurisdiction and if he is entitled to his liberty under the law, it should not be denied to him on a consideration of expediency,' wrote Justice Satyanarayana Rao. 'The Judiciary is, after all, another limb of the same Government and it is as much the duty of the executive as that of anybody else, to maintain the dignity of this court and to see that its prestige is not lowered in the eyes of the public.'[2]

Justice Raghava Rao, who wrote a separate opinion, was even more damning in his assessment. He found particular merit in Nambyar's argument that the power, under the Constitution, to issue a writ of habeas corpus conferred upon the high court as well as upon the Supreme Court is something so absolutely sacrosanct that no legislation could prejudicially affect it, nor could the executive seek shelter of a piece of legislation prejudicially affecting it.

His conclusion was majestic, serving, as it did, as a glorious vindication of Nambyar's arguments. 'I cannot help recalling to my mind Lord Mansfield's famous judgment reversing the outlawry of Wilkes in 1768,' wrote Justice Raghava Rao. 'As that noble and learned Lord there did, so may we not here, from the responsible seats which we have been called upon to fill, and what is more, to fulfil, by virtue of our appointments, proclaim in solemn tones from this sacred shrine of justice. The Constitution does not allow reasons of State to influence our judgment, "*Fiat Justitia ruat caelum.*"'[3] (Let justice be done though the heavens fall.)

In many ways, this judgment of the Madras High Court could be seen as embodying Nambyar's more general philosophy of good democratic governance: that the rule of law was sacrosanct and a failure to abide by its diktats was incurable, even in the face of what the State might regard as exceptional circumstances.

* * *

Months before Nambyar took up Gopalan's cause for the second time in the Madras High Court, he had argued, in the court's hallowed Hall No.1, before a full bench comprising the Chief Justice P.V. Rajamannar, Justices Satyanarayana Rao and Viswanatha Sastri, a case of equally important constitutional purport. This was a matter of particular personal importance to V.G. Row, as it concerned the ban imposed by the State of Madras on the People's Education Society. The body, in which Row served as general secretary, had been registered in November 1947, months after Independence, and had as its objects: (a) to encourage, promote, diffuse and popularize useful knowledge in all sciences and more especially social science; (b) to encourage, promote, diffuse and popularize political education among people; (c) to encourage, promote and popularize the study and understanding of all social and political problems and bring about social and political reforms; and (d) to promote, encourage and popularize art, literature and drama.

Though these purposes appeared benign, on 10 March 1950, the Government of Madras issued an order, G.O. No. Ms. 1517 Public (General) Department, declaring under Section 16, Criminal Law Amendment Act, 1908, the People's Education Society as an unlawful association.

In court, the government filed an affidavit supporting its order and asserted that the society was, in reality, a propaganda organization of the Madras branch of the Communist Party and was formed by the leading communists of Madras, its first secretary being M.R. Venkataraman, who was also the secretary of the Madras Committee of the Communist Party of India (CPI). The government claimed, accordingly, that the funds collected by the People's Education Society were being funnelled to the CPI and were being put to spurious use.

Interestingly, although V.G. Row had approached the high court in April 1950, his petition was ultimately heard and decided in September that year, a few months after the Supreme Court had delivered its verdict in the *A.K. Gopalan* case. Row's case, therefore, had to be decided in the backdrop of an amendment made by the Government of Madras to the Indian Criminal Law Amendment Act, 1908, a move intended at overcoming some of the effects of the judgment in *Gopalan*. An 'unlawful association' was now defined in Section 15(2), among other things, as one 'which has been declared by the State Govt. by notification in the Official Gazette to be unlawful on the ground that such association (i) constitutes a danger to the public peace, or (ii) has interfered or interferes with the maintenance of public order or has such interference for its object, or (iii) has interfered or interferes with the administration of the law or has such interference for its object.'

Further, the amendment mandated that a notification issued under Section 15 declaring an association to be unlawful should specify the ground on which it was issued, the reasons for its issue and any other particulars that had a bearing on why it was necessary. The notification, the amendment said, must also fix a reasonable period for the association's members to present a representation to the state government objecting to the declaration. These objections were to be considered by an advisory board that had the power to direct the government to cancel the declaration.

Since the amendments had come into force by the time Row's case was taken up for arguments, Nambyar predicated his arguments on different grounds, and among others that in any event the amending legislation violated Articles 14 and 19 of the Constitution and, hence, had to be struck down. This argument was critical to understanding the relationship between the State and its citizens, and it remains relevant to date.

Article 14 states, 'The State shall not deny to any person equality before the law or the equal protection of the laws within the territory of India.'

According to Nambyar, the law defining and criminalizing unlawful associations breached both the guarantee of equality before the law and the equal protection of the laws. In Nambyar's argument, while a guarantee of due process flowed from Articles 19 and 21, the specific guarantee of equality in Article 14 must neither be underestimated nor rendered nugatory. The article demanded, in his belief, that all legislation treat persons equally both in the privileges they conferred and in the liabilities that they imposed. The Criminal Law Amendment Act, according to him, failed to do this.

Nambyar contended that the law made unreasonable and undesirable classifications and distinctions between one kind of unlawful association and another. He drew a contradistinction between Sections 120-A, 120-B, 141 and 151 of the Indian Penal Code, all of which dealt with associations of persons whose objects and purposes were heinous and that while in those cases the accused had a right to be tried in accordance with the ordinary laws of criminal procedure, and the right to engage counsel, cross-examine witnesses, lead rebutting evidence and address arguments in open court, those rights were denied to persons whose associations were declared unlawful by way of a mere declaration under the Criminal Law Amendment. This distinction drawn between the two statutes, Nambyar asserted, was tantamount to both a denial of equality before the law and the equal protection of the laws.

One must remember that this was September 1950—barely a few months after the Indian Constitution had been adopted and India's Supreme Court had hitherto not had an opportunity to expound its jurisprudence on Article 14. In making an argument predicated on equality, Nambyar, therefore, had to look for support for his propositions from somewhere beyond Indian jurisprudence. Much as he had done in *Gopalan's* case, Nambyar relied primarily on American case law, citing decisions such as *Barbier v. Connelly*,

113 US 27 (1885), *Yick Wo v. Hopkins*, 118 US 356 (1886) and *Smyth v. Ames*, 169 US 466 (1898). The citations rolled off his tongue, as a marker of the supreme, and often original, research that he did. Using these cases, Nambyar argued, as Justice Viswanatha Sastri recounts, that the phrase 'equal protection of the laws' necessarily involved and implied, one, an exclusion of arbitrariness, two, ensuring just access to courts, and three, freedom from deprivation of personal liberty or property except as the result of a conviction by the ordinary courts of the land.

The argument, as we can see, was far ahead of its time in India. The idea that arbitrary state action could militate against a guarantee of equality didn't subsume the country's constitutional jurisprudence until much later. Even today, forfeiture of property in the absence of due process is condoned; it isn't seen as a violation of the equal protection clause. Instead, our courts have tended to compartmentalize these issues into narrow positivist confines that have had the effect of gravely prejudicing citizens' civil liberties. Nambyar realized very early that the courts had to fashion a form of ethical thinking that would place liberty and freedom above the coercive influences of the State.

That a legislation that is arbitrary, in and of itself, or which promotes arbitrary executive action could be in violation of Article 14 wasn't thought, at the time, as plausible. In that sense, Nambyar's arguments served as a precursor to a doctrine of equality that the Supreme Court would come to accept in the years to come, and which would become an almost self-evident proposition in Indian Constitutional Law. But, in 1950, an argument predicated purely on arbitrary state power as constituting a violation of the right to equality was far too ahead of its time and was rejected by the Madras High Court.

6

Piercing the Dark Shadows of Preventive Detention: *S. Krishnan v. The State of Madras*

The reaction to the Supreme Court's judgment in *Gopalan* among the intelligentsia of the time was somewhat curious and divided. In Granville Austin's words, both the Act under question and the Supreme Court's ruling on it 'aroused apprehensions'. The *Times of India*, for instance, was concerned by the 'notes of hesitancy' in the opinions that upheld the Act; later, in an editorial on 31 May 1950, the newspaper lamented the absence of unanimity in the court's verdict, which, according to it, not only detracted from the court's authority but also caused a sense of 'bewilderment and consternation in the public mind'. Shortly before the verdict in *Gopalan* had been rendered, Homi Modi, the then governor of Uttar Pradesh, had written to President Rajendra Prasad, expressing his contempt for the legislation and the manner of the orders passed under it: together the law and its application had the effect, he said, quoting from Justice Sen of the Calcutta High Court, of converting the judiciary into 'a legislature with limited powers' and the executive into 'a judiciary whose decisions were to be final'. Modi also deplored the 'frame of mind', that pervaded the nation at the time, a mindset of repression that, he believed, simply militated against the Constitution's aims and ambitions.[1]

The *Statesman* was more guarded in its view on the Preventive Detention Act, 1950 and its execution; the public, it said, was likely in support of the statute, but the government, it warned, ought to be careful in not using the law 'merely to promote the convenience of officials'[2]. The *Hindustan Times* was, however, more expansive in its support of the legislation and the court's verdict in *Gopalan*. In the meantime, throughout India, based on the decision in *Gopalan*, a slew of habeas corpus petitions, challenging orders of detention made under various legislations, were heard by the high courts. One of those who filed such a petition was Mohan Kumaramangalam, who was arrested on 24 June 1950 by police at Bombay (present-day Mumbai) where he and his wife had been invited to stay for a day. Thereafter, despite his wife having filed a writ petition in the Bombay High Court, Kumaramangalam was transferred to the State of Madras, for detention at the Central Jail, Vellore. This came after a telegram was sent from Bombay to Madras:

> Secret. No. S. C. II/991-I. Shri Surendra Mohan Kumaramangalam, top-ranking communist of Madras, has been arrested and detained by Bombay Police. Arrest was effected mainly because he was wanted by Madras Police for detention. There is not much specific material to form basis of grounds to sustain his detention in Bombay. Bombay Government, therefore, propose to transfer him to Madras and solicits Madras Government's consent under Section 2(1) of Transfer of Detained Persons Act, 1949. Intimation of consent and also name and place of jail in Madras to which Shri Kumaramangalam should be transferred may please be sent by wire.[3]

On 7 July, the chief secretary to the Government of Madras, in turn, sent a telegram to the Government of Bombay communicating the Madras government's consent to have Kumaramangalam transferred to its state. After this order was effectuated and after Kumaramangalam had been transferred to Vellore Jail, the commissioner of police, Bombay, cancelled the order of detention. However, despite this order having being communicated to the jail authorities in Vellore, Kumaramangalam remained lodged in prison.

Thereafter, on 12 July, Kumaramangalam was served with a fresh order of detention that had purportedly been issued on 18 April by the commissioner of police, Madras, in the exercise of the powers conferred on him under the 1950 Act that had largely been upheld in the *Gopalan* case. Against this order of detention, Kumaramangalam made an application to the Madras High Court for the issuance of a writ of habeas corpus, directing the Madras government to produce him before this court and set him at liberty.

Before a bench of the Madras High Court comprising Justices P. Govinda Menon and Basheer Ahmed Sayeed, it was Nambyar who pleaded Kumaramangalam's case. He made several salient arguments, pointing out that it was not open to the Bombay police to pass an order under the Preventive Detention Act, 1950, detaining a person who was residing outside Bombay. To make this argument, Nambyar, as was often his wont, relied on decided cases from countries abroad. He argued that whatever might have been the structure of the Government of India and the provinces before the coming into existence of the independent Republic of India, from 26 January 1950 onwards there could be little doubt that the territory of India consisted of a union of autonomous constituent states. The powers between these states, he claimed, were tautly divided. He invited the court's attention to similarly organized states in Canada and Australia, and, in particular, to the decisions of the courts in *Royal Bank of Canada v. Rex*, and *Merchant Service Guild of Australasia v. Commonwealth Steamship Owners Association*. Even in the United States, Nambyar pointed out, the conditions were similar, something that was clearly evident from Willoughby's textbook on the Constitution of the United States of America. The State of Bombay, he therefore claimed, could not for the purpose of the Preventive Detention Act, 1950, pass orders detaining a person found within its territory for his activities outside that state or direct that such a person be interned outside the State of Bombay.

The court agreed with Nambyar. 'It seems to us, therefore, that when the Commissioner of Police, Bombay, arrested the petitioner as he was wanted by the Madras Police for detention,' the judgment said, 'the arrest was illegal, and the petitioner's detention was also illegal.'[4]

But Nambyar's success was nonetheless on narrow technical grounds. The court also held that 'Had it been a case where as a result of the order of release issued by the Government of Bombay, the petitioner had been released and re-arrested in pursuance to an order of detention passed by the Government, we would not have held that such an order of detention is illegal because on the materials placed before us it seems to us that the grounds of detention afford sufficient justification for the action of the Government of Madras.'[5]

This statement from the Madras High Court summed up the Preventive Detention Act. The Supreme Court, in upholding the statute in *Gopalan*, had clearly given its imprimatur to a draconian legislation. It did not matter that Kumaramangalam had not committed any crime at the time of his detention. This is clear from the judgment's citing, with approval, of possibly the Federal Court's final reported verdict in *Machindar Shivji v. The King*:

> The grounds communicated to the appellant stated, inter alia, that he was working [with] the communist party of India 'which is spreading its doctrine of violence in different parts of the country, fomenting industrial strikes, causing agrarian unrest, rendering life and property insecure, and trying to seize power by violence' and that he was assisting and associating with a named prominent member of the party who had 'gone underground' . . .
>
> It was said that the communist party not having been banned in the Province, the appellant's alleged membership of that party, even if true, could not, in the absence of any allegation of acts or conduct on his part suggesting that he was acting or was likely 'to act in a manner prejudicial to public safety, be regarded as a ground for satisfaction under Section 2 (1) (a). We cannot

accede to this contention. While mere belief in or acceptance of any political ideology may not be a ground for detention under the Act, affiliation to a party which is alleged to be spreading its 'doctrine of violence rendering life and property insecure and trying to seize power by violence' may, in certain circumstances, lead to an inference that the person concerned is likely to act in a manner prejudicial to the public safety, order or tranquillity. The fact that the party had not been outlawed is immaterial, that being a matter of expedience . . .[6]

It was clear, therefore, that there was more than a kernel of truth in the aphoristic observations of Justice Sen, on how the preventive law had converted the judiciary into 'a legislature with limited powers' and the executive into 'a judiciary whose decisions were to be final'. In expressly prohibiting the courts from examining the necessity for these orders of detention and leaving them purely in the hands of the executive's subjective satisfaction, the law certainly militated against widely accepted notions of due process. As David Bayley, an American law professor, observed later, it was 'almost impossible to determine exactly what the authorities consider[ed] either a "violent activity" or a "threat"', since both of these were 'catch-all terms'. What's more, the statements of grounds for detention, which were submitted to all the detenus, were never made public. Those cases in which the statements containing the grounds of detention came out in public, only served to highlight the arbitrariness inherent in the law. Bayley cited one such instance, where one Asutosh Lahire was arrested in New Delhi and where the following reasons were furnished to him by the government:

You came to Delhi on March 27, 1950, and held a press conference in which you gave a highly exaggerated version of happenings in Bengal and East Bengal. It is understood that since after [sic] the press conference your activities have continued to be of a nature inciting communal passions. It has also come to notice that your activities during your stay in West Bengal had also been of

a communal nature. Your activities in the present atmosphere in
Delhi are likely to create hatred between different communities
which may lead to disturbance of public peace and order.[7]

Yet, supported by the Supreme Court's backing for this law, despite
a background of simmering dissent, Parliament felt emboldened
enough to extend the applicability of the Preventive Detention
Act for another year, by passing legislation on 19 February 1951.
Incidentally, as Granville Austin points out, it was on the day when
the President gave his assent to this new law, on 22 February, that the
Madras High Court released Gopalan, finding his order of detention
to be vague and indefinite and, therefore, illegal. After hearing of
Gopalan's immediate arrest on release by the high court, within a few
feet from the court premises, Nehru is reported to have written to
C. Rajagopalachari, who had become home minister on Vallabhbhai
Patel's death in 1950, that the arrest 'within a few yards of the high
court building gives one a shock . . . [and creates] a good deal of
prejudice against us.'[8]

These comments from Nehru came close on the heels of
Rajagopalachari's words in Parliament ardently supporting an
extension of the Preventive Detention Act. 'Stern and ruthless'
action was needed, Rajagopalachari had said,[9] against 'mischievous
and violent elements'. While conceding that the 'normal principle
of criminal justice' was certainly infringed by the Act, matters of
prevention, he added, did not permit 'the same amount of correctness
in evidence as we can demand when a prosecutor alleges overt acts in
proving an attempt or an abetment of a specific crime.' The violent
elements that Rajagopalachari was referring to here were not only
'communalists and black-marketeers,' but also those like Gopalan,
avowed communists, containing within them a streak of what the
state deemed, 'fanatical' radicalism.

The amending Act, which was brought into force on 22 February
1951, substituted the year '1952' for '1951' in the Preventive
Detention Act, 1950 and extended its operation till 31 March 1952.

As a result of this extension, orders of detention continued against several persons, who were otherwise entitled to be released on the Act's expiry. These persons, including one of the prominent leaders of the Communist Party at the time, S. Krishnan, took the challenge to the Supreme Court. They questioned the constitutional validity of the amending Act, on the ground that it ran counter to the fundamental right guaranteed under Article 22(4), which stipulated that 'No law providing for preventive detention shall authorise the detention of a person for a longer period than three months.' Their lawyer in the Supreme Court was, once again, Nambyar.

* * *

The Indian Supreme Court does not maintain a publicly available record of its proceedings; what we have before us are only the final judgments rendered by the court. While these may contain the basic kernel of the arguments put forward by the counsel, the vigour and precision in a lawyer's arguments are left to our imagination. With Nambyar, however, especially in matters involving a threat to civil liberties, it's easy to envision the passion in his arguments. 'A new Constitution demands a new philosophy of life,' he had written in a paper in the same year that the Supreme Court heard arguments in S. Krishnan's petition.

> Yet it is doubtful whether many of us, lawyers, legislators or judges have fully wrenched ourselves from the fetters of the past and tuned ourselves to the freedom of the present. In an age of legislative supremacy, born of the doctrine of omnipotence of Parliament, no citizen could claim any fundamental right. For the essence of a fundamental right lay in the paramountcy of the right over the Legislature of the land. Nevertheless, though over a year has passed since the promulgation of the new Constitution, the civil servant, the administrator and the Government still function apparently oblivious of the deep changes wrought in the mechanism of Government. Legislative enactments are still passed, rules and

orders made as if the old British regime still continued without the slightest effort to adjust themselves to the new order; and when such Acts or orders end up before the High Court with the issue of a Writ Rule Nisi and a Rule absolute, the offender throws up his hands in despair and blames fundamental rights as the source of all evils in the country.[10]

In pleading Krishnan's case, therefore, Nambyar wasn't merely representing the cause of yet another client. On the contrary, he was making arguments on first principles, on the supremacy of fundamental rights, ideals which he held so near to his heart. To him, as he would read later that year at the Madras State Lawyers' Conference at Calicut, the clauses on preventive detention in the fundamental rights chapter were really an abrogation of due process, a sinister ploy to thwart liberty, to overcome apparent governmental difficulties. 'Detention without trial has been an unavoidable necessity in the stress of war,' he said. And further,

> But detention without trial in times of peace is reminiscent of the Spanish Inquisition and Louis XIV, the Bastille, and the Concentration Camp, Buchenwauld and Siberia. In no civilised country in the world does arbitrary detention obtain as the normal feature of everyday life. And the history of Fascism, Nazism and Communism has necessitated the setting up of a Committee of the U.N.O. to frame a World Charter of Human Rights binding on every State. No amount of fine phrasing can disguise the fact that preventive detention without trial is utterly repugnant to the universal conscience of civilized mankind.[11]

Nambyar, quite naturally, couldn't make his submissions in court by resorting to rhetoric of this kind. He had to tailor his arguments within the confines of the Constitution, whatever may have been the unreasonableness of its contents.

Article 22(4) of the Constitution, for Nambyar, placed a specific limit on the legislative power of Parliament and state legislatures in respect of preventive detention laws, in that no law could authorize the detention of a person for a period longer than three months without the intervention of an advisory board and without obtaining its opinion within three months. Since the amending Act authorized detention for a period longer than three months without the opinion of the advisory board having been obtained within such a period, with respect to persons who had already been detained under the previously subsisting legislation, the amendment, Nambyar alleged, infringed Article 22(4). What is more, the law made by Parliament, in exercise of the powers conferred on it under Article 22(7), fixing a maximum period of one year for detention in certain cases, without obtaining the opinion of the advisory board, had now effectively become a part of the fundamental right conferred under Article 22(4). Sections 9 and 12 of the amended Act, to Nambyar, therefore contravened this fundamental right, since they authorized detention of persons who had been detained under the subsisting legislation for a period longer than one year. Next, Nambyar argued that Parliament had no authority to alter the period of one year, prescribed by it by virtue of the authority given to it under Article 22(7)(b), in a manner that affected the cases of persons who were previously detained under the 1950 Act.

Finally, and perhaps most forcefully, Nambyar told the court, in no uncertain terms, that the Constitution does not envisage detention for an indefinite period and since the amended statute failed to provide for a maximum period of detention, its language and spirit militated against the Constitution in every manner possible.

Attorney General Setalvad's reply was brief. He contended that if the petitioners had been released on 22 February 1951 and re-arrested and detained immediately thereafter under the amended Act, such detention would have been valid and that Parliament had, in its wisdom, merely used a different mode of proceeding with orders of detention. In the alternative, Setalvad also argued that, in any event, the amended provisions could be sustained under Article 22(4)(b), which in *A.K. Gopalan* had been held to be a distinct and independent provision authorizing preventive detention for periods longer than three months in accordance with a parliamentary law under sub-clauses (a) and (b) of Article 22(7). He further argued that when testing the *vires* of legislation, the legislature's intent is immaterial—when a preventive detention law provides for an advisory board, that doesn't necessarily mean that such a law must conform to sub-clause (a) of Article 22(4); it can still be upheld if it fulfils the conditions prescribed in sub-clause (b). The 'and' in sub-clause (b), according to Setalvad, had to be understood in a disjunctive sense.

To support this view, Nambyar cited Lord Cairns's aphoristic observations in *Julius v. Bishop*, a House of Lords judgment from 1880. 'Where a power is deposited with a public officer for the purpose of being used for the benefit of a person, that power ought to be exercised.' Section 11 of the amended Act allowed for indefinite detentions, which was to the obvious disadvantage of a detainee. Where the Constitution enabled a law to set a maximum period, Parliament's refusal to utilize this option, according to Nambyar, rendered Section 11 ultra vires.

A majority of the court, barring Justice Bose who wrote a lucid dissent of some verve and vigour, agreed with the government. It was in Justice Bose's dissenting opinion that Nambyar's attack on the amendments came to bloom. 'I am ploughing a lonely furrow that, fortunately, will not much matter,' wrote Bose. But the brooding spirit of his dissent, to borrow from Justice Charles Evans Hughes's iconic phrasing, remains alive to this day. Justice Bose agreed with Nambyar that Article 22(4) *does* confer a fundamental right to not be detained beyond a certain period. He held that the extent of that period may vary, but the maximum limit is, in the first instance, three months or, alternatively, the period fixed by Parliament under sub-clause (b) of clause (7).

Justice Bose made several subtle yet pivotal observations. He also laid down an approach of interpreting the Constitution, which Nambyar would have doubtless endorsed:

Brush aside for a moment the pettifogging of the law and forget for the nonce all the learned disputations about this and that, and 'and' or 'or', or 'may' and 'must'. Look past the mere verbiage of the words and penetrate deep into the heart and spirit of the Constitution. What sort of State are we intended to be? Have we not here been given a way of life, the right to individual freedom, the utmost the State can confer in that respect consistent with its own safety? Is not the sanctity of the individual recognised and emphasised again and again? Is not our Constitution in violent contrast to those of States where the State is everything and the individual but a slave or a serf to serve the will of those who for the time being wield almost absolute power? I have no doubts on this score. I hold it therefore to be our duty, when there is ambiguity or doubt about the construction of any clause in this chapter on fundamental rights, to resolve it in favour of the freedoms which have been so solemnly stressed . . . Read the provisions which circumscribe the powers of Parliament and prevent it from being supreme. What does it all add up to? How can it be doubted that the stress throughout is on the freedoms conferred and that the limitations placed on them are but regrettable necessities.[12]

Summarizing his opinion, Bose accepted that his was not the only interpretation to the questions at hand. However, he sided with the petitioners' plea and expanded on Nambyar's arguments to the extent that he did for one chief reason. In a matter concerning a fundamental right, when the full possibility and content of the right has been examined and settled, and if the scope for a difference in opinion still persists, 'the interpretation which favours the subject must always be used because the right has been conferred upon him and it is the right which has been made fundamental, not the fetters and limitations with which it may be circumscribed by legislative action.'[13]

Nambyar may not have won this case, but his arguments carried the day, and in Justice Bose's dissent they found an elucidation that Nambyar would have surely hoped would appeal to the intelligence of a future day.

7

The Right to Property and Parliamentary Powers to Abridge the Fundamental Rights: The First, Fourth and Seventeenth Constitutional Amendments

'Now would I give a thousand furlongs of sea for an acre of barren ground', famously cried Gonzalo, in William Shakespeare's *The Tempest*. Though Gonzalo's sudden fondness for land was motivated by what he believed to be his imminent death in a storm at sea, there can be no doubt that the human race has always placed tremendous value in the holding and owning of private property. In 1789, the French National Assembly asserted in its 'Declaration of the Rights of Man and the Citizen' that the purpose behind the existence of any political association was to preserve the 'natural and imprescriptible rights of man.' These rights, it went on, were '. . . liberty, property, security and resistance to oppression.'[1]

In 1984, the German agronomist Theodor Bergmann wrote in the introduction to his book on agrarian relations in India that 'India's modern history is closely and in different ways connected with the battle for ownership and utilization of agricultural land. That seems natural in a country, where the overwhelming majority of the population lives on the land and from farming and the whole internal and export economy is still largely dependent on the production of this sector.'[2] Indeed, in India, the evolution of the right to property constitutes one of the most tumultuous areas of our constitutional history, caused by a heady combination of the historical realities of the land tenure system, followed by the economic decisions of the British Raj, the compulsions and lessons learnt by the Independence movement and perhaps most importantly, the new Supreme Court of India, which was to proceed on a path towards shaping its institutional identity in the Indian polity.

First recognized in pre-Independence times in the Government of India Act, 1935, the right to property became a fundamental right in Part III of the new Constitution of India, then lost its status as a fundamental right and finally emerged in its present form a constitutional right,[3] though not a fundamental one. The trajectory of the right to property is also the one which was most deeply and personally intertwined with M.K. Nambyar's own life, and in many ways Nambyar's personal history and the history of his people brings to bear the major themes and key developments in the journey of the right to property.

Most historians concur that the turbulence around the right to property was caused by the post-Independence government's fervent desire to carry out the arduous task of undoing the economic and social damage of the colonial period. This was a task that the government believed could only be achieved by undertaking a vast exercise of redistribution of wealth and land relations, which necessitated the upending of legal and social arrangements that had existed for centuries. These moves were opposed staunchly by the new Supreme Court of India, which viewed the executive ingress into the arena of property rights to be deeply opposed to notions of individual liberty and to the existing regime of land tenures.

Nambyar's home state of Kerala had its own landlord-tenant system, i.e. the jenmi system. The jenmis had the full proprietary rights in the land and permitted the tillers of the soil to work the land in exchange for a share of the produce. The system was a complex one, but broadly speaking it was as follows: the uppermost castes who were absolute owners of the land and were known as 'jenmis', would generally mortgage their land to an intermediary class of persons, who were known as *kanamkars,* in security for money which would be paid to the jenmi. This money would be the substantial share of the revenue derived from the cultivation of the land. The kanamkars in turn would employ cultivators or *verumpattoms* who were the real tillers of the soil, who received the lowest revenue from the land which they worked. In some cases, too, there were no intermediaries, and the cultivator was in a direct relationship with the jenmi.[4] Much before the coming into force of the Constitution of India, the freedom struggle and even the very idea of India in its modern form took shape, the issue of property rights was the cause of much social foment in the Malabar region. If one were to travel back in time, a century prior to even Nambyar's birth in 1898, one would find the beginning of a period of great unrest in Kerala, centred on the system of land tenures and collection of revenue therefrom. In fact, the Moplah rebellions and the caste-based struggles that occurred in Kerala had much to do with the fervent endeavour of the tenants and tillers of the soil to stake what they believed to be their rightful claim to the fruits of the land which they worked, but which did not belong to them and belonged instead to the landlord classes. It would not be a stretch therefore to imagine that the system into which Nambyar was born, i.e. a landlord family, would in some way impact his thinking on the subject of property rights.

In 1939, a committee was set up to recommend changes to the Malabar Tenancy Act, and by this time, Nambyar, a well-respected and well-known lawyer of the Malabar region was called to give evidence before the committee. Nambyar, a great believer in individual freedoms, was also the son of a wealthy landlord, and what he said before the committee makes for fascinating reading. Unlike many modern-day socialist writers, who have excoriated the unfairness of the jenmi system, Nambyar had a different view and felt that the landlords too had suffered a great deal.[5] Further, on the question of the need to reform the law so as to create a balance between landlord and tenant, Nambyar was even clearer as to where he stood:

> . . . it cannot in fairness be one-sided. It cannot benefit the tenant at the expense of the landlords, or the landlord at the expense of the tenant. Social justice demands that the scales be held even. Nor do I imagine would the Committee countenance any suggestions that would involve the complete expropriation of all vested rights. There may of course be exponents of Marxist views to whom the only legislation that may be attempted is to nationalise all land and give the toiling farmer the full fruits of the sweat of his brow. Possibly such views may be right. But I do not think the Committee at present would be inclined to entertain, much less canvas suggestions that would alter the fundamental frame work of society as at present constituted.

Nambyar, therefore, saw the system of landlord–tenant as essential and fundamental to society as he knew it, and was not of the view that this relationship was one which could be easily upset. Though it was clear that he felt there was an element of unfairness in the lot of the tenant, he was clearly not of the mind that this justified a complete overhaul of the system. In some ways, one can reconcile his view on the right to property easily with his views on personal liberty. For him, the individual was supreme, and the rights of the individual, be they civil rights of life and liberty or the right to property, deserved equal protection. How he reconciled these views with the coming into force of the new Constitution, with its avowedly socialist leaning, carries interesting insights into his personality.

The report of the Malabar Tenancy Committee came to be published in 1940, and a few short years later, India was to achieve independence. The right to property, already protected statutorily in the Land Acquisition Act, 1894, was also placed in Article 299 of the Government of India Act, 1935, which provided for the deprivation of property only subject to the payment of compensation.

Finally, when the draft of the Indian Constitution was being discussed, its provisions on the right to property were among the most hotly debated. As Granville Austin notes in his book *The Indian Constitution: Cornerstone of a Nation*,[6] this debate took place over more than two and a half years, and was arguably more intense than any other issue, except perhaps the discussions over the choice of the country's official languages. The two competing claims that were being debated were, on the one hand, the eagerness of the Constitution makers to create in India a true welfare State, one which could further the country's topmost agenda, i.e. the complete eradication of poverty. This, several prominent members of the Constituent Assembly felt, could only be done inter-alia through a redistribution of wealth, i.e. private property and the abolition of the *zamindari* system. On the other hand was the equally urgent need to ensure that the civil and political liberties of the Indian populace were well and truly protected from any kind of State excess. Both these requirements arose from India's brutal experience with British colonialism, which resulted not only in the decimation of the country's economy, but which had also subjected its people to the brutal whims of an arbitrary and capricious State. The Government, therefore, could not be granted unfettered power to deprive landowners of their private property.

Though M.K. Nambyar's role in the debate on the right to property only came in at a much later point in the history of the Constitutional provision, he was, in a way, the embodiment of these two paradoxical lines of thinking. As his arguments in the preventive detention cases, and indeed in his approach throughout his career, would show, he was a firm believer in the notions of fairness and the importance of human dignity. This aspect of his personality could surely not have countenanced the continued economic suffering of vast swathes of the Indian population. On the other hand, he himself was from a family of landlords and certainly saw significant justification in their side of the argument as well. How Nambyar, as a lawyer, chose ultimately to balance his views became evident in the various arguments that he put forth while dealing with the right to property cases and makes for interesting reading.

Like Nambyar, the Constituent Assembly had its work cut out to balance the scales between the need to redistribute wealth and the rights of the existing landowners. As Austin notes in his other seminal work *Working a Democratic Constitution*, both Rajendra Prasad and Sarvepalli Radhakrishnan agreed on this. The government's aim, President Prasad had said, was 'to end poverty . . . to abolish distinction and exploitation'.[7] The vice-president, Radhakrishnan, had called 'for the removal of all social disabilities . . . of man-made inequalities and injustices and [to] provide for all equality of opportunity.'[8] This thinking, as Austin noted, was best brought out in an op-ed in the *Hindustan Times* by K. Santhanam, who wrote that the meaning of the social revolution that the Constitution was to engineer was to get India 'out of medievalism based on birth, religion, custom and community and reconstruct her social structure on modern foundations of law, individual merit and secular education.'[9]

While there was consensus on the fundamental basis of the proposed social revolution, the means to achieve this was still under debate. The main source of tension surrounded the element of compensation that was to be paid to the zamindars, in exchange for their land. Nehru preferred, as Austin noted, a minimal level of compensation, while Prasad leaned towards the zamindars, who had worked hard to lobby him.[10] The Biharis had concentrated on their statesman Prasad by telling him that to deny them of their lands without paying them a just compensation would be contrary to promises made. Patel wanted compensation to be fair and just, but wanted the matter to remain outside the Constitution, fearing judicial review over every expropriation of land made by the State.[11]

Ultimately, in August 1949, the founders agreed on the compromise—on what would become Article 31 of the Constitution. This provision was made in addition to Article 19(1)(f), which provided to citizens a general freedom to acquire, hold or dispose of property, except when the State made laws imposing reasonable restrictions in public interest. Article 31 additionally buttressed this right by declaring that no person could be deprived of their property except by authority of law. Additionally, clause 2 to Article 31 made it clear that no property could be taken possession of or acquired for public purpose by the State under any law unless such law provided for a just compensation to the landowner.

In hindsight it seems obvious that the provision would immediately be the area of tremendous conflict between the courts and the government, but in the early days of independence, it was clear that the tussle that was soon to be set off was to some extent unanticipated. The founders, at the time at least, were satisfied with what they had made. Even K.M. Munshi, who had initially preferred that India adopts a wider, more liberal right to property clause, was satisfied with the provision. If the legislature lays down genuine principles of compensation, the court would not, he said, 'substitute their own sense of fairness for that of Parliament' and 'they will not judge the adequacy of compensation from the standard of market value; they will not question the judgment of Parliament unless the inadequacy is so gross as to be tantamount to a fraud on the fundamental right to own property.'[12] Prime Minister Nehru was also, as Austin wrote, rather buoyant. 'On a proper construction of the clause,' he informed the Assembly, lawyers had told him that 'normally speaking the judiciary should not and does not come in.'[13]

Nothing, of course, could have been further from the truth. As the scholar Burt Neuborne puts it, 'Unlike the relatively mild challenge posed by efforts to alter the language of the free speech protections of article 19, the issue of property proved quite tumultuous. The repeated collisions between the Supreme Court's protection of fundamental rights of property, guaranteed by articles 31 and parliament's early efforts to pass economic reform legislation, resulted in the first serious challenge to judicial protection of fundamental rights.'[14]

The government, desperate to protect its laws from interference by the courts, thought of various devices to be introduced into the Constitution to exclude judicial review of land reforms legislation.

In its original form, Article 19(1)(f) guaranteed to all citizens a fundamental right to acquire, hold and dispose of property, subject however to reasonable restrictions that may be made by the government in public interest. Article 31, on the other hand, provided that any state acquisition of property can only be made through the enactment of a valid law, to achieve a public purpose and on payment of compensation. According to the zamindars, their property was being expropriated from them without paying them a just compensation, and, further, these laws also did not serve any public purpose, and, therefore, the legislation was liable to be declared unconstitutional. They also argued that the laws unreasonably discriminated between certain classes of landlords and, as a result, also violated the right to equality pledged by Article 14.

The Patna High Court agreed with the zamindars, while the Allahabad and Bhopal High Courts found otherwise. Appeals were filed against each of these judgments, and there were also a number of other petitions filed directly in the Supreme Court challenging many of these laws. Before these cases could be heard, however, the Union government—fearing that these statutes could be upended—resorted to what would in later years become its favourite trick: a constitutional amendment through Article 368.

The First Amendment of the Constitution introduced two new articles and added a new schedule to the document: Article 31A provided that 'no law providing for the acquisition by the state of any estate or of any rights therein or for the extinguishment or modification of any such rights' would be deemed void on the ground that it abrogates or abridges any of the fundamental rights. Accordingly, in one fell swoop, as Nambyar would put it, all fundamental rights became unavailable to zamindars. In addition, Article 31B was also introduced. This provided that no provision of any law in the newly introduced Ninth Schedule could be challenged on the ground that it abrogated or abridged any of the fundamental rights. Into this Ninth Schedule, the amendment placed some thirteen different laws, including the Bihar Land Reform Act, which the Patna High Court had struck down.

Bihar's zamindars, from whom land had been taken away through the Bihar Land Reform Act, challenged the validity of the First Amendment of the Constitution in the Supreme Court, in *Sri Sankari Prasad Singh Deo v. Union of India*. The challenge was made on various grounds, but the court was unmoved. Justice Patanjali Sastry, who wrote the judgment on behalf of himself, Chief Justice Kania and Justices Mukherjea, Das and Chandrasekhara Aiyar, held that a constitutional amendment was not law within the meaning of Article 13(2) and therefore fundamental rights were not outside the scope of the amending power. However, the court did clarify that whenever government acquired property, it ought to pay a full and just compensation to the landowner. Although Article 31 of the Indian Constitution used the word 'compensation' and not 'just compensation' like its American counterpart, the court found that the word 'compensation' envisaged the payment of the fair equivalent in money value of the property taken. The result was that any deprivation in property by the government was liable to be paid for in full money value.

The government's response to the Supreme Court's judgment in *Sankari Prasad* was typical; it brought out an amending law: the Constitution's Fourth Amendment, substituting Article 31 with new language. This amendment brought about two significant changes: one, it declared that mere deprivation of property would not constitute an acquisition of property unless the ownership of the property was transferred to the State or a corporation owned by the State; and two, it declared that no law or acquisition could be challenged on the ground that compensation provided by the law was inadequate. What this meant was that the government could acquire private property on payment of even a meagre sum of money, say, even 1 per cent of its value in the market.

The impact of these amendments was felt acutely in the south of India as well. The Fourth Amendment to the Constitution of India caused significant consternation among the landholding classes of Kerala society. As Nambyar observed in his talk at the Bangalore conference,[15] when this Fourth Amendment Bill was before the select committee of Parliament, proceedings were already afoot at the Madras High Court to challenge the validity of the Malabar Tenancy Act on the ground that the legislation infringed Articles 14, 19 and 31. Although there was no reference at all to jenmam property in Malabar or Kerala within the Fourth Amendment Bill, there were deep concerns among those in power that if the challenge before the Madras High Court failed, the petitioners might approach the Supreme Court. Overnight, therefore, in the *explanation* to the word 'estate' in the Fourth Amendment, a reference was made to jenmam properties in the states of Madras and Travancore–Cochin. As a result, when the Fourth Amendment emerged, jenmam property had become an estate, thus placing it beyond review by the courts of the abolition of jenmam rights.

* * *

On 27 April 1955, the Fourth Amendment to the Constitution officially came into force. The amendment was being made on account of the Supreme Court's various interventions. The deprivation of property referred to in clause (1) of Article 31, the government believed, was to be construed in the widest possible sense, in a manner that would include any curtailment of a right to property. It was believed that the Supreme Court's judgments had made it compulsory to pay compensation under clause 2 to Article 31 even when the right to property was merely restricted by a regulatory provision of law without such restriction being accompanied by an acquisition or actually taking possession of that or any other property right by the State. It was, therefore, considered necessary to make clear the ambit of the State's power of compulsory acquisition and requisitioning of private property, and distinguish this power from cases where the operation of regulatory or prohibitory laws of the State results in mere 'deprivation of property'.

Under the new regime, therefore, any person could be deprived of his or her property if a law was enacted for the purpose. On the other hand, if the government were to acquire a person's land, although the person was to be compensated for such acquisition, the government was under no obligation to pay the owner an amount equivalent to the market value of the land. Article 19(5), which provided to citizens the right to acquire, hold and dispose of property still stood, but, as Nambyar put it, the possession of property now 'lay entirely at the will and mercy of the Government'.[16] So long as the government enacted a law, and provided for compensation—any amount, howsoever feeble—the owner had no remedy.

No doubt, even after the Fourth Amendment, the Constitution continued to insist that land could be taken only for a 'public purpose'. But, once again, as Nambyar was keen to point out, the words 'public purpose' partook a rather elastic connotation. Whatever was deemed by the State to advance the general interests of the community at large was construed as constituting public purpose. For example, the acquisition of land for a cooperative society for the construction of houses for the society's members was deemed to be a public purpose, even though both the direct and indirect beneficiaries of such an acquisition was only the society's members and not the general public. Acquisition of lands for a company that manufactured refrigerators, as Nambyar wrote, was also deemed to constitute a public purpose.[17] The lines, he said, between what was public and what was private, in a welfare state, were always very thin—welfare of even one citizen may well be termed as the welfare of the State. And in Madras, he wrote, there was a housing scheme under which land was compulsorily acquired to provide for dwelling houses. Therefore, the words 'public purpose' scarcely served as a check against arbitrary acquisition.[18]

Nambyar was of the view that despite its evident inequities, public opinion was somehow not alive to the dangers of the Fourth Amendment, until its provisions began to influence legislation across the country. The definition of the word 'estate' was now so wide that land included not only those belonging to the rich zamindars, jagirs and inams, but also included every species of landed property that could be called 'estate' by law. For example, Nambyar pointed out, in the state of Bombay, every yard of land constituted an estate. And soon almost all state governments enacted ceiling legislation, and under the guise of agrarian reform, lands of citizens in excess of an arbitrarily fixed limit were being wrested away and were being distributed to the landless and occasionally to others too, in return for little or no compensation.

For years, the middle classes had thought of land as an immovable investment. But now, in an instant, the most immovable of assets was made eminently movable. Petitions filed in the courts were of no avail. The bar contained in Article 31A, as introduced through the Fourth Amendment, served as an unassailable shield against challenges made to the legislation under Articles 14, 19 and 31.

Every political party in power at the time, Nambyar wrote, took advantage of the newly amended Article 31. The colonial-era Land Acquisition Act of 1894 was amended by many states, making the law especially draconian, denying the citizens compensation equivalent to the market value of the land that was being acquired, much less a solatium on the amount. The bar imposed by Article 31A meant that none of the ceiling legislation could be properly challenged. Between 1955 and 1964, the court interpreted the term 'estate' expansively, and upheld a series of legislation that sought to invalidate intermediary rights. For example, in *Atma Ram v. The State of Punjab*,[19] a 1959 judgment, the court held that the expression 'rights' in an estate encompassed within its ambit not merely horizontal divisions, but also vertical divisions, and included, therefore, not only the rights hitherto enjoyed by proprietors and sub-proprietors, but also lower-grade tenants, like *ryots* or under-ryots.[20]

This was the prevailing set of circumstances under which the Kerala Agrarian Relations Act was enacted in 1960. It was precisely fearing legislation of this kind that P.P. Ananthanarayana Aiyer had thought it fit to petition Prime Minister Nehru through a letter dated 31 October 1958. Aiyer, who had retired as a professor after a stint at the University of Rangoon and a short service with the Burmese government, had returned to his native village in Kerala to take up agriculture. 'It may be somewhat odd,' he wrote in his letter to Nehru, 'that a retired College Professor should turn a farmer—but I can claim to have made good.' Owning a small parcel of land, Aiyer rented out portions to small agricultural labourers, and his technique, he believed, not only helped him in sustaining himself but also improved the larger project of agriculture in the country. The landlord, Aiyer believed, had been wrongly portrayed 'as the one class responsible for the ills of the land.' Aiyer believed that a declaration of support from Nehru to landowners such as himself would 'deliver confidence and strength to the large farming community that will reflect in increased agricultural production in the land. The landowners and agricultural associations [will] then launch on their own a drive for the cent per cent increase in agricultural produce that we all look forward to.'[21]

In 1961, at the peak of the ongoing struggle between the executive, legislature and the judiciary over the right to property, the state of Kerala passed the Kerala Agrarian Reforms Act, whose primary aim was to impose a ceiling on estate lands held under the *ryotwari* system, reduce the compensation payable on acquisition of such land and thereafter 'assign the land to the cultivating tenants or to the landless or to those with small amounts of land.'[22]

At the time of the enactment, the most widely prevalent system of landholding in many parts of the state of Kerala was the ryotwari settlement. Under this system, the holders of ryotwari *pattas* (or lease deeds) held land on lease from the government, subject to the payment of land revenue, as opposed to the other common Kerala land tenure system—i.e. the jenmi system, where the jenmis were the owners of the land (discussed earlier in this book). The leases were usually of thirty years and it was open to the leaseholder or ryotwari *pattadar* to sell, mortgage or gift the land to another person, with the further transferee becoming liable to pay the land revenue. The only condition for holding of the lease was the regular payment of the land revenue.

Ryotwari pattadars in turn gave sub-leases to several persons who lived and worked on the land. The lessee of a ryotwari pattadar had only those rights conferred under the sub-lease and was 'a sub-tenant at-will liable to ejectment at the end of each year.'[23] Thus, under the prevailing system, the ryotwari pattadar was virtually a landlord, and the actual tillers of the soil had limited rights on the land that they worked. It was this seemingly iniquitous system that the Kerala Agrarian Reforms Act sought to do away with.

The constitutional validity of the Kerala Agrarian Reforms Act, 1961, was challenged swiftly by the ryotwari pattadars of areca nut and pepper plantations in the erstwhile South Canara district in the case of *Karimbil Kunhikoman v. The State of Kerala.*[24]

At the time when the case was argued in the Supreme Court, Article 31A had already been brought into the Constitution and provided that certain laws described therein, which provided for the compulsory acquisition of land, could not be challenged for having violated fundamental rights. Further, certain laws that provided for the compulsory acquisition of estate lands were immune from challenge on the anvil of certain fundamental rights. The question, therefore, was whether the Kerala Agrarian Reforms Act, 1961, was one such law. For if the landowners could demonstrate that the Act did not fall under Article 31A, the Act could be subjected to scrutiny for violating fundamental rights such as the right to equality and the right to property.

The two petitioners were Purushothaman Nambudiri and Karimbil Kunhikoman, both of whom were represented in court by Nambyar. The petitioners were from a region in Kerala, which was originally in the South Canara district of the state of Madras. The area came to be a part of the state of Kerala after the States Reorganisation Act of 1956. Specifically, their lands were located in the Hosdurg and Kasaragod taluks. The petitioners held large areas of land, a major part of which was held by them as ryotwari pattadars of Madras under the Board's Standing Orders of that state. Nambyar incidentally was himself born and raised in the Kasaragod taluk, and his arguments in the case were likely fuelled both by professional integrity and his own personal ideological proclivity.

In these lands owned by them, the petitioners, as the court observed in its eventual judgment, operated areca, pepper and rubber plantations. Nambyar attacked the law on several fronts. One, the bill which had become an Act, he said, had lapsed before it was assented to by the President, since the legislative assembly that had introduced the Bill had dissolved. Two, the law was a piece of colourable legislation, in that it was beyond the scope of the state government's powers. Three, and this is critical, the properties of the petitioners who were ryotwari pattadars were not estates within the meaning of Article 31A of the Constitution, and therefore the law was not immunized by the bar imposed through the Fourth Amendment. Four, the law exempted plantations of tea, coffee, rubber and cardamom from certain provisions, but a similar exemption had not been granted to areca and pepper plantations and was therefore discriminatory and in violation of the equal protection clause. Five, the manner in which the ceiling had been fixed by the law was arbitrary and discriminatory. And six, the compensation payable under the Act was reduced progressively in proportion to the extent of landowning, and, therefore, violated the equal protection clause.

On three primary grounds, the court agreed with Nambyar. It ruled that in exempting coffee, tea, rubber and cardamom plantations alone, without sufficient cause and basis, the law offended the guarantee of equality contained in Article 14 of the Constitution. What's more, fixing unequal amounts of compensation based on the extent of landowning, the court believed, was unjust and indefensible. 'The only thing we can see is that because a person is possibly richer he must be paid less for the same type of land while a person who is poorer must be paid more,' wrote Justice Wanchoo. According to him:

> This kind of discrimination in the payment of compensation cannot in our opinion be possibly justified on the objects and purposes of the Act. The object and purpose of the Act, as we have already said, is to grant rights to cultivating tenants so that they may improve their lands resulting in larger production to the benefit of the national economy. Secondly, the object of the Act is to provide land for the landless and to those who may have little land by taking excess land from those who have large tracts of lands so that peasant proprietorship may increase with consequent increase in production due to greater interest of the cultivator in the soil. But these objects have no rational relation which would justify the making of different cuts from the purchase price or the market value for the purpose of giving compensation to those whose interests are being acquired under the Act.[25]

Finally, a ryot, as Nambyar had argued, also possessed the right to sell, mortgage, gift or lease the land in his place for revenue. Further, the lessee of a ryotwari pattadar had no rights other than those conferred under the lease and was generally a sub-tenant at-will liable to ejectment at the end of each year. And most significantly, although a ryotwari pattadar was virtually like a proprietor and had many of the advantages of such a proprietor, he could still relinquish or abandon his land in favour of the government. Therefore, the word 'estate', the court held, could not include within its meaning ryot land and the Act could not be used to acquire lands belonging to the petitioners.

Much as the argument on the status of ryotwari pattadars proved hugely influential, there perhaps wasn't sufficient basis for it given the actual workings of such landowners. But the ultimate decision, shaped by the ingenuity of Nambyar's contention, struck a dagger blow to the government's plans.

From his later writings, it was clear that M.K. Nambyar felt that the object of the Act was to not only take away the landlord's land and give it to the tenant, but also to take away land from those who have holdings beyond an arbitrarily fixed ceiling and give those lands away to others. This, the law sought to achieve through, what he described as, 'several shifts and contrivances'. The statute fixed a specified date on which the right, title and interest of the landlord over his land would cease and vest in the government, only for the government to thereafter transfer the property to the tenant. Similarly, on an appointed day, any land held over and above the ceiling fixed would vest with the government, for the purposes of assignment to others. This, Nambyar warned, was nothing but a thinly veiled device to provide the legislative process with a façade of sanctity. In reality, he saw the law as institutionalizing the naked deprivation of a citizen's property. He also saw the law as disregarding the individual as a unit for fixing the limit of the ceiling. While it could well be granted that a person should forgo the freedom to remain joint to effectuate the Act, he didn't quite see how the shares of each person could be adjusted for the purposes of giving effect to the arbitrarily fixed ceiling.[26]

In court, however, his arguments were as clinical as they were persuasive, without ideological flourish and the Supreme Court accepted them. The Court accepted his submissions and took the view that since the Act of 1908 was an existing law dealing with landlord tenures of Madras, the word 'estate' could only have the meaning assigned to it by that Act. Once it held that the word 'estate' could not include ryotwari land in South Canara, the Kerala Agrarian Reforms Act, 1961, could not be said to be a law protected under

Article 31A, and therefore was open to being tested for violating fundamental rights. The Court further observed:[27]

> Considering, however, that the Act of 1908 was in force all over the State of Madras but did not apply to lands held on ryotwari settlement and contained a definition of the word 'estate' which was also applicable throughout the State of Madras except the areas indicated above, it is clear that in the existing law relating to land-tenures the word 'estate' did not include the lands of ryotwari pattadars, however valuable might be their rights in lands as they eventually came to be recognised.

Once it had held that the law was not protected under Article 31A, the Supreme Court took the next step and accepted Nambyar's further argument that the law inasmuch as it applied only to areca nut and pepper plantations and not to cardamom, rubber and coffee plantation violated the right to equality, and accordingly the law came to be struck down.

The fallout of the judgment was swift, with Parliament wasting no time in enacting the Constitution's Seventeenth Amendment Act, in 1964, and Nambyar was clearly displeased if not anguished by the move.

'Next to life, in the hierarchy of human rights, comes property,' he declared in an address to the Conference of Southern States on the Seventeenth Amendment of the Constitution, in Bangalore. The Statement of Objects and Reasons that accompanied the Seventeenth Amendment to the Constitution of India, provided as follows:[28]

> ... It is, therefore, proposed to amend the definition of 'estate' in article 31A of the Constitution by including therein, lands held under ryotwari settlement and also other lands in respect of which provisions are normally made in land reform enactments. It is further proposed to provide that where any law makes a provision for the acquisition by the State of any estate and where any land comprised therein is held by a person under his personal cultivation, it shall not

be lawful for the State to acquire any such land as is within the ceiling limit applicable to him under any law for the time being in force or any building or structure standing thereon or appurtenant thereto, unless the law relating to the acquisition of such land, building or structure provides for payment of compensation at a rate not less than the market value thereof.

2. It is also proposed to amend the Ninth Schedule by including therein certain State enactments relating to land reform in order to remove any uncertainty or doubt that may arise in regard to their validity.

Thus, the Amendment sought to bring lands held under ryotwari settlement within the fold of the term 'estate', and permit acquisition of such lands as were above the ceiling limit. The Amendment also sought to place the Kerala Agrarian Reforms Act, 1961, which Nambyar had successfully challenged, into the Ninth Schedule of the Constitution, thereby making it immune from any fundamental-rights challenge.

Nambyar firmly believed the proposed amendment at the time, if enacted as law, portended significant damage to the rule of law. The purpose of the address, therefore, was to point out what Nambyar thought were severe deficiencies in the Union government's proposal, deficiencies which hit at one of the cornerstones of liberty. The amendment itself, in Nambyar's belief, was a culmination of a retrograde twelve years in which the working of India's Constitution had been dented by a deep commitment to what he viewed as palpable injustice.

When this proposed amendment was on the anvil, Nambyar fervently wrote and spoke against it. 'What the Bill . . . purports to do is to bring ryotwari lands within the fold of an estate and thus within the bar of Article 31A,' he told the audience at the Conference of the Southern States in Bangalore, on 6 August 1963. 'To call ryotwari an estate is a contradiction in terms. The Bill seeks to secure immunity to all legislative measures relating to land situate anywhere in India from any challenge.'[29]

To say that Nambyar was flabbergasted by the government's measures would be to put it lightly. He simply saw no reason why a citizen, minor or major, married or unmarried, should be deprived of what he holds, so as to find himself without a source of livelihood. He saw the amending Act as securing all the 'vices of a Communist society without any of its virtues—of security of food or of work, or of medical attention.' In disregarding the individual as the unit—something which the Constitution, he believed, was decidedly premised on—the law engineered a grave injustice and an irredeemable injury.

In trying to expound his views on the illegality of these laws, time and again, Nambyar returned to his core belief in the inviolability of fundamental rights. He saw Articles 14, 19 and 31, in particular, as constituting the strongest bulwark of a citizen in the enjoyment of his property. Without these liberties, he believed, a citizen would be exposed to the terrific dangers of absolutism and despotism.

The Seventeenth Amendment not only sought to amend Article 31A to make its bar stronger and more far-reaching, but also sought to include within the Ninth Schedule more than forty state enactments, with a view to removing any 'uncertainty or doubt that may arise in regard to their validity'. As Nambyar was at pains to point out, this legislation was not only immune from the various checks imposed by Articles 14, 19 and 21 but also other fundamental rights including Article 26. In one fell swoop, the Seventeenth Amendment, he pointed out, would remove laws from the peril of attack under any fundamental right. Could there be a scarier proposition? Could there be a greater threat to India's democratic fabric?

'In the Constitution, Articles 14, 19(5) and 31 still continue to exist; but they will not be available against legislative and executive excesses against a citizen's land,' Nambyar cautioned the conference's audience.

Why this should be done, it is not far to seek. Over all the lands in India, the party in power desires to have its strangle-hold for absolute and unquestioned disposition, undeterred by 'Fundamental rights' and unhampered by judicial review. Law is but the handmaiden of policy; and the Legislature is only a machinery to register the policy of the party in power, or, in the ultimate analysis, the will of the few who are in control of the reins.[30]

'Kochunni's case opened a new vista of constitutional interpretation,' wrote Nambyar of the judgment. 'Every fundamental right was equally sacrosanct. A law to be valid should run the gamut of each and every fundamental right.' These lines also embody in many ways Nambyar's larger philosophy, his outlook towards democracy and constitutionalism. To him, 'constitutional pattern' ought not to yield to 'socialistic pattern'. Slogans of socialism, he believed, had to operate within the larger and greater objectives of the Preamble.[31]

Ultimately, Nambyar's vision was guided by a commitment to an array of civil liberties—these included a right to freedom not only over the physical body but also over property. 'If the progress of the country demands a new social order in which all property has to be taken and redistributed,' he wrote, 'the Constitution allows such course provided it could be demonstrated before a Court that it is reasonable, that is in the interests of the general public and that it subserves the common good.' But the Constitution as it was originally drafted, he believed, also demanded that properties acquired should be paid for and not expropriated without compensation. Only then would the laws of acquisition conform to the 'principle of justice which is consecrated in the Preamble and in article 38 of the Directive principles.'[32]

Articles 31A and 31B were framed in his belief with the avowed purpose of eliminating inequality. But he saw taking property without paying adequate compensation as antithetical to this idea. 'The ink on the paper on which the Constitution was written was hardly dry, when those in power began infiltrating alien ideas into the Constitution, contaminating the great objectives consecrated therein,' he wrote. 'The Constitution as originally conceived and framed was not given a fair trial.' And for that faithlessness to the Constitution, he added, 'the country has to pay a terrible price.'[33]

If the First and Fourth Amendments had sought to undermine the basis of the constitutional guarantees of a right to property, the Seventeenth Amendment had sought to altogether eviscerate the chapter on fundamental rights. The consequences, as Nambyar saw it, were plainly apparent: no land law made by the legislature, howsoever harsh, oppressive or unjust, howsoever arbitrary, discriminatory or confiscatory, could ever be righted by a court of law; any injury, howsoever grave, could never be redressed.

The question, then, when the Seventeenth Amendment ultimately came to be enacted was simple: could a constitutional amendment nullify a fundamental right?

In Nambyar's belief, the Constitution's makers had before them several different models of governance, and they quite consciously chose the American model, deciding to improve on it by taking into account India's own cultural and social history. To that end, the Constitution bestowed on an independent judiciary the power to interpret the Constitution and strike down legislative enactments that were repugnant to any of its provisions. The makers, Nambyar wrote, were deeply cognizant of the fact that 'the tyranny of the many is as bad if not worse than the tyranny of an individual'[34] and to that end, certain basic human rights had to necessarily be made inviolable by constitutional diktat. India's constitutional aims were so clear that 'no Constitution in the world has sought to guarantee the freedom of the citizen in language so clear and explicit,'[35] wrote Nambyar.

Ultimately, the question for Indian constitutional lawyers and political theorists thrown up by the tussle over the right to property was whether the fundamental rights, explicitly guaranteed by the Constitution, could be taken away by way of constitutional amendments. Like most other constitutions, India's Constitution too provided for a machinery for amendment. This procedure was found in Article 368. Plainly read, at the time, Article 368 stated that an amendment to the Constitution may be initiated 'only by the introduction of a Bill for the purpose in either House of Parliament'. It further stipulated that such a Bill must be passed by a majority of the total membership of that House and by a majority of not less than two-thirds of the members of that House present and voting, before it is presented to the President for his assent. Further, with respect to certain provisions of the Constitution, apart from Parliament's sanction, the further endorsement of at least one-half of the states through legislative resolutions was made mandatory.

It was clear, therefore, that a specific machinery was put in place to amend the Constitution where Parliament thought it necessary. But could this device be used to render nugatory the guarantee of fundamental rights that the Constitution's makers had considered so essential to India's democratic project? To that end, the ensuing question was whether laws made under Article 368 were, like any other piece of legislation, subject to the rigours of Article 13(2). This clause stipulated that any law made in contravention of the fundamental rights guaranteed in the Constitution shall be void.

Nambyar thought that attempts to avoid the applicability of the fundamental rights were an affront to the rule of law, to the majesty of the original constitutional promises. Almost every time the highest court in the land declared a law invalid, the Government emerged with a constitutional amendment to undo the effects of such a judgment. The executive, wrote Nambyar, appeared to 'tell the Supreme Court "if you dare to strike down any Act, we will strike down your decision"'. He saw the replacement of a fundamental right through a constitutional amendment as bringing the entire Constitution into disrepute, and its 'organs into contempt'. There is, he added, 'for such palpable high-handed disregard of the Organic Law of a State, hardly any parallel'.[36]

And so, it was with the Seventeenth Amendment too. Not only was the bar imposed by Article 31A strengthened by expanding the definition of what constituted an 'estate' (a consequence of the

Supreme Court's judgment in *Karimbil Kunhikoman*), a plethora of state enactments were also placed into the Ninth Schedule immunizing them from challenges under Article 13(2). The effect was evident: the fundamental rights to equality, to freedom of ownership of property, and against dispossession of property, would now be rendered nugatory. Or, as Nambyar put it, the amendment sought to 'secure immunity to all legislative measures relating to land situate anywhere in India from any challenge.' Nambyar found the incorporation device of Article 31B, as Fali S. Nariman wrote in his autobiography *Before Memory Fades*, 'a striking proof of the failure of the Indian Parliament to conform to the Constitution under which it was elected.'[37]

The Seventeenth Amendment was first challenged before the Supreme Court in *Sajjan Singh v. The State of Rajasthan*.[38] Technically, here, the only question before the court was whether the procedure prescribed in the proviso to Article 368 had been followed in enacting the Seventeenth Amendment. But because the question over the correctness of the judgment in *Sankari Prasad* was also urged by certain counsel, the court also briefly looked into whether a constitutional amendment could abrogate a fundamental right. The judgment in *Sajjan Singh* was, however, not unanimous. Two out of the five judges, Justices M. Hidayatullah and J.R. Mudholkar, wrote separate, dissenting opinions.

According to the majority, it was clear from a bare reading of the text of Article 368 that Parliament possessed the power to amend any provision of the Constitution, including those guaranteeing fundamental rights in Part III. 'In our opinion, the expression "amendment" of the Constitution plainly and unambiguously means amendment of all the provisions of the Constitution,' wrote Chief Justice Gajendragadkar. 'It would, we think, be unreasonable to suggest that what Art. 368 provides is only the mechanics of the procedure to be followed in amending the Constitution without indicating which provisions of the Constitution can be amended and which cannot. Such a restrictive construction of the substantive part of Art. 368 would be clearly untenable.' What is more, a constitutional amendment, the majority said, would not constitute a law within the meaning of Article 13(2). Had the framers intended so, 'they would have taken the precaution of making a clear provision in that behalf.'[39]

The dissenting opinions were rather more guarded about the idea that the power conferred under Article 368 was plenary in nature, that there were no limits to Parliament's authority to amend the Constitution. In words that have since come to occupy something of an iconic status, Justice Hidayatullah wrote, 'The Constitution gives so many assurances in Part III that it would be difficult to think that they were the play things of a special majority. To hold this would mean prima facie that the most solemn parts of our Constitution stand on the same footing as any other provision and even on a less firm ground than one on which the articles mentioned in the proviso stand.'[40]

How could it be permissible that an explicit constitutional guarantee be withered away through the simple process of a parliamentary amendment? While Nambyar firmly supposed that certain provisions were beyond the scope of Parliament's amending power he was also deeply conscious that the law on the subject, the precedent laid down by the Supreme Court, was decidedly against his beliefs, at least for the time being.

8

I.C. Golak Nath v. The State of Punjab: Laying the Foundations of the Basic Structure

Round about the same time as the judgment in *Sajjan Singh*, when two dissenting opinions were questioning the basis for Parliament possessing an unlimited power of amendment, Professor Dieter Conrad, a German who was then teaching at the Heidelberg University's South Asia Institute, was delivering a lecture to the law faculty at Banaras Hindu University. Germany's history with Hitler and Nazism had made Conrad acutely aware of the undemocratic predispositions of even democratically elected leaders—that the very processes of a democracy could be used to remove the structures on which the republic stands.

Conrad's lecture was titled 'Implied Limitations of the Amending Power'. In his talk, Conrad warned that the Supreme Court in cases that it had decided until then had perhaps been influenced by the fact that it hadn't yet been confronted with any extreme constitutional amendment. But it was the duty of the jurist, he added, 'to anticipate extreme cases of conflict, and sometimes only extreme tests reveal the true nature of a legal concept.'[1]

To that end, he pondered if Parliament could by a two-thirds majority, as prescribed in Article 368, amend Article 1 of the Constitution and divide India into two states of Tamil Nadu and Hindustan. 'Could a constitutional amendment abolish Article 21, to the effect that forthwith a person could be deprived of his life or personal liberty without authorisation of law? ... Could the amending power be used to abolish the Constitution and reintroduce, let us say, the rule of a Mughal emperor or of the Crown of England?'[2]

The government, in such cases, may well conform to the procedure prescribed in the Constitution; it may well possess the required two-thirds majority needed to pass such an amendment, but did it possess the power to alter what was really the basic structure of the Constitution? In asking these questions, Conrad was borrowing heavily from the German experience. Indeed, Germany's Constitution expressly barred amendments to the provisions concerning the country's federal structure and the 'basic principles' laid down in Articles 1 to 20.

The question, therefore, was very much still alive in the minds of legal practitioners, academics and, as evinced by the dissenting opinions in *Sajjan Singh,* the minds of the judges of the Supreme Court as well. It was certainly still alive in the mind of M.K. Nambyar.

Although the Supreme Court in *Sajjan Singh* had found the Seventeenth Amendment to be validly made, the dissenting judgments of Justices Hidayatullah and Mudholkar had provided landowners with a glimmer of hope; it had opened up an avenue for a fresh challenge. A group of rich landlords from Punjab were willing to stake their chances. They were the son, daughter and granddaughters of a Henry Golak Nath, who had died on 30 July 1953. Henry Golak Nath was the son of Golak Nath Chatterji, who, in historian Granville Austin's recounting, had been disgraced by his Kuleen Brahmin family for having converted to Christianity. Austin recounts that Chatterji had left Bengal in the mid-nineteenth century and had reportedly walked across the whole of north India to Punjab, where he joined up with the Scottish American Presbyterian Mission.

Early Years

M.K. Nambyar (MKN) on the day of h is graduation from the
Kumbakonam Arts College.

Students at Kumbakonam Arts College with their principal, Statham.
MKN wears a tie and is seated third from left, in the first row.

MKN and classmates graduating from the London School
of Economics (LSE).

MKN on his return from London as a barrister.

Following the Return from London

MKN's house in Mangalore where he lived as public prosecutor.

MKN in his Austin convertible with family.

Echikkanom Tharuvaad House.

From right: MKN with his brothers-in-law: K.K. Nambyar, Dr P.C. Nambyar and Dr K.C. Nambyar.

MKN with his family. From left: MKN, Nalini and Kalyani
Amma (seated). Sivan, Venu, Gopi, Ramkumar, Malini and
Mohan (standing).

MKN and his wife, Kalyani, on their foreign tour.

MKN in a jovial mood at the wedding of his junior, Manivannan.

MKN sharing a light moment with V.K. Krishna Menon,
then defence minister.

MKN felicitates Lord and Lady Denning at the Madras
Bar Association.

Law Minister Shanti Bhushan unveiling MKN's photograph at the
Madras Bar Association.

MKN, aged about sixty years, with his wife, Kalyani Amma.

MKN.

Portrait of MKN put up at the office of the Sourashtra Dharma
Paribalana Committee, Kumbakonam.

The family gets together for a photo outside the Chennai House.

In Jalandhar, where Chatterji eventually stationed himself, he became the first Indian in the country to be ordained as a Presbyterian minister. Going on to marry a Kashmiri woman, the couple had several children, and one among the many was Henry Golak Nath. Golak Nath, who had received his divinity degree in 1879 from Princeton Theological Seminary in the United States, on his return took his father's place as a minister. Together with his brother William, Golak Nath acquired some 500 acres of farmland in the region.[3]

But, in 1962, the financial commissioner of the Jalandhar Division held that the petitioners, that is the legal heirs of Henry Golak Nath, held some 418 standard acres and 9-1/4 units above what they were entitled to hold under the Punjab Security of Land Tenures Act X of 1953. But Inder Golak Nath and the others, who by now had inherited only thirty acres, as a result of the law, argued that this finding infringed their right to equality under Article 14 and their right to hold property under Article 19(1)(f). They first went to the Punjab High Court in 1965, but when that failed, they knocked on the doors of the Supreme Court, this time under Article 32, seeking a direction, among other things, that the Constitution (First Amendment) Act 1951, the Constitution (Fourth Amendment) Act, 1955, the Constitution (Seventeenth Amendment) Act, 1964, insofar as these amendments affected their fundamental rights, were unconstitutional and inoperative and for a direction that the Punjab Act of 1953 was void as it violated Articles 14 and 19(1)(f) of the Constitution.

This argument was always going to be a difficult one to sustain. Given the precedent that weighed heavily against the petitioners—the judgments of constitution benches in *Sankari Prasad* and *Sajjan Singh*—Nambyar, Fali Nariman writes, wasn't hopeful of even securing an admission of his petition. He thought there was every chance that the case would be dismissed at its very threshold, that the Supreme Court wouldn't so much as care to look at the deeper arguments assailing the amendment's validity. But to Nambyar's surprise, not only was his petition admitted, it was also referred immediately to a full court of permanent judges serving at the time, a bench of eleven judges. Once the reference was made, Nambyar's confidence soared. He believed it was a matter of destiny, especially since the then Chief Justice, Koka Subba Rao, was of a similar bent of mind.

Nambyar had witnessed the Supreme Court closely during Subba Rao's tenure. As a puisne judge, Subba Rao was a regular dissenter. He had an abiding concern for, and commitment to, fundamental rights. As George Gabdois noted, Subba Rao wrote forty-two sole dissenting opinions, more than any other judge before or since, and invariably every one of them was in support of a private party's claim against a governmental action. So dear was his love for fundamental rights that Chief Justice S.R. Das, during his farewell address in September 1959, jokingly said: 'Then we have Brother Subba Rao who is extremely unhappy because all our fundamental rights are going to the dogs on account of some ill-conceived judgments of his colleagues which require reconsideration.' Although this was a statement made in the lighter vein, it had more than an element of accuracy to it, for Justice Subba Rao genuinely believed that a number of the Supreme Court's judgments in its first decade were regressive.

During arguments, though, as Nariman recounts,[4] although many individual judges made interventions, there were two of them—sitting respectively at the far ends of the bench—who were difficult to read because they scarcely spoke: Justice C.A. Vaidialingam and Justice J.K. Mitter. There was substantial banter among the junior lawyers in court and friendly bets were exchanged on which one of these judges might speak first. But more critically, lawyers arguing in the court were perplexed as to which way these judges might rule. As it happened, it was Justice Mitter who was the first to speak out: 'which page,' he apparently asked a counsel who was reading out from a law report. Justice Vaidialingam, on the other hand, was quiet throughout, not uttering a single word during the course of the whole hearing. Yet, as Nariman writes, Nambyar was confident that Vaidialingam would rule in favour of the petitioners, because he believed the judge shared Subba Rao's larger world view.

Oral hearings in the case stretched for twenty-two working days, something of a record at the time. Although Nambyar was the lead counsel and almost every junior briefed in the case was keen that he commence arguments, R.V.S. Mani, a 'loquacious advocate from Nagpur', in Nariman's telling, refused to yield, and insisted that he argue first, since his petition was apparently the first to be numbered by the court's registry. Mani began, Nariman says, in the following manner: 'My first proposition, My Lords, is . . .' and after each of the judges wrote down his first proposition, he laboured on, 'my second proposition, My Lords, is, . . .' until Justice J.C. Shah lost patience. Throwing his pencil down from the bench, Shah reportedly said, 'No more—you give it to us all in writing.'[5]

But Nambyar would enjoy a longer leash. Before the hearings, he had sought permission from Professor Conrad, through his letter of 20 October 1966, to use the manuscript of his lecture at Banaras Hindu University as part of his presentation before the Supreme Court. In a matter of few days, Conrad acceded to Nambyar's request with the condition that the manuscript be presented to the court in its entirety.

Using Conrad's lecture as his basis, Nambyar made a series of arguments, which find reflection in Subba Rao's ultimate judgment. The arguments had a certain elegance to them, in their simplicity and in their coherence. One, the Constitution, Nambyar told the court, is intended to be permanent and it cannot therefore be amended in a manner that would injure, maim or destroy its basic structure, its indestructible character. Two, the word 'amendment', he added, ought to imply an addition or change within the lines of the original instrument, which will allow the instruments of the State to carry out the Constitution's purposes more efficiently, and it cannot be construed in a manner that would enable Parliament to destroy the document's permanent character. Three, the fundamental rights enlisted in Part III of the Constitution are a part of the Constitution's basic structure and any power to amend can only be used to preserve these rights and not eliminate them. Four, the limitations of the amending power are implied in the terms of Article 368 itself, because it does not use words (at the time) such as 'repeal' or 're-enact', which were used in other parts in the context of mere legislative enactments. Five, speeches delivered in the Constituent Assembly by Jawaharlal Nehru and Dr Ambedkar showcase clearly that it was never the framers' intention to allow Parliament to repeal a fundamental right. That an amendment moved by H.M. Kamath to expressly permit such a power was withdrawn before Article 368 was ultimately adopted, lent further support to this proposition. Six, Part III of the Constitution was a self-contained code and it was flexible enough to meet the changing needs of the country. Seven, while Article 368 provides for the procedure to amend the Constitution, the power itself stems from Articles 245, 246 and 248, which are subject to the rigours of a fundamental rights challenge. Eight, the definition of 'law' in Article 13(2) includes a constitutional amendment. And nine, the Seventeenth Amendment takes away the power of the high courts and therefore ought to have been sanctioned by at least half of the state legislatures.

Subba Rao didn't rule precisely as Nambyar and the other counsel for the petitioners might have wanted him to. But he did hold the Seventeenth Amendment unconstitutional to the extent that it abridged fundamental rights. This was because, in his belief, the power to amend the Constitution stemmed solely from Articles 245, 246 and 248 and therefore even a constitutional amendment was a 'law' amenable to the Constitution's fundamental rights. Yet, the court did not strike down the Seventeenth Amendment, since at the time it was made it was believed, based on the court's earlier judgments, that it was valid to abridge a fundamental right by way of an amendment. To overcome this rather peculiar problem, Subba Rao borrowed the doctrine of prospective overruling from America. Through this he held the Seventeenth Amendment to be valid, but denied to Parliament the power from that date onwards to amend the Constitution in such a manner that would change or alter any of the provisions of Part III.

During the course of the hearings, the then Advocate General for the State of Madras, the charismatic Mohan Kumaramangalam, warned Chief Justice Subba Rao—in what Nariman describes as a somewhat 'intemperate' address—of the 'grave consequences' that would follow if the petitions were allowed. It would, Kumaramangalam said, likely lead to a revolution. At the hearing itself, Subba Rao gently smiled and said nothing. But in his judgment, Subba Rao markedly rebutted these suggestions:

> It was said that if the provisions of the Constitution could not be amended it would lead to revolution. We have not said that the provisions of the Constitution cannot be amended but what we have said is that they cannot be amended so as to take away or abridge the fundamental rights. Nor can we appreciate the argument that all the agrarian reforms which the Parliament in power wants to effectuate cannot be brought about without amending the fundamental rights. It was exactly to prevent this attitude and to protect the rights of the people that the fundamental rights were inserted in the Constitution. If it is the duty of the Parliament to enforce the directive principles, it is equally its duty to enforce them without infringing the fundamental rights. The Constitution-makers thought that it could be done and we also think that the directive principles can reasonably be enforced within the self-regulatory machinery provided by Part III. Indeed both Parts III and IV of the Constitution form an integrated scheme and is elastic enough to respond to the changing needs of the society. The verdict of the Parliament on the scope of the law of social control of fundamental rights is not final, but justiciable. If not so, the whole scheme of the Constitution will break. What we cannot understand is how the enforcement of the provisions of the Constitution can bring about a revolution. History shows that revolutions are brought about not by the majorities but by the minorities and some time by military coups. The existence of an all comprehensive amending power cannot prevent revolutions, if

there is chaos in the country brought about by misrule or abuse of power. On the other hand, such a restrictive power gives stability to the country and prevents it from passing under a totalitarian or dictatorial regime. We cannot obviously base our decision on such hypothetical or extraordinary situations which may be brought about with or without amendments. Indeed, a Constitution is only permanent and not eternal. There is nothing to choose between destruction by amendment or by revolution, the former is brought about by totalitarian rule, which cannot brook constitutional checks and the other by the discontentment brought about by misrule. If either happens, the constitution will be a scrap of paper. Such considerations are out of place in construing the provisions of the Constitution by a court of law.[6]

Once again, in Subba Rao's rousing words, there is more than a hint of Nambyar's basal philosophy. That every fundamental right was equally sacrosanct. That for a law to be valid it should run the gamut of each and every fundamental right. That in furthering the directive principles, the government should not forget that it exists to subserve the common good. That there are certain rights, as Justice Samuel Miller wrote all those years ago, which in every free government must be beyond the control of the State.

Subba Rao's powers of persuasion meant that four other judges on the bench, including his former junior Justice Vaidialingam joined his opinion. But five judges—Justices Wanchoo, Bachawat, Ramaswami, Bhargava and Mitter—dissented and affirmed the principles laid down in *Sankari Prasad* and *Sajjan Singh*, holding that Parliament's power to amend the Constitution was plenary and unlimited. It was left ultimately to Justice Hidayatullah to cast the deciding vote. Hidayatullah, remember, had dissented in *Sajjan Singh* too. In contrast to Subba Rao, he held that although the power to amend the Constitution stemmed from Article 368, that power did not extend to the amendment of a fundamental right. Such a view, he thought, would render Article 13(2) nugatory. An amending statute under Article 368 too was a law, in his belief, under Article 13(2), and therefore while Parliament otherwise enjoyed plenary power to amend the Constitution it could not abridge, contravene or abrogate a fundamental right.

Golak Nath, despite Subba Rao and Hidayatullah's ruling that fundamental rights were beyond the Parliament's power to amend the Constitution, was far from a perfect decision. For all of Subba Rao's intrinsic belief in the power of fundamental rights, his opinion was decidedly flawed, in that he failed to understand (this was perhaps intentional and strategic) that Article 368 provided a constituent power, that constitutional amendments could never be akin to an ordinary parliamentary law. Granville Austin, for example, noted that Subba Rao was unquestionably influenced by Conrad's formulation, which Nambyar presented to the court with customary clarity, but he did not go along with the view for the fear that it might leave open an avenue for Parliament to continue to remove fundamental rights, which it considered to be beyond the scope of the Constitution's purported basic structure. These fears were no doubt scarcely ill-founded, as history has since shown us, but they also mean that his opinion ultimately failed to provide a constitutionally justifiable answer to the question of whether there could be any real and effective checks on Parliament's power.

The judgment in *Golak Nath*, as the scholar Manoj Mate has shown us, received a lukewarm response not only from members of the legal profession but from the press too. The *Indian Express* and the *Hindustan Times* supported Subba Rao's opinion, but *The Hindu* and the *Statesman* were more guarded. The *Statesman* argued that the court's decision had brought in a 'rigidity in the Constitution' (the *Statesman*, New Delhi, 1 March 1967). *The Hindu* argued that 'many will be inclined to argue that the supremacy of parliament in legislating for the needs of a changing society should not be unduly hampered by judicial interpretations of constitutional provisions in terms of a rigid framework. After all, the basic safeguards for citizens in a democracy are the vigilance exercised by a live public opinion and the periodic accountability of ministers and legislators to the electorate.'

Predictably, the decision in *Golak Nath* created ruptures in political circles. Mate's recounting of the events makes for interesting reading. Some five weeks after the judgment, Nath Pai, an MP from the Samyukta Socialist Party (SSP), introduced a bill in Parliament with a view to overturning the decision in *Golak Nath*. Quick on the heels of the bill's introduction, a conference titled 'Fundamental Rights and Constitutional Amendment' under the stewardship of L.M. Singhvi was organized, in which a number of senior lawyers and senior members of the political class participated. At the conference, *Golak Nath* came in for substantial criticism. The former Attorney General M.C. Setalvad, for instance, said that if one were to consider the dissenting opinions delivered in the case, the total weight of opinion in support of Parliament's unlimited power to amend the Constitution was thirteen judges to eight. Senior advocate N.C. Chatterjee bemoaned the fact that the court in *Golak Nath* had simply ignored the vital distinction between ordinary legislative power and Parliament's constituent power.

Ultimately, Golak *Nath's* amendment didn't come to fruition, but Parliament, under Indira Gandhi's prime ministership, did introduce the Twenty-fourth and Twenty-fifth Amendments to the Constitution in a bid to reassert Parliament's sovereignty by negating the impact of *Golak Nath*. Through the former amendment, Parliament granted itself absolute authority to amend the Constitution, including the power to make amendments by way of addition, variation or *repeal* of any provision of the Constitution, including those that guaranteed fundamental rights. Through the latter amendment, the right to property was further curtailed by, among other things, amending Article 31 to ensure that the compensation fixed for expropriation of property was taken out of the scope of judicial review.

Curiously one of those affected by these amendments was Kesavananda Bharati Sripadagalvaru, a senior pontiff and head of the 'Edneer Mutt'—a Hindu institution situated in Edneer, a village in the Kasaragod district of Kerala, incidentally the same district from which Nambyar hailed. But by the time these developments took place, Nambyar was in the autumn of his life and was not well enough to travel to New Delhi to address arguments. Kesavananda Bharati did, however, meet Nambyar, and solicited his advice. Although Nambyar helped settle some of the early pleadings that formed part of a constitutional challenge that would culminate in a decision of shattering proportions, he referred the mutt to Nani Palkhivala who with his characteristic brilliance would lead arguments in the court. At the time when Nambyar settled the petition in March 1970, the Twenty-fourth, Twenty-fifth, Twenty-sixth and Twenty-ninth amendments, which were later made the subject of challenge had not yet been passed, and so Nambyar's inputs were confined to the challenge to the local Kerala Law.

In *Kesavananda*, Nambyar's arguments on implied limitations ultimately found favour with the court, though expertly argued by Nani Palkhivala, who, of course, richly deserves every credit for the judgment, and for having convinced the court to accept the doctrine. The court ruled through the slimmest of 7:6 majorities that the power to amend the Constitution could not be exercised in a manner that damaged the Constitution's basic structure. In the absence of a precedent from any other Commonwealth nation, where an amendment had been subject to the rigours of judicial review, Nambyar, in *Golak Nath*, thought it fit to rely on the German experience, which he believed carried with it a number of important lessons. Were Parliament's powers considered infinite, he argued, the parliamentary executive could be removed, fundamental rights could be abrogated, and, in effect, what was a sovereign democratic republic could be converted into a totalitarian regime. The court in *Golak Nath* didn't quite think it necessary to go this far. But in *Kesavananda*, it was this formulation of Nambyar's that shaped Justice H.R. Khanna's legendary, controlling opinion, which tipped the balance in favour of the petitioners.

- 50 -

37.   The petitioner therefore humbly prays
that this Hon'ble Court may be pleased to-

   a) Declare that the Kerala Land
      Reforms Act, 1963 (Act I of
      1964) as amended by the Kerala
      Land Reforms (Amendment) Act,
      1969 (Act XXXV of 1969) is un-
      constitutional, ultra vires
      and void;

   b) Issue a writ of Mandamus or any
      other appropriate writ, order or
      direction directing the state of
      Kerala to forbear from enforcing
      the provisions of the said Act;
      and

   c) Pass such further or other orders
      as may be deemed just and proper
      in the circumstances of the case.
      AND THE PETITIONERS SHALL AS IN
      DUTY BOUND EVER PRAY.

DRAWN BY:
SHRI N.A. SUBRAMANIAN
ADVOCATE

SETTLED BY:
SHRI M.K. NAMBYAR
SENIOR ADVOCATE SUPREME COURT.

FILED BY:
J.B. DADACHANJI & CO.,
ADVOCATES SUPREME COURT
NEW DELHI.

FILED ON: MARCH 1970.

Extract of the writ petition settled by M.K. Nambyar for His Holiness
Sri Kesavananda Bharti Sripadgalvaru

Justice Khanna conceded that it wasn't possible to subscribe
to everything in Conrad's arguments, but this much, he said, was
true: 'Any amending body organized within the statutory scheme,
howsoever verbally unlimited its power, cannot by its very structure
change the fundamental pillars supporting its Constitutional

authority.' Yet, the limitation, wrote Justice Khanna, wasn't as much implicit from a reading of the Constitution as a whole as it was evident from the very meaning of the word 'amendment'. According to him, what could emerge out of an amendment was only an altered form of the existing Constitution and not an altogether new and radical Constitution.[7]

Khanna's holding, in a nutshell, exemplified what Nambyar had argued so forcefully in *Golak Nath*. As Soli Sorabjee would later write, the stand adopted by Nambyar and the arguments advanced by him, 'apart from reflecting his deep research, study and erudition' were also 'evidence of his farsightedness'. Nambyar always had within him a basic dislike for the powers of majoritarianism. He intuitively believed that allowing Parliament plenary powers to amend the Constitution would lead towards a sure path of totalitarianism. A new constitution, he believed, demanded a new philosophy of life. He intuitively saw the grant of an unlimited amending power as militating against that need for a new philosophy. Unlimited power of any kind, he thought, was anathema to democracy. And, in Conrad's lecture, he found the theoretical backing for his intrinsic beliefs. In *Golak Nath* he was able to apply Conrad's theory to a ready problem, to show the court that how it answers questions over Parliament's powers to amend the Constitution was likely to have a far-reaching impact not merely on the case before it but on the future of India's democracy.

9

The March of the Law: Nambyar, the Constitutional 'Colossus'

Orson Welles, one of the most influential filmmakers of his time, once said, 'There is no biography so interesting as the one in which the biographer is present.' Welles was probably correct. It is but obvious that a biography suffers several disadvantages that an autobiography does not, and in a prolific career that spanned over five decades, there would undoubtedly have been numerous insights and anecdotes that M.K. Nambyar might have shared, had he chosen to tell the story of his own life. Unfortunately, this material is not available to third persons, even to members of his family and for this reason, while Nambyar argued a multitude of hugely significant cases both at the Supreme Court and the various high courts of India, and while some of his important cases have been analysed in the pages of this book, it has not been possible to delve into great detail about many of the others, though they too were extremely important. Be that as it may, no account of M.K. Nambyar's life would be complete without making at least an attempt at giving the reader a sense of his stature, and some notion of the volume and importance of his life's work.

At the height of his career, M.K. Nambyar was one of the most sought-after senior advocates in India. For an idea of scale, one need only consider the fact that there are several hundred reported cases (to say nothing of the cases that went unreported) where he is credited as the arguing counsel. These cases were argued at the Supreme Court of India, and the various high courts, particularly those of Madras, Kerala, Karnataka, Andhra Pradesh, Gujarat, Punjab and Haryana, Allahabad and Calcutta, and do not even include the cases where judgments were not reported, or those that took place before the trial courts. He advanced arguments before at least twenty-one constitution benches of the Supreme Court, two of which were eleven-judge benches. Indeed, M.K. Nambyar in his prime was such a popular choice of lawyer, that a fairly comprehensive textbook on the provisions of the Constitution of India could be published out of his cases alone.

Apart from the landmark cases of *A.K. Gopalan, Golak Nath*, etc., which have been discussed in the preceding pages, Nambyar also argued in the *Privy Purses* case challenging the abolition of privy purses by the Government of India, *Bennett Coleman* challenging the news print control order, on the right to religion conferred by the Constitution on minority Hindu groups in Venkatramana Devaru's case, and numerous other cases on the right to property (*Deep Chand*), administrative law (*Gulapalli Nageshwar Rao, Radheyshyam Khare)*, taxation (*D. Cawasji*), election law, on the powers, privileges and immunities of state legislatures, etc., all of which are considered to be landmarks within the legal profession.

His clients ranged from Chief Minister K. Kamaraj Nadar; Chief Minister M. Karunanidhi; P. Srinivasan, deputy speaker of the Tamil Nadu Legislative Assembly; Murasoli Maran; Raja Sir M.A. Muthiah Chettiar, the famous banker and politician; Kavalaparra Moopil Nair (the head of one of the four chief dynasties of the Nairs); P.C. Purushothama Reddiar, the famed stage actor; M.R. Radha, and numerous other successful industrialists, religious leaders and politicians, including, of course, several prominent left-wing politicians, such as A.K. Gopalan, V.G. Row, Mohan Kumaramangalam and others.

What made Nambyar such a popular choice? One can only say that some lawyers possess the ability to innovate, some possess the skill of brilliant oratory, and some a deep learning. While Nambyar certainly had the former two attributes, what set him apart was the depth of his academic knowledge, discernible irrespective of the nature of the case that he argued or the forum where it was argued. The knowledge that he possessed from his years of study in India and abroad shaped his arguments and lent to them the conviction that can only come from a true scholarly belief in the principles he espoused.

Though he is exceedingly well known for his challenges to preventive detention and for numerous other cases on the fundamental freedoms, areas of life and personal liberty were, however, by no means the only areas that Nambyar was considered to be an expert. Extremely comfortable in administrative law, as it was a subject in which he had obtained his master's degree in England, Nambyar's career fortuitously saw him involved in numerous challenges to various administrative decisions of the government in the high courts and also at the Supreme Court of India. Many of these cases were brought on behalf of motor vehicle operators who were applying for permits from the state government and had run into some or the other legal hurdle. As the motor vehicle business was one of the most lucrative of the time, and since by the time of *Gopalan*, Nambyar was a household name, the operators felt that a lawyer of Nambyar's standing would be best suited to defend their legal interests.

In 1958, eight years after *A.K. Gopalan*, Nambyar, who was by then a regular face in the Supreme Court of India, appeared before two constitution benches of the Supreme Court in two very important cases on aspects of administrative law. The first, and indeed, one of his most famous cases on natural justice, that of *Gulapalli Nageshwar Rao v. Andhra Pradesh State Road Transport Corporation*,[1] saw Nambyar appearing for none other than a group of motor vehicle operators who had been denied permits after a hearing was granted to them by the state government. While the hearing was conducted by the State Transport Secretary, the ultimate decision on grant or refusal of permit was taken by the chief minister. This, Nambyar argued, would render the hearing an empty formality. The five-judge bench of the Supreme Court agreed with Nambyar and set aside the government's decision stating:

> This divided responsibility is destructive of the concept of judicial hearing. Such a procedure defeats the object of personal hearing. Personal hearing enables the authority concerned to watch the demeanour of the witnesses and clear up his doubts during the course of the arguments, and the party appearing to persuade the authority by reasoned argument to accept his point of view. If one person hears and another decides, then personal hearing becomes an empty formality. We therefore hold that the said procedure followed in this case also offends another basic principle of judicial procedure.

Gulapalli Nageshwar Rao is still considered a landmark in administrative law on this aspect. The second case of 1958 was that of *Radheyshyam Khare v. The State of Madhya Pradesh*,[2] where Nambyar appeared for the Municipal Committee of Dhamtari in Madhya Pradesh and its president, Radheyshyam Khare. Though Nambyar lost the case, his arguments compelled the Supreme Court to examine the difference between an administrative act and a quasi-judicial act for the purposes of judicial review, and the court, referring to the voluminous foreign material cited at the Bar, laid down the following test, which also remains good law: '. . . the body of persons (1) must have legal authority, (2) to determine questions affecting the rights of parties, and (3) must have the duty to act judicially.'[3] In the high courts too, Nambyar would appear numerous times in cases involving principles of administrative law, citing foreign material from England, the United States and other countries to bolster his arguments. For example, in *The State of Madras v. Shanmuga Oil Mills*,[4] Nambyar argued before the Madras High Court that the Madras Market Crop Rules, which gave an unfettered discretion to the executive to fix the rates of tax, was excessive delegation of legislative powers and would be wholly illegal. The Madras High Court agreed with Nambyar, and held that as the delegation in question possessed 'no limits', it therefore would be invalid.

In 1951, the trustee of the Guruvayur temple approached Nambyar to appear for him in a challenge to the provisions of the Madras Hindu Religious Endowments Act, 1951. The Act as enacted, provided for the administration and control of all manner of Hindu religious endowments by the government through a Commissioner of Endowments, thus depriving the Hindu religious endowments of significant autonomy. Several bodies filed writ petitions in the Madras High Court, including the trustee of the Guruvayur temple, with one of the prominent among them being the Shirur Mutt. Considering his stature, M.K. Nambyar was the first petitioner to argue, and the persuasiveness of his arguments was made crystal clear by the following observations of the High Court:

> Mr. M.K. Nambiyar who appeared for the trustee of the Guruvayur temple argued his petition first and Mr. Alladi Krishnaswami Aiyar and the learned Advocate-General replied to that petition after which the petition relating to Guruvayur temple was allowed to be withdrawn as the Government agreed to cancel the decision to notify the temple and to permit the trustee to function. The arguments addressed by Mr. Nambiyar were adopted by the petitioners in the remaining petitions and they further supplemented the arguments addressed by Mr. Nambiyar . . .[5]

After hearing Nambyar and the other learned advocates, the Madras High Court struck down twenty sections of the Madras Hindu Religious Endowments Act, holding that they violated the fundamental right to property guaranteed under Article 19(1)(f). Among these provisions were those granting powers to the Commissioner to enter into the properties of the endowment, inspect the moveable and immoveable properties, tax the endowment and also take steps to assume complete control of the administration of the endowment for a period of five years, if felt necessary. The judgment was later challenged in the Supreme Court in *Commissioner, Hindu Religious Endowments, Madras v. Sri Lakshmindra Thirtha Swamiar of Sri Shirur Mutt*,[6] where the Supreme Court upheld the Madras High Court judgment with respect to twelve sections, but upheld the validity of the other eight sections. Impressed by his arguments for the trustee of Guruvayur, which shaped the high court decision, Nambyar was briefed to appear even before the Supreme Court though his client, i.e. the Guruvayur temple, thanks to his arguments, had succeeded in the high court decision.

In the same year and around the same time that Nambyar argued the challenge to the Madras Hindu Religious Endowments Act, 1951, for the trustee of the Guruvayur temple, Nambyar was also approached by the trustees of the Shri Venkataramana temple and its endowments, who were aggrieved by the application of the said Act to them.

Unlike in the case of the Guruvayur temple, the argument that was advanced by Nambyar for the Venkataramana temple in the case of *Devaraja Shenoy v. The State of Madras*[7] was that the temple belonged to members of the *Gowd Saraswath* Brahmin community, which formed a 'religious denomination' under the Constitution. Article 26 grants to all religious denominations the fundamental freedom to manage their own religious affairs, and thus, Nambyar argued, the Act offended this freedom of the Gowd Saraswath community, and the high court agreed. Though the state government did file an appeal against the judgment to the Supreme Court, the appeal was not pressed and ultimately came to be withdrawn.[8]

The very next year, Nambyar would again appear for the Gowd Saraswath community, this time canvassing a far more controversial proposition. Perhaps emboldened by their success in *Devraj Shenoy's* case, the community was back in court to challenge the Madras Temple Entry Authorisation Act, 1947, on the ground of a violation of Articles 25 and 26 of the Constitution of India so far as the Gowd Saraswaths were concerned. The Act, which threw open the doors of all temples notified under it to all sections of Hindu society, had the support of Article 25(2)(b) of the Constitution of India, which expressly permitted the State to 'make any law for . . . throwing open of Hindu religious institutions of a public character to all classes and sections of Hindus.' The Madras law, which was by all accounts extremely progressive and was specifically aimed at ending caste discrimination in matters of religious worship, was now being applied by the state government to the Sri Venkataramanaswami temple at Moolky, Mangalore. Though Nambyar certainly was in support of such progressive measures, he felt that the Gowd Saraswath community had a deserving cause. This was possibly on account of the fact that Nambyar himself had spent so much of his life in Mangalore that he was surely aware of the customs and practices of Moolky Petah and their unique claim to the Sri Venkataramanaswami temple. In Nambyar's argument, the temple in question belonged exclusively to the Gowd Saraswath Brahmins residents of three villages—Mannampady, Karnad and Bappanad, collectively known as 'Moolky Petah', and that the said Brahmins were migrants from Goa, Konkan and also from other places in South Kanara District who had settled down in these villages. As they were treated as aliens by other Hindus, they did not dine and inter-marry with other local Brahmins. They also had their own distinctive rituals and separate spiritual heads, with the management of the temple at all times being carried on by the members of the community resident in Moolky Petah. This Nambyar said would make them a religious denomination, a point that he had already successfully argued in *Devaraja Shenoy's* case and therefore Article 26, which provided complete freedom to religious denominations to manage their own affairs, would render the application of the Temple Entry Act ultravires the Constitution of India.

The Madras High Court did not agree with Nambyar, and in a strongly worded judgment held that the right to manage religious affairs protected by Article 26 could not ever be said to mean the right to exclude other persons from worshipping. In fact, the right to freely practise religion was guaranteed by another article of the Constitution, Article 25. The residents of Moolky Petah did not give up at the high court however, and took their appeal to the Supreme Court, where M.K. Nambyar once again led the arguments. Taking the Court painstakingly through the history of the Gowd Saraswath community, Nambyar argued that Article 26 gave denominations the right to exclude persons from worshipping at specific locations, and interestingly, unlike the Madras High Court, the Supreme Court agreed. This placed the Supreme Court in a quandary as on the one hand, it was faced with Article 26, which appeared to permit religious denominations from excluding persons from their places of worship, and on the other hand there was Article 25, which expressly permitted the State to make a law throwing open places of worship to all. To get out of the apparent deadlock, the Court held:

> The result then is that there are two provisions of equal authority, neither of them being subject to the other. The question is how the apparent conflict between them is to be resolved. The rule of construction is well settled that when there are in an enactment two provisions which cannot be reconciled with each other, they should be so interpreted that, if possible, effect could be given to both. This is what is known as the rule of harmonious construction.[9]

Applying the rule of harmonious construction, the Court held that the relevant sub-clause of Article 26 would necessarily have to be subject to the relevant sub-clause of Article 25, because only such a construction would ensure that both Articles of the Constitution could be given effect to. Thus, the rights given to religious denominations by Article 26 would not extend to those matters covered by Article 25(2)(b), i.e. a law intended to throw open public temples to all sections of Hindus. The judgment in *Sri Venkatramana Devaru & Anr. v. The State of Mysore* was delivered by a bench of five judges of the Supreme Court and is still considered to be a landmark on the rights conferred under Articles 25 and 26 of the Constitution of India. One would not know however, what Nambyar, who was an inwardly, though not demonstratively religious man, and a strong believer in personal liberty, felt about the judgment.

In 1957, Nambyar was approached by the Sourashtra Dharma Paripalana Committee, the trustees of two temples, the Sri Varadaraja Perumal temple and the Sri Veda Narayana Perumal temple at Kumbakonam. The Sourashtra community was a group of persons, originally from the Saurashtra region in present day Gujarat, who had migrated and settled down in various parts of Tamil Nadu, including Kumbakonam, where Nambyar had studied in the Government College. As a result, Nambyar was familiar with the community and their practices, and when he learnt that the Deputy Commissioner, Hindu Religious and Charitable Endowments had issued them a notice seeking to take over the administration of the temple, Nambyar agreed to represent their cause before the Madras High Court. Nambyar successfully argued that the Sourashtra Community was a religious denomination and therefore protected by Article 26 of the Constitution, and the trustees were able to maintain their autonomy in managing the temples. Though the judgment itself was not reported, it was referred to in another judgment on a similar issue by the Madras High Court, which agreed with its conclusions noting that the Sourashtra Community was a religious denomination.[10] The trustees were full of gratitude to Nambyar, particularly for the reason that he had charged them no fee, and every year on Onam, they sent him eight feet of silk dhoti, four feet of silk *angavastram* as well as six feet of white silk saree for his wife, Kalyani Nambyar. This practice continued every year till his death.

Nambyar was also famous for his arguments in various right-to-property cases. One set of cases, of course, dealt with the rights of landholders, which has been set out extensively earlier in this book, but Nambyar would also argue several cases on behalf of the holders of various industrial and commercial undertakings, who faced the prospect of losing their businesses or revenue in terms of various nationalization schemes. The judgments in several of these cases became landmarks. In *Deep Chand v. The State of Uttar Pradesh*,[11] the Government of Uttar Pradesh sought to prohibit private stage carriage operators from plying on certain routes in the state despite having done so for a number of years and under valid permits issued to them under the Motor Vehicles Act, 1939. The state government had passed its own legislation, after obtaining the assent of the President, which stipulated that on certain routes, only government stage carriages would be permitted. Nambyar challenged the UP Act on several grounds, among which were that the UP Act was in fact a law that deprived the petitioners of their property without compensation and was therefore violative of Article 31 of the Constitution of India. Accordingly, to Nambyar, after the coming into force of the Constitution of India, any law which was inconsistent with the fundamental rights was void *ab initio*. The judgment debated important issues, including the applicability of the 'doctrine of eclipse' to laws passed after the coming into force of the Constitution of India and agreed with Nambyar's arguments.

In *West Ramnad Electricity Company v. The State of Madras*[12] Nambyar would argue on behalf of the appellant that the Madras Electric Supply Undertakings (Acquisition) Act, 1954, which provided for the compulsory acquisition of electrical undertakings, was violative of Article 31, inasmuch as the Act did not authorize the payment of compensation commensurate with the undertaking sought to be acquired. The court, however, did not agree. Nambyar made similar arguments before the various high courts as well, some successful and some not. In the ultimate analysis, Nambyar was clearly swimming against the tide, which was pushing towards a larger governmental presence in industrial establishments.

As Nambyar would point out many times to different courts, Article 19(1)(f) granted the fundamental right to all citizens to acquire, hold and dispose of property, subject only to reasonable restrictions that may be imposed by law in the interests of the general public. Article 31(1), which was again a part of the Fundamental Rights chapter, declared that no person shall be deprived of his property save by authority of law. Article 31(2) further provided that no property moveable or immoveable could be taken possession of or acquired for public purpose by the State under any law unless such law provided for a just compensation to the landowner. Collectively, Article 19—which was restricted only to citizens—and Article 31 secured to the people a fundamental right to property.

The right to property, therefore, for Nambyar, had evolved through the ages into constituting a basic framework of a civilized society. But it is difficult to gauge how much his own background influenced his thinking on these matters. Nambyar's broadly libertarian views may not have been the prevailing thought of those who occupied the Constituent Assembly. Indeed, the place of property rights in constituting a framework for society was in substantial doubt at the time. However, the Constitution was ultimately a product of compromise, an understanding between people who thought differently about how India ought to be organized, how its institutions ought to function. The property rights clauses eventually reflected this conflict, providing to us a paradox of sorts.

But, still, Nambyar did not quite see any inherent rift between a guarantee of a right to property and the State's quest to drive society towards greater equality. Indeed, he recognized that the inviolability of private property is by no means absolute under the

Indian Constitution. The power of eminent domain, generally considered to be an incident of sovereignty in all civilized states, was embodied in Article 31(2) of the Constitution, after all. This gave to the State the authority to take private property for public purposes. The articles that granted a fundamental right to property equally made those rights amenable to public welfare. Therefore, Nambyar recognized that the Constitution allowed for property to be taken and redistributed. That if the progress of the country demanded a new social order, a redistribution of property was permitted as long as it could be demonstrated to a court of law that such a course was in the interests of the general public and that it subserved the common good. But this power came with an important caveat: that any property taken should be paid for; to not compensate for a taking, in Nambyar's belief, would infringe the principles of justice enshrined in the Preamble to the Constitution. For him, social justice had to be predicated on fairness and any laws made in furtherance of these objectives had to, for Nambyar, be subject to the fundamental rights contained in Part III. As long as the mandates of Articles 19(1)(f) and 31 were met, any programme for social justice would be fair and reasonable.

Yet, to glean a lawyer's political philosophy or beliefs purely from the cases that he might have argued and the causes that he might have represented can be an exercise fraught with difficulty. After all, a lawyer is sometimes morally obligated to advance arguments quite opposed to his own personal and political views. In this, the arc of Nambyar's career may not seem particularly unusual. He appeared for people avowedly on the Left, such as A.K. Gopalan, Mohan Kumaramangalam and S. Krishnan, among others, in civil liberties cases of different kinds, particularly involving issues of preventive detention. He also appeared for people on the other end of the political and social spectrum—rich landlords, for instance—whose right to property, he argued, stood transgressed by the State's policy of land redistribution. The questions are: is there a conflict here? Do his appearances across the political spectrum indicate that Nambyar was simply doing his job as a lawyer, taking up cases for clients who approached him with briefs of different kinds? Or do they indicate an anomaly in politics, where Nambyar himself was unsure where he truly belonged?

When one reads Nambyar's writings in conjunction with the arguments that he advanced, it becomes clear that Nambyar did, in fact, possess a strong political attitude. The cases he pleaded weren't merely a product of his lawyerly obligations, but they also flowed from a larger philosophical underpinning. His ideology wasn't quite classically libertarian as we might presume at first blush, with pure freedom from any interference, and nothing else, at the core of his beliefs, where a person's civil rights—such as the right against unlawful detention—are on par with a person's right to hold property. On the other hand, Nambyar's political philosophy was far more nuanced, influenced no doubt by his own upbringing, but also shaped by his education, both in India and especially in the United Kingdom. He was neither strongly libertarian nor did he lean himself to the socialist thinking of those on the Left whom he often represented. Instead, he was guided by an ideology that ran down the centre of these two conflicting thoughts, guided as it were by a basic belief in the freedom of man—this thread, as the reader would see, guided his arguments irrespective of the aspect of law he argued.

Nowhere was Nambyar's belief in personal liberty more evident than in the preventive detention cases of *A.K. Gopalan, S. Krishnan,* etc. Yet, these were not the only landmark cases on the subject that Nambyar would argue, and with each case, he displayed his commitment to the various facets of personal liberty. 'Life, Liberty and Property,' Nambyar wrote, 'are the basic Rights of Man.'[13] The guarantees embodied in the Constitution of the United States, which pledged that these rights shall not be deprived except with due process of law, and the promises made in the French Declaration of the Rights of Man, which proclaimed them to be the natural and imprescriptible rights of man, possessed, for Nambyar, a sense of majesty about them. They were words that he found especially rousing and inspirational. It stimulated in him a profound belief in constitutionalism, in the rule of law as a weapon against all arbitrariness, against all manner of repressive State conduct. To him, the fundamental function of the court was to serve as the voice of the Constitution, to offer protection to individuals against the encroachment of their rights by the State.

Nambyar thought it puzzling that the same men who had fought so valiantly against the British for freedom, when placed in a position of power, tended to militate against the very freedoms that they once held so dear. 'Indeed, it is an interesting paradox that those who were loudest in their insistence on the inclusion of fundamental rights in the Constitution,' he wrote, 'are now among their most bitter opponents.'[14] Apparently, he had in mind the issues surrounding the right to property as well as the inclusion of preventive detention into the Constitution. That freedom to think, to act, to speak, to live, constituted the core of Nambyar's personal and political philosophy. This belief in freedom from State interference did not mean that Nambyar was unmindful in any way of social and economic inequality, or that he believed that the State had no role to play in alleviating the imbalance between different classes and castes of people. Far from it, and whenever he argued cases on the subject, he strived to strike a balance between these two competing claims.

As soon as Nambyar shifted over to the Madras High Court, it became evident to most people who heard him argue that his academic knowledge on various legal subjects was extremely deep. While *A.K. Gopalan* is one of his best-known cases, in fact, prior to *Gopalan,* Nambyar would argue another case before the Madras High Court where he set out his vision for Article 21 of the Constitution of India. In *M.R. Venkatraman v. The Commissioner of Police, Madras*[15] Nambyar challenged the preventive detention of the petitioner on the grounds of Article 19 and 21. Nambyar argued for the first time that Article 21, which said that no person could be deprived of his life and personal liberty except by 'procedure established by law', conferred a right similar to that held by the US Supreme Court under the Fourteenth Amendment to the US Constitution. The Fourteenth Amendment in the Constitution of the United States stated that no person could be deprived of life, liberty or property except by the 'due process of law'. In terms of the 'due process' clause, the US Supreme Court had arrogated to itself an unlimited power to declare a law invalid if according to the majority of the Judges of the Supreme Court that law was unreasonable.[16] The question therefore, was whether the phrase 'procedure established by law' meant that the government could prescribe any procedure however unfair the court felt it to be as long as it was legislatively competent to do so, or whether the phrase implied that the procedure itself had to be inherently fair as in the case of the Constitution of the United States. Nambyar fervently argued for the latter, and interestingly, one of the two judges agreed, stating in his opining that:[17]

> My conclusion therefore is that the expression 'according to procedure established) by law' means a procedure fixed in accordance with legislative enactment passed by the Parliament or the State Legislature which does not offend or is revolting to, notions and ideas of dignity of the human being and is neither indecent, unconscionable or repugnant to civilized beliefs.

While the other judge found it unnecessary to go into the question in the facts of the case, the judges for different reasons concurred that the detention of the petitioner was illegal and Nambyar had thus secured his first victory on a critical interpretation of Article 21. The victory, of course, was short-lived, and as discussed in earlier pages of this book, just a couple of months later, the Supreme Court would reject Nambyar's argument on this point in *A.K. Gopalan*, holding that Article 21 placed no limits on the kind of procedure the legislature could enact for the purpose of depriving a person of life, liberty and property. Nambyar, however, did not give up on his vision of Article 21 and Article 19, even though the Supreme

Court at the time appeared to disagree with him. Around the same time that he argued *Gopalan* before the Supreme Court, V.G. Row, who was deeply impressed with the learning that Nambyar displayed in his arguments, had also entrusted Nambyar with another equally important case at the Madras High Court.

What had happened was that the Madras Government, which was clearly engaged in a crackdown on members of the left-wing movement, had declared the People's Education Society (a well-known communist organization of which Row was the general secretary) an unlawful organization. Of course, this situation could not be countenanced and Nambyar moved swiftly to challenge the section under which the declaration was issued on the grounds of violation of Articles 14 and 19 of the new Constitution of India. That section, i.e. Section 16, of the Indian Criminal Law Amendment Act, 1931, permitted the banning of an organization if the provincial government was of 'the opinion that any association that interferes or has for its object interference with the administration of the law or with the maintenance of law & order, or that it constitutes a danger to the public peace, the Provincial Govt. may, by notification in the official Gazette, declare such association to be unlawful'.

There was, of course, now a development, for though the case had been filed prior to the decision in *Gopalan,* by the time it was argued, the judgment was in fact delivered and proved hugely significant, for the Supreme Court had not only interpreted Article 21 but had also interpreted Article 19 in the following terms:[18]

> The net result is that the unlimited legislative power given by Art. 246 read with the different legislative lists in Sch. VII is cut down by the provisions of Art. 19 & all laws made by the State with respect to these rights must in order to be valid observe these limitations. Whether any law has in fact transgressed these limitations is to be ascertained by the Ct. & if in its view the restrictions imposed by the law are greater than what is permitted by cls. (2) to (6), whichever is applicable the Ct. will declare the same to be unconstitutional &, therefore, void under Art. 13.

In *Gopalan*, though the court had ruled decisively that Article 21 gave no scope to the court to assess the fairness or reasonableness of the procedure enacted to deprive personal liberty, it appeared to have left open the question so far as Article 19 was concerned. In his arguments in the *V.G. Row* case therefore, Nambyar made a spirited attempt to limit the effect of the ruling in *Gopalan* and argued that at least so far as Article 19 was concerned, the court in interpreting the restrictions imposed by Clauses (2) to (6) of Article 19 would have an identical power to that of the American Supreme Court under the 'Due Process of Law clause'. The majority of the full bench of the Madras High Court did not accept this contention and held that while the court could examine whether the law was reasonable or not, if it found the law to be permitted by Clauses (2) to (6) of Article 19, then it would have no choice but to uphold it, whether or not even the judges themselves found the provision unreasonable.[19] The court also did not find that Section 16 violated Row's right to freedom of speech and expression, though ultimately, however, it agreed with Nambyar that the law did violate Row's right to freedom of association protected under Article 19(1)(c) because it neither provided for communication of the grounds for banning nor had a mechanism for appeal. Additionally, inasmuch as the law created different categories of unlawful associations with some subjected to a harsher procedure than others, the right to equality under Article 14 also stood violated. When reading the judgment, one gets the feeling that courts were perhaps of the view that something was wrong with such restrictive laws, but was not, after *Gopalan*, prepared to go the full mile, as Nambyar sought to persuade them to do.

Just a few months later, Nambyar, clearly undeterred, was again before another full bench of the Madras High Court in *W.N. Srinivasa Bhatt v. The State of Madras*,[20] appearing this time for the keeper of a printing press, the Avanti Press at Rajamahendrawaram, East Godavari District. This time, the petitioners were seeking to quash orders issued under the Indian Press (Emergency Powers) Act,

1931. Avanti Press had published a Telugu book which, according to the government, contained passages that violated Section 4 of the Act, which proscribed material that had the effect of 'inciting to or encouraging commission of an offence of murder or any cognizable offence involving violence'. For such violation, the Act directed payment of security by the publisher, to deter him from publishing such material, and even permitted seizure of the press itself. Nambyar argued that this was a clear violation of the petitioner's freedom of speech and expression protected by Article 19(1)(a), as the restrictions contemplated under Article 19(2)[21] were only to the extent that the law prohibiting free speech related to 'libel, slander, defamation, contempt of Court or any matter which offends against decency or morality or which undermines the security of, or tends to overthrow, the State'. Thus, Nambyar argued, Section 4 of the Act was overbroad, going far beyond the restrictions on free speech permitted by Clause (2) of Article 19. He also argued that demanding security from the printer of the press amounted to pre-censorship, as the printer would then be deterred from publishing material at all. Two judges of the court disagreed and dismissed Nambyar's petition, and took the view that 'No reasonable person could hold that, to make criminal the counselling of murder or the commission of offences involving violence, would be an unconstitutional restriction of the right of "freedom of speech and expression".'[22]

Undaunted by these setbacks, Nambyar would repeatedly argue his interpretation of Articles 19 and 21 in a variety of different cases and began to see some success. In 1954, in a case called *Venugopal, In Re*,[23] Nambyar successfully argued before the Madras High Court that Section 49-A of the Madras City Police Act, which criminalized the publication of any material relating to information likely to facilitate wagering or betting on horse races, violated Article 19(1)(a). Here, the high court was called upon to examine the phrase 'decency or morality', which was one of the permissible grounds of restrictions on free speech occurring in Article 19(2). Interestingly, the high court appeared to make a slightly progressive departure from its view in *W.N. Srinivasa Bhatt's* case, and posed the following question to itself:

> . . . what is the morality or decency in respect of which the Legislature can seek to impose reasonable restrictions. Is it what the legislative mind considers moral or decent, or is it something which has to be determined by standards of universal acceptance and accord?[24]

Unlike in *Bhatt,* where the court felt that its powers to interpret even the reasonableness of the restriction under Clauses (2) to (6) of Article 19, four years on from the decision, the court was prepared to agree with a judgment of the Bombay High Court, which held that 'the morality referred to in Art. 19(2) is not the ad hoc morality created by the State Legislature. It is a morality which is accepted by all the world or at least throughout the length and breadth of India.'[25] The case was a significant step forward for Nambyar's interpretation of the Constitution, and he continued to press on with his attempts at widening the ambit of Articles 19 and 21, in a series of cases throughout his career. Each judgment is a wonderful exposition on the subject and unfortunately there are too many to examine. What is clear, however, is that this was the area that Nambyar was most passionate about, and he worked hard to convince the courts of his beliefs on the basic rights of all persons. If *A.K. Gopalan* was his first major constitutional case, then it is fitting that the last landmark case that he argued was also on the subject of freedom—this time of the press in *Bennett Coleman v. Union of India,*[26] and by that time, i.e. the early 1970s, the Supreme Court, which had been so hesitant initially, had accepted many of the ideas that Nambyar had initially pressed before the courts. In a variety of judgments, unconnected to Nambyar, the court had accepted the view that freedom of the press was an essential component of Article 19(1)(a). In *Bennett Coleman*, Nambyar challenged the Newsprint Policy (put in place by an increasingly authoritarian Indira Gandhi), which placed numerous restrictions on circulation, number of pages, access to financial resources, etc. Nani Palkhiwala brilliantly argued on freedom of the press, while Nambyar argued on the freedom of the press to carry on its business. In a thumping judgment, the Supreme Court struck down the policy and in the words of the famous Indian Constitutional scholar, M.P. Jain, the judgment was 'a landmark in the history of citizens' civil rights in India'.[27]

Nambyar's final victory in the area of personal liberty would come a few years after his death, when the Supreme Court in *Maneka Gandhi v. Union of India*[28] agreed with what Nambyar had argued so passionately before it two decades earlier, that the 'procedure established by law' in Article 21 of the Constitution of India did not mean just any procedure, but one which was 'fair, just and reasonable'. Thus, in the ultimate analysis, one can only say that the mark that Nambyar left on the Constitution of India is both indelible as well as undeniable.

Epilogue

The story of M.K. Nambyar is the story of a man from a small town who forsook the easy life of a landlord's son and forged his own path to become one of the most accomplished and well-known lawyers of his time.

To say that law was an uncommon choice for people from Nambyar's background is an understatement. Yet by sheer dint of hard work and a small amount of luck, he was able to propel himself from the small town of Mangalore first, to the Madras High Court and eventually to the national stage. Advocate V.P. Krishnan Nambiar, who knew Nambyar well, said that he could 'recall the quiet dignity, the unostentatious humility and mellowed wisdom of M.K. Nambiar as a migrant scotfoot from the muffassil, rubbing shoulders with some of the front rank lawyers of the Madras Bar of those days, from whom he was soon to wrest his place as the leading constitutional lawyer and jurist of erudition and eminence'.

At the peak of his career, Nambyar was appearing in virtually every major constitutional litigation in the country, several of which were in the Supreme Court of India. In the Madras High Court, which he had made his home, he was regarded as one of the top lawyers appearing in a range of civil, criminal and commercial cases. He would routinely travel to other high courts as well and was in the Supreme Court regularly for many constitutional cases of the moment.

The Full Court Reference held by the Supreme Court of India in Nambyar's memory is testament to the giant that he was. The then Attorney General Niren De said:

Most of the cases in which he appeared, beginning from Gopalan's case, involved important constitutional issues and it can be said, without exaggeration, that Nambyar's arguments assisted this Court a great deal in the interpretation of several Articles of the Constitution, particularly those relating to fundamental rights. Until his death, he was perhaps, the most erudite Constitutional Lawyer in the country.[1]

Chief Justice of India Justice A.N. Ray had this to say:

He belonged to that school of lawyers who are guided by dignity and discipline in professional life. He always wanted to rectify his knowledge by reading matters which would enliven law. He was a lawyer whose arguments struck a balance between rigidity on the one hand and formlessness on the other . . . Nambyar was by nature of a scholastic bond of mind. He would make intensive preparation of cases before he would appear in court. He would get to the roots and principles of law. He would make an incisive study of case law. The result of his industry was apparent when he presented his case before the Court . . . It is a matter of great pride and honour that he had become a legend in his own lifetime. As I said earlier, he is a man who believes in maintaining the dignity of the legal profession and follows the tradition handed down by the legal giants of yesteryears. To say that Mr. Nambyar was a lawyer par excellence would be a gross under-statement.[2]

M.K. Nambyar was so many things. He was simultaneously a driven and extremely successful professional, but also a family man, deeply committed to his wife and children. He was a firm defender of the fundamental rights to equality, and to life and personal liberty, yet he fought equally for the right to property—being himself from a family of landlords. He was known to be a quiet person, and despite his success, remarkably humble. His former junior and the late senior advocate M.N. Krishnamani fondly recalled Nambyar's great love for the south Indian breakfast item, idli. Nambyar once told

Krishnamani: 'Do you know, of all the food items which one I like the most? It is idli. How delicious, how fine, how harmless and yet how simple? A healthy man can take it and even a sick person can take it, isn't it?'[3]

In those days, the rearing of the children was left entirely to the women of the house. Therefore, he did not have much of a role to play in the upbringing of his children, and to them he seemed a distant figure to be revered. In fact, it was only when his sons were in their forties that he, for the first time, sat down with them and had a small glass of whisky. Despite the formal nature of his relationship with his children, he was a huge source of financial and psychological support to them. They could always and often did look up to him whenever they required financial support, whether for going abroad for higher studies or for performing the marriages of their daughters or even for building their own houses. All this he was able to do thanks to the successful nature of his practice.

His children recall fondly some of the lighter moments with their father. Ever immersed in his work, he was habituated to answering questions put to him around the house, with his mind diverted elsewhere. The children always knew that when they heard Nambyar repeat the word 'splendid' in response to whatever was said to him, their father, though physically present, was most likely lost in the next legal argument that he would have to deliver. One day, a guest paid a courtesy call at home and at a certain point in the conversation, Nambyar probably was diverted. The guest brought up the unfortunate news of the death of a dear relative, to which Nambyar promptly replied, 'Splendid, splendid.'

There were other lighter moments. In his early years of practice in the Madras High Court, Nambyar had an occasion to appear for a very famous Tamil stage actor, by the name of M.R. Radha. The script of one of his plays had been proscribed. Nambyar, appearing for M.R. Radha, asserted the actor's right to freedom of speech and succeeded in having the ban lifted. Radha was grateful to him and therefore insisted upon Nambyar being a chief guest at one of his most famous plays *Ratha Kaneer*. *Ratha Kaneer* tells the story of an extremely rich person (played by M.R. Radha) who, having just returned from England, abandons his extremely traditional Indian wife and falls in love with a prostitute.

In the play, the infatuated man gives away most of his wealth to his mistress and takes up permanent residence with her. Having lost his wealth and most of his loved ones, Fate strikes one more fatal blow, afflicting him with leprosy, whereupon his fickle mistress promptly throws him out of the house. Nambyar was seated in the front row, in the middle, and during the intermission, was escorted to the green room to meet all the actors. When he returned to his seat, Radha's assistant came to him with a metal glass, and when Nambyar asked what it was, he was told whisky. Nambyar was shocked and said, 'take it away, take it away'. Nevertheless, he immensely enjoyed the play. At least till the police arrived at the theatre to arrest Radha. Radha, in his guttural voice, shouted at the police, 'How dare you arrest me? Do you know who my lawyer is? It is Nambyar!' and pointed to Nambyar who was seated in the front row. Being the self-effacing person that he was, Nambyar squirmed in his seat!

Nambyar had a sense of humour, which he even displayed in court. In an incident shared by M.N. Krishnamani, Nambyar had asked him to research a particular proposition of law: 'an unintelligible order of a quasi-judicial authority can be quashed through issuance of a writ of certiorari.'

Krishnamani recollects that he hunted and hunted for such a judgment, but could not find any such case. Finally, he found an old English judgment which he believed would be of assistance and showed it to Nambyar. The latter read the judgment and remarked 'Very good!' The next day while arguing, he told the court: 'I had asked my junior to get me a case law on this point. He has ably got one directly on the point.'

He then read out the relevant passage from the judgment which said: 'When the proposition is obvious, it will be difficult to get a case-law on it.' Needless to say, the judges and everyone in the court were greatly amused.

Nambyar was a religious man, but not demonstrative of it. On the birthday of each child, one page of the Ramayana would be opened at random and that page was said to portend the future of the child in the coming year. Thereafter, the boy would be given eight annas (sixteen annas in those days made a rupee) and dispatched to the nearby Kadiri temple, where the eight annas would have to be deposited with the priest, who would then perform a small puja for blessing the child.

Among the very many hurdles that Nambyar had to get over for arguing cases, the most significant personal hurdle was asthma, which he had from childhood. This was no ordinary asthma because frequently he was temporarily incapacitated by bouts of wheezing. The first relief that he obtained was when cortisone became available in London. On learning of the availability of the drug, he straightaway had it imported and began to use it. But the suffering was such that he continued to experiment with various cures and must have tried virtually every stated cure for this disease. In one instance, he travelled to Hyderabad, where thousands of persons gather on a particular day each year to be given a live fish to swallow, which is believed to permanently rid one of asthma. Nambyar with a police escort, which was made available to him, cut through the crowd to reach the family that had the small fish in a huge cauldron. They ask you to open your mouth and quickly thrust in the fish, which wriggles down your gullet. He also tried several ayurvedic and other alternative therapies in the hope of curing himself. But none of these had any effect whatsoever on Nambyar and he continued to depend on cortisone, which proved to be his lifelong saviour till he passed away.

M.K. Nambyar was born at the end of the nineteenth century and passed away on 18th December 1975 after a brief illness. He was a totally self-made person. From what was then a small village where he was born to a town, Mangalore, and then to the capital of the Madras State, to finally rise in stature, to be decorated as a legend of the law and a great constitutional lawyer, is indeed a life fulfilled.

Acknowledgements

I would like to acknowledge the contributions and support of T.V. Krishnan, Suhrith Parthasarathy and Suhasini Sen. I would also like to gratefully acknowledge K. Madhavan, M.K. Nambyar's stepbrother. Without them the publication of this book would not have been possible.

T.V. Krishnan, who is no more, possessed a deep personal knowledge of the region and had meticulously researched M.K. Nambyar's life in the tharuvaads; he brought to life information which even the living members of my family did not know or recollect. These portions of the book, including those of M.K. Nambyar's early professional life are almost entirely his contribution. My uncle, K. Madhavan's, fascinating book was invaluable in unearthing many stories and background material regarding M.K. Nambyar's childhood and early family life.

Similarly, with regard to M.K. Nambyar's professional life, the cases he handled and their historical background, it was the in-depth research by Suhrith Parthasarthy, a well-known lawyer in the Madras High Court, that enabled the inclusion of these portions in this book. Suhrith, who is a successful lawyer and writer, was also responsible for drafting the majority of the chapters relating to M.K. Nambyar's professional life. His contribution was invaluable.

Suhasini Sen was responsible for many of the chapters including historical research on Nambyar's life in Kerala, as well as certain chapters relating to his cases and career. She undertook the entire responsibility of seeing the publication of the book through its various stages.

I have to thank my siblings, K.C. Mohan, K.K. Gopinath and Malini Gopalan for their invaluable inputs.

K.K. Venugopal

Appendix

LIFE – A LAWYER'S VIEW

(By M.K. Nambyar, LL.M. (Lond.) Barrister-at-Law)

Between a scientist and a lawyer the difference is deep. One deals with the laws of inert matter, the other with the laws of human conduct. But while matter at rest or in motion is always subject to its determinate laws, man does not always move in subservience to any law. Human conduct is unpredictable.

A lawyer has his life and being in the life and being of his fellowmen. Whether in his chambers or in the courts, he is confronted every day with the problems of human conduct and human endeavour, with the springs of man's actions, his greed and his despair, with the drama of birth and death in its infinite variations, and with the mystery of human behaviour in all its complexity.

For thirty years, I have been at the Bar. For thirty years, I have watched the stream of life with its eddies and whirlpools flowing past beside me in the courts.

I have practised in every kind of court, civil and criminal, from the lowest to the highest, before the smallest magistrate and before the Judicial Committee of the Privy Council, from a munsif's court to the Supreme Court of India. For nine years, I was a public prosecutor.

I am not speaking just of the uncertainty of a final judgment in any case. A judge is not a slot machine, where on the same facts and the same law the same judgment will follow. But more intriguing is the direction of events in cases coming before the courts—from conception through execution and down to their final end. What I have been struck with again and again is the play of the unforeseen in the most carefully planned incident and the hand of the unseen, inexplicable and unaccountable.

Not long back, an unusual story was unfolded in a sessions court. The prosecution case was this: In a village not far off from a coastal town, the boats of a powerful landholder were burned in the night. Suspicion fell on a recalcitrant tenant who had been forcibly evicted by the landlord a few weeks earlier. But there was no evidence to sustain a criminal complaint against him. The only course left to the landholder was to wreak private vendetta. But the tenant had disappeared from the village. Emissaries were sent far and near in search of the victim of this vendetta. He was finally traced, lured into a cavern, plied with drinks and trapped in a waiting motor car. The car then drove off towards a thick forest ten or twelve miles away. The assassins in the car were impatient to do away with him. He was hammered and throttled.

But the car had to pass through a crowded bazaar on its way to the forest. It was about eight in the night. The shops were just closing. But right in the midst of the bazaar, the car came to a sudden halt. Petrol had run out. From the depths of the car came the cry of the half-dead man: 'I am being killed.' People gathered. Lanterns were raised. Someone from the car shouted that the man was mad and that he was being taken to a temple for a cure. The driver jumped out with a can of petrol, filled the tank and drove away.

But those who had gathered around the car grew suspicious. Information about it was carried to a neighbouring gentleman. Two cars were sent to chase it from two different directions, one with a sub-inspector of police who happened to be camping nearby. The fleeing car was eventually traced, empty and abandoned, but with the telltale stains of blood and a hammer. Next day, the dead body was found not far from the road. Those in the car who had been identified were tried and sentenced to death or to transportation for life.

If the car had not stopped at the time and place that it did but had reached its intended destination unimpeded, the victim should have been buried in the depths of the forest and the murder in all probability should never have been out.

Such events are not rare. Man prides himself on the most careful planning. But something goes wrong. How? Why? None can tell.

Now, here is a strange case of a missing Jain. He was a youngster of twenty-four or twenty-five, rich, newlywed, flashing in diamond earrings and silk shirts. Unfortunately, he kept bad company. Quite often he used to leave his home in the village for weeks together for the attractions of town life. For some time, his absence was not noticed. Then, his people grew anxious. No one knew where he had gone. It took a month or two for the matter to be reported to the police. A smart police sub-inspector started the investigation. For days he drew a blank. Then, one day, when he tackled an erstwhile companion of the missing man, a strange story came to light. Under the pretext of taking him to a festival, this man and three others took him at night through a lonely road and beat him to death for his diamond earrings and gold . . . They buried him on the summit of a distant hill. The sub-inspector was taken to the spot. A few bones lay strewn about, which the wild animals which infested the jungle had left behind. The only properties that could be recovered were the young Jain's shirt and sandals, both of which had been made to order.

There were indications that the confession was true. But the confession would be retracted at trial, and no court would enter a conviction without satisfactory proof of the *corpus delicti*. Could the bones be established as those of the missing Jain? The chemical examiner to whom the bones were sent had opined that he could not say whether they were of a man or a woman. With such evidence, the only alternative for the prosecution was to withdraw the case.

On the morning the trial was to commence, I had a brain wave. Among the bones recovered, there were the humerus, one part of an arm and a few bones of a foot. From these, could it be possible for medical science to arrive at the height of the man and the length of his arm and his foot? In England I knew there were instances of a body being reconstructed from a few bones. The shirt and the sandals furnished important data for verification. And the wife could state with precision the height of her husband.

When the court assembled, I moved for a reference of these questions to the professor of medical jurisprudence at Madras. Everyone smiled. It was a forlorn hope. Anyway, the bones were sent to the expert for examination.

Within a few days, the answers came. There was a scientific formula from which the height of a man could be deduced from the length of the humerus. The arm and the foot were reconstructed. The measurements of each were given. They tallied almost exactly with the sleeve of the shirt, the sandals and the height of the man given by the wife.

What was more, the professor of medical jurisprudence had made a new discovery. Among the bones was a mandible—a jaw bone. This bone revealed, according to the professor, that the face had a slight disfiguration, with a projecting underjaw.

That opinion would cut both ways. If the missing man had no such feature, then the mandible was not his and the whole prosecution case was false. If otherwise, the proof of identity was complete and unassailable.

But there was no mention at all in the evidence collected by the police that the unfortunate Jain suffered from any such malformation. If any witness now swore to the same, it was open to the grave suspicion that it had been got up to conform to the expert opinion. Confronted with the new problem, I summoned the police officer and asked him to secure a photograph of the missing Jain. That was the only safe course to follow. He agreed to try. Within a few days he turned up with a group photograph obtained from the school the man had attended as a boy. And there it was—the projecting underjaw, clear and well defined.

In due course, the trial commenced. The professor of medical jurisprudence was examined as a witness in court. The height, the foot, the arm and the mandible of the man all accorded with the shirt and sleeve, the sandals, the photograph and the wife's evidence. The coincidence were too many to be rejected. Conviction followed. All the accused were sentenced to be hanged, and the sentence was confirmed by the high court.

These appertain, no doubt, to the realm of criminal law. But civil cases also afford similar instances. Let me recount just one. The Marumakkathayam Act, as originally enacted, contained one defect. By some oversight the Act had been so phrased as to exclude children by a wife who died prior to the passing of the Act from inheriting from their father. One such suit was filed in a court and dismissed. The defeated party came up to file an appeal. I dissuaded him. The law was clear. But the party would not listen. His logic was simple. If he was the son of his father, no one could deny him the right to his father's inheritance. At last I yielded. If he wanted to throw away good money in pursuit of a shadow, it was entirely his affair. The appeal was filed on some other grounds. The decision under the Act was not impugned. It could not be impugned.

When, two years later, the appeal was taken up for argument, I was caught up in another court and I passed the papers to my junior. The next morning my young friend, the junior, met me. He had argued that the trial court was wrong in its view that under the Marumakkathayam Act the son by a predeceased wife could not inherit from the father. The court, he told me, was inclined to agree with him. But the learned judge discovered that I hadn't taken the ground even in my appeal memo. Was it an inadvertence? Or was it deliberate? Anyway, would I be free to attend his court that day?

I smiled. I was rather busy. I wanted to explain that the identical point had been considered by the high court and decided against us. My young friend was not quite familiar with Marumakkathayam law. Where ignorance was bliss it was folly to be wise. It told him that I would attend his court immediately I was free, and explain.

But curiously enough, I could not get released from the court wherein I was engaged. The learned judge, who resumed the hearing of the appeal, would not wait and felt so convinced of my junior's contention that he proceeded to judgment immediately. The decree of the lower court was reversed and my client won.

The judgment was absolutely wrong. When the party met me later, I assured him that he would lose in the high court in the event of a second appeal. He didn't mind. And, as anticipated, the second appeal was filed. In the high court the result was foregone.

But within a few months a strange thing happened. A proposal came from the government to amend the Marumakkathayam Act to remove this identical anomaly, with retrospective effect. I was amazed at the new turn of events. Eventually, the amendment was carried. The second appeal came for hearing in due course and was dismissed in view of the new amendment. Inheritance from the father for a child from a woman who had died before the Act became a settled fact.

Had the appeal never been filed, the trial court's decree should have become final and left untouched by the new amendment. Or, had I been enabled to appear at its hearing, I shouldn't have hesitated to do my duty by the court and explained the true position of the law as it stood, however disastrous it might have been to my client.

It is easy to multiply instances. No one for a moment can minimize the importance of human endeavour in the march of events, whether in courts of law or elsewhere. By thought, word and deed, man shapes the course of the future. His life is largely his own making. And not merely his own life, but even the world around him in which he moves and has his being is shaped by his aspiration, his ambition and achievements.

And yet, through the web of life of each one of us runs an unseen thread, which shoots an unexpected ray into the pattern of our existence. The turning points in one's life have often been fashioned by formative forces of something unforeseen, something unaccountable, something inexplicable, beyond our reach and beyond our comprehension. Life to me is still a mystery. My will is my own. My acts are of course mine. I sit in the frail bark of my body and steer with all my might. But I find I am neither the master of my vessel nor the captain of its decisive direction. For, the momentum of its movements has often been gathered from the impact of the unknown.

THE CONTOURS OF THE CONSTITUTION

(By M.K. Nambyar, LL.M. (Lond.) Barrister-at-Law)

On 26 January 1950, one epoch in India's history closed and another commenced. British power in India had grown from commerce to conquest, and in the process of two centuries had welded a subcontinent into an empire under the suzerainty of a common Crown. But with the impact of Western culture and ideals began the rise of Indian nationalism; and the last fifty years have witnessed the spectacular cavalcade of the march of a nation to its pre-ordained destiny. Of the story of the great struggle for freedom, of the triumph of Indian nationalism over the forces of British imperialism, of the withdrawal of British power from India, and of the proclamation of the new Republic, history furnishes no parallel. From the ashes of the old a new state has risen, with new ideals and a new Constitution.

Every system of government that is born of revolution, violent or non-violent, bears the indelible impress of the impulses of its being. It mirrors the struggles of the past in its provisions to ensure the security of the future. It represents the aspirations, achievements and ambitions of a people. No Constitution is merely a collection of clauses, or the handiwork of skilled draftsmanship. It is an organic growth springing from the forces of natural vitality, and changing in colour and content in the process of time.

To know what the Constitution is, we have to know what it was. To understand the present, we have to recall the past. Under British suzerainty, the subcontinent of India stood comprised of two Indias—Indian India and British India—one composed of 'Native' States, the other of British provinces. In the first, in juridical theory, the ruler was the sovereign of his State, the fountainhead of all legislative, executive and judicial powers, and the liege-lord of his subjects. In fact and in form, the pattern of government that obtained in most of the States was an unfeigned despotism, though in a few of the 'enlightened' States it was sought to be redeemed by the setting up of a legislature of nominated or partly nominated and partly elected representatives of the people, which could however be overborne at the pleasure of the ruler. The will of the ruler was thus the law of the land, whether expressed in the form of a <u>fiat</u> or a <u>firman</u> or a regulation. His territory was no British territory and his subjects not British subjects: nevertheless, his subservience to the Paramountcy remained always paramount; and the whispers of the Resident were command which no ruler could dare disobey. External relations were, of course, centred completely in the hands of the Paramount power. War and peace were matters of exclusive concern of the common suzerain. In any view, the people of the States had no part nor lot in the governance of their country.

British India, however, presented a slightly different picture. It was subject to the sovereignty of Parliament and the imperium of the British Crown. But India awoke from her bondage. The Morley Minto Reforms of 1909, the Montford experiment in diarchy in the Indian provinces in 1919 and the Government of India Act of 1935 represent the gradual efforts to meet the growing demands of a nation that had found its soul. But the Constitution Act of 1935 still retained the tentacles of Whitehall. It sought to grant autonomy to the nine Governors of the provinces but gave them no freedom. The area of government was partitioned into three domains, one reserved to the discretion of the Governor into which ministers may not enter but may be overborne, and the third left to ministerial responsibility. In matters of discretion and individual judgement, the Governor was subject to the superintendence of the Governor-General, who in turn was subject to the superintendence of the Secretary of State. Even the attenuated autonomy was uncertain in its duration; for at the bid of the Governor under the notorious Section 93 of the Act, he could resume the reins of power entirely into his hands, and supersede the legislature and the ministry. Nor was there even a semblance of responsibility at the Centre. At Delhi, the government was manned entirely by the nominees of Whitehall, with the Governor-General at its head, but subservient in all matters to the control and superintendence of the Secretary of State. The framework of the constitutional structure thus rested in its apex at Whitehall. It derived its legal source and political sustenance from the British Parliament.

Both Indian India and British India lay under the heels of the foreigner. If they were united, they were united only in common bondage to the Crown. And the governance of both lay rooted in despotism, whether of an individual ruler or of a multitudinous assembly called Parliament. For in either of the two Indias, the people had no effective voice in the administration of their country. The responsibility for their well-being lay, in the ultimate analysis, not in their hands but elsewhere, either in a prince or in Parliament.

This was the old order; and the older order has changed. Today India is free. We have cut asunder the bonds of our bondage and freed ourselves from the foreign yoke. The Indian is no longer a slave in his own country and despised outside. He can now walk with his head held high at home, or abroad. India has taken her place in the comity of nations, in her own right as a sovereign State. Embassies have been opened in important capitals; and her voice is listened to with respect in the councils of the world. She is fast moving into the leadership of the continent of Asia; and international forces decisive of the fate of the world are slowly shifting from Europe to Asia. Soon, India is likely to forge ahead into a world power.

That has been the first and foremost sequel to the people of India constituting 'India into a Sovereign Democratic Republic'. Not the less spectacular or striking has been the great internal changes wrought by the Constitution. Indian nationalism had created the vision of India as the common mother, with her head pillowed on the snowy heights of the Himalayas, her arms stretched across the Indus and the Ganges, and her feet washed by the waters of the Cape. The Partition of 1947 left her maimed and mutilated: nevertheless she has emerged from the ordeal far stronger and more vigorous than at any time in her history. It was the proud boast of Lord Canning that what the Moguls never completed and the Marathas never contemplated the British had achieved. But even the British attained only unity, not union, and unity of suzerainty, not the union of States. Indian India and British India have now been integrated into India, that is, Bharat, a Union of states. The Constituent States have now been welded into a federal polity with legislative, executive and judicial powers over the units and the Union. The President of India is the supreme head of the Union. Within its assigned fields, Parliament at Delhi can legislate for the entire territories comprised in India. And the writs of the Supreme Court now run to every corner of the country. For the first time in history, India has become a nation with a common territory, common government and common citizenship. The magnitude of that achievement is the highest tribute to Indian nationalism and the wise statesmanship of its leaders. For, without such unity the break-up of the British rule in India should have followed the same course as the break-up of the Mogul rule in India. A fragmented India should have been the greatest menace to her new-won freedom.

What the Constitution further ensures is a democratic Republic. The divine right of the people has replaced the divine right of the princes and omnipotence of the British Parliament. Adult franchise and responsible government have made the people the fountain of all power. It is for them to choose their representatives in the legislature, and through them the persons who may be entrusted with the reins of the government. In Part A, in states which are the counterparts of the old British Indian provinces, a Governor still continues as the head of the state: while in Part B, states which are the survivors of the old Indian States, the Rajapramukh is the ruler. But whether called a Governor or a Rajapramukh, he is only the Constitutional head of his state; and in a scheme of responsible government his position is assimilated to that of the King in England, who, in the language of Lord Coke, is but 'a dignified hieroglyphic'. No President, Governor or Rajapramukh may act save on the advice of his ministers. He is bound to summon the leaders of the major party in the legislature to form his government; for without legislative sanctions no taxes may be levied, nor expenditure incurred. The control of the purse has shifted to the chosen of the people; and should the government of the day fail to retain the confidence of the legislature an appeal to the electorate is inevitable. The sovereignty of the people has thus become the basic postulate of the political philosophy of the Constitution.

One unique feature of the Constitution is the mechanism by which elementary human rights are secured to the citizen against infringement by the legislative or the executive bodies of the State. Every civilized country in the world has sought to solve the conflict between individual liberty and social control in different ways. In England, there are no fundamental rights. There, Parliament is free and the judiciary is bound: but a vigilant public opinion safeguards the subject against legislative excesses; and the enforcement of the rule of law by courts protects him from executive illegalities. In France and in Switzerland, fundamental rights have been enacted as part of the Constitution; but if the French Parliament or the Swiss Federal Legislature should enact any law in conflict with these rights, the courts have no power to strike them down as invalid. In these countries, such provisions are largely considered as copy-book maxims, the infringement of which is not amenable to judicial control. In the United States, however, it is different. The rights of the individual enshrined in the Constitution are enforceable by courts. Though the Constitution has not expressly so enacted, judicial interpretation has vested in courts the right and the duty to annul legislative enactments which are repugnant to any of its provisions. Recognizing that the tyranny of the many is as bad if not worse than the tyranny of an individual, some of the basic human rights have been made inviolable by the legislatures and governments of the units and the Union. On the American model the Constitution of India has improved. Equality before the law and equal protection of laws are assured. The . . . freedoms, speech, assembly, association, movement, residence, property and profession are separately enumerated, and the ambit of permissible legislation under each head is again defined. Untouchability, the curse of India, is abolished. Preventive detention is hedged in by limitations. Religious freedom is expressly secured. And the right to constitutional remedies is specifically guaranteed by empowering the Supreme Court to issue writs or orders for enforcement of the fundamental rights. Legislation by Parliament or by the State is made subservient to the fundamental rights of the citizens; and all laws, present and future, which abridge or abrogate these rights, are expressly declared void. No Constitution in the world has sought to guarantee the freedom of the citizen in language so clear and explicit, or to secure his rights beyond the chances of judicial interpretation. So long as no declaration of emergency is made, the fundamental rights are an integral part of the organic law of the land and cannot be imperilled by legislative or executive acts.

The creation of a 'Sovereign Democratic Republic securing the unity of the Nation', and 'Justice, Liberty, Equality and Fraternity' for the citizen are thus the conscious aim and purpose of the Constitution, as proclaimed in the Preamble. Words more inspiring cannot be found in any other organic instrument. They hold within themselves both a prayer and a promise. It may be that the text of the Constitution may here and there be open to happier phrasing. But no one who is familiar with the leading Constitutions of the world can fail to be impressed with the range of its vision, the loftiness of its ideals and the details of its provisions to effectuate its purpose. There is no brighter chapter in India's history than that which was heralded by the Constitution on 26 January 1950. Blessed are they who saw the dawn of their country's freedom. And yet it must be owned that it is not merely the machine that matters so much as the method of its working. Nor, in a democracy, is it permissible to look up to the steering of the Constitution only to those at the helm. The foundation of democracy is freedom; and eternal vigilance is the watchword of liberty. Those who are called to power are but the chosen of the people. They come of the people, and reflect but the character and the aspirations of the people. The experience of the past is the guide for the future. The inertia, apathy and indifference of its inhabitants made India a prey to invasion and misrule for centuries. Constitutions are but instruments to secure individual happiness and national prosperity. If we endeavour to live up to the ideals of our Constitution, the Constitution will surely lead us to our glorious destiny.

THE FRAMEWORK OF THE NEW CONSTITUTION

(By M.K. Nambyar, LL.M (Lond.), Barrister-at-Law)

Every constitutional settlement is a child of the circumstances in which it is made, and the Cabinet Mission's proposal can hardly be understood except in the context of the conflicting currents in India's political life. After years of struggle for Indian independence, Indian nationalism was confronted by fissiparous obstacles from within. What Lord Morley had feared in the grant of communal electorates as the sowing of the dragon's teeth had come to realization in the sprouting of claims for communal States. No one during the ten long years of making of the present Constitution had ever thought of suggesting the creation of a Muslim state as the objective of Muslim aspirations. Yet, within two years of the functioning of provincial autonomy under the Constitution Act of 1935, the slogan of Pakistan had become the goal of the Muslim League. The cry gained momentum in a few years. No settlement of India's independence was possible without the division of India. To such a course Indian nationalism could never agree. The unity of India was paramount, fundamental and inviolable. The Cripps Mission in 1942 and the Wavell Conference in 1945 found no agreement on any basic essentials. Direct talks between the leaders of the main parties in 1945 were of no avail to bridge the ever-widening gulf between them. It was in this impasse that the Cabinet delegation endeavoured to explore all avenues for a settlement in the Tripartite Conference at Simla. It failed, as could easily have been foretold. It attempted the impossible. But from the welter of conflicting proposals and counter-proposals emerged the Cabinet Mission's Plan, which sought to synthesize the hostile ideologies into a common framework. The Plan, it is insisted, is neither an award nor a document of legal validity. It is only a recommendation, but a recommendation voicing the views of His Majesty's government.

The claim of the Muslim League party, in substance, rested on the constitution of the six provinces of the Punjab, the

North-West Frontier Province, Baluchistan, Sind, Bengal and Assam into a sovereign State of Pakistan, and the rest of the provinces into Hindustan. The two States were then to enter, not into a federal Union, but into a treaty to provide for matters of common concern, like defence, external affairs and communications necessary for defence.

What was envisaged was the setting up of a joint agency or a confederation. But if a central executive or legislature was formed instead, parity of representation to the two sovereign groups in the government was insisted. Since two sovereign States had to come into being, two Constituent Assemblies were the necessary postulates of the Muslim League's demand. To the Indian National Congress, there could be neither Pakistan nor Hindustan but one India in which the provinces and States could be welded into an organic federal Union. The area of its authority could be restricted to defence, external affairs and communications. But provinces which desired joint economic or administrative planning in any sphere could cede to the Centre optional subjects in addition to these to secure the advantage of common legislation.

A careful scrutiny of the Pakistan demand revealed to the Mission its inherent antithesis, no less than the grave dangers to India's security and defence. The six provinces of the proposed Pakistan do not share even the essential element of continuity. The eastern and western provinces are divided by 700 miles. The Muslim population in all the six provinces only totals a bare majority of 51.69 per cent, while the province of Assam, Western Bengal, and Ambala and Jullunder divisions in the Punjab have predominantly non-Muslim populations. Logically, the compulsion of these areas into Pakistan would have no justification. Their exclusion would equally reduce Pakistan to insignificance. From the point of view of security, the division of the country into two, or in effect three, independent zones, would render the defence of either State ineffective. The Cabinet Mission was therefore constrained to reject a sovereign, separate Pakistan, and this led to the inevitable conclusion that the interests of the country demanded a central federal Union of the States and provinces in India.

The federal Union's authority was to be confirmed only to the three subjects, and all others, including residuary subjects, were reserved to the provinces.

The Congress proposal of cession of optional subjects did not, however, appeal to the Mission. The Cabinet Mission observes:

> Apart from the difficulty of working such a scheme, we do not consider that it would be fair to deny to other Provinces which do not desire to take the optional subjects at the Centre, the right to form themselves into a group for a similar purpose. This would indeed be no more than the exercise of their autonomous powers in a particular way.

The Cabinet Mission, therefore, devised a system of grouping of provinces for joint collaboration on the optional subjects and provided against Muslim fears of a perpetual Hindu majority rule at the Centre by requiring for the decision of any major communal issue in the federal legislature a majority vote of the representatives present and voting of each of the two major communities as well as of a majority of all the members present and voting.

The plan evolved is laid in a six-step basic formula, which it is best to set out at length to appreciate its full significance:

1. There should be a Union of India, embracing both British India and the States, which should deal with the following subjects: Foreign Affairs, Defence and Communications; and should have the powers necessary to raise the finances required for the above subjects.

2. The Union should have an Executive and Legislature constituted from British Indian and States representatives. Any question raising a major communal issue in the Legislature should require for its decision a majority of the representatives present and voting of each of the two major communities as well as a majority of all the members present and voting.

3. All subjects other than the Union subjects and all residuary powers should vest in the Provinces.
4. The States will retain all subjects and powers other than those ceded to the Union.
5. Provinces should be free to form Groups with Executives and Legislatures, and each Group could determine the Provincial subjects to be taken in common.
6. The constitutions of the Union and of the Groups should contain a provision whereby any Province could, by a majority vote of its Legislative Assembly, call for a reconsideration of the terms of the constitution after an initial period of two years and at ten-yearly intervals thereafter.

The machinery devised to bring the Constitution into being is only a single Constituent Assembly, to split itself into three sections, A, B and C. The Punjab, the North-West Frontier Province, Sind and Baluchistan are grouped into 'B', Bengal and Assam into 'C' and the rest of the provinces into 'A'. Each section is to design the Constitution for each province included in its fold, and 'shall also decide whether any group constitution shall be set up for those Provinces, and, if so, with what Provincial subjects the Groups should deal'. Since the members of the Constituent Assembly are to be chosen by the present legislative assemblies, which are not fully representative, each province is given the freedom to opt itself out of the group if the new legislature to be constituted under the new Constitution should so decide. The principle of self-determination in the creation of Pakistan or Hindustan is thus effectuated in two ways; firstly, by granting each sectional Constituent Assembly—not each unit of that section—the independence to determine whether the component provinces of that section shall form into a Union or not; secondly, by vesting in each province the right to secede from the group it may have been forced into by the chances of a majority vote in the sectional Constituent Assembly. The formation of Pakistan or Hindustan is thus left to the will of the people of a province and not to its compulsory membership of a particular section of the Constituent Assembly. It is open to any section to refuse to group; but if it does [agree to], the grouping is not final, but subject to revision by the new legislative assemblies of the constituent units . . .

. . . The last act of the Union Constituent Assembly is to negotiate a treaty with the United Kingdom to provide for matters arising out of the transfer of power. The prime minister, Attlee, and also the Cabinet Mission, have made it plain beyond the shadow of doubt that India is free to remain within or without the empire.

Such then is the outline of the Constitution that is proposed by the Cabinet Mission with the approval of His Majesty's government. Even a cursory observer familiar with the complexities of the Indian problem cannot fail to be impressed with the spirit of sincerity and helpfulness animating the entire plan. A new Constitution represents a new endeavour at governmental organization. While it may be articulate of the struggles of the past, it equally sets the horizon to the strivings of the future. If these bounds can expand with the expanding needs of the people, the Constitution may endure. Else it must perish. A Constitution must therefore see fulfilment in fulfilling the organic impulses of national life.

It is in contrast with the experiments of the past that the proposals of the present can be judged. The cry of Indian nationalism for full self-government that grew strident in the first world war was sought to be satisfied by the introduction of diarchy in the provinces and the association of representative legislature with the bureaucracy at the Centre. The historic struggle of 1929 to 1932, and the mass civil disobedience and non-violent rebellion in wide areas culminated in the Round Table Conferences and, finally, in the enactment of the Constitution of 1935. It was 'made in England'. It was purely the product of a Conservative Parliament, and the handiwork of British draftsmanship.

It broke up the unitary State of British India, which had been so functioning from the year of the Regulating Act, endowed the provinces with complete autonomy and provided for a federation of the British provinces and Indian States under the Crown. Not the least important feature of the Constitution was the scheme of safeguards woven into the fabric of the fundamental law.

The federation so devised never came into being. The States looked and looked before they leaped, and never leaped. Diarchy, which had been decried in the provincial structure, was, however, planted at the Centre. Defence, external and ecclesiastical affairs were excluded from popular control and vested solely in the Governor-General, to be administered by him at his discretion with the aid of his nominees, called counsellors. In the provinces, in theory, the whole area of government was transferred to ministerial hands.

The dynamics of responsible government, it is well known, lie in the control over the purse by the chosen of the people and the consequent control of the powers of the King by the representatives of the nation. The King reigns but does not govern. The discretionary rights of the Crown in the Constitution are, therefore, vested in the ministerial heads, giving rise to the maxim that the prerogatives of the King have become the privileges of the people. And wherever Parliamentary system obtains, whether in the Dominions like Australia or Canada or in the colonies like Southern Rhodesia, the discretionary powers of the King's representatives, either a Governor or a Governor-General, whether in summoning and dissolving the Parliament or in the appointment and dismissal of ministers or in the assent to the bills or in connection with any other matter appertaining to the administration, are discharged in accordance with the advice tendered by the ministry. No King who wishes to retain his crown and throne can dare disregard the advice of his ministers; and in 1932, Prime Minister De Valera established Constitutional precedent in compelling the dismissal of his Governor-General in acting counter to his wishes in what was after all a very minor matter. But all this rests on usage, not on formal law.

Suspicion and mistrust of British imperialism constrained the Constituent Assembly of the newly formed Eire to enact those conventions into the Constitution Act of 1922 so that the Governor

General may not refuse the advice of his ministry. Suspicion and distrust of Indian nationalism impelled British imperialism to a similar course, to enact express clauses in the Government of India Act of 1935 excluding the applicability of such conventions in the discharge of the functions of the King's representative in all vital matters. The Act enjoins the Governor and the Governor-General to be aided by ministerial advice, except in so far as he is required by the Act to exercise his functions in his discretion or individual judgement. With respect to a large number of important matters, the Governor and the Governor-General are directed to act in their discretion or individual judgement. The entire area of governmental authority in the provinces and in the federal Centre, exclusive of the three reserved subjects, is partitioned into three domains: Firstly, a domain in the Governor's or Governor-General's discretion into which ministers are debarred from entering; secondly, the domain of his individual judgement into which ministers may enter but may be overborne; and lastly the domain of ministerial action in which ministerial advice prevails. Diarchy disappeared, but triarchy appeared in a more insidious and all-pervasive form. In so far as he is directed to act in his discretion or individual judgement, the Governor is subordinate to the Governor-General, and the Governor-General to the Secretary of State for India and through him to the Parliament. By a series of provisions, each is empowered to control the day-to-day administration, invested with special responsibilities in matters affecting the State, and armed and equipped with the necessary funds and authority over the civil service to carry out his behests. In each lies the discretionary right to summon, prorogue or dissolve the assembly, sanction introduction to a large number of bills, arrest further movement of the legislative anvil, and assent, refuse or reserve consideration of the bills so passed. With regard to a large part of the finance, each is independent of legislative grants; in respect of items of expenditure relating to his own special responsibilities, each has the means to secure the necessary revenues despite the refusal of the assembly. Finally, though each is only a creature of the Constitution, each is endowed with the power of life and death over the Constitution. At his edict, under Section 93, the country passes from democracy to dictatorship. Not even Henry VIII, who could legislate by proclamation, in virtue of the Statute of Proclamation, owned powers half as plenary or as drastic as that vested in the constitutional heads by the Government of India Act, 1935.

But this is not all. To avoid all possibilities of freedom from these constitutional shackles, further fetters were forced, preventing any legal repeal of these provisions in so far as they related to the Governor-General's powers in the federal scheme. A federation is an indestructible Union; by the very nature of its creation it is unalterable, save as provided for by the compact that brings it into being. Section 6(5) of the Government of India Act 1935 enables Parliament to amend the provisions mentioned in the second schedule to the Act without affecting the federal Union. The second schedule details not merely what may but also what may not be amended. The discretionary powers of the Governor-General, the superintendence of the Secretary of State from Whitehall, and almost the entire armoury in the Constitution that makes the Governor-General the master of his government, and through him the Secretary of State, are preserved inviolate against parliamentary revision. The steel frame of the old despotism which Indian nationalism strived so long to supplant is continued in all its terrific strength; and what has been hardly noticed even in India is that it is sought to be perpetuated for ever. For, not even Parliament has any legal authority over the federation of India, except to the extent that the constitution itself has conferred. The federal Union of India is not a union of purely British Indian provinces and non-British States came into being; Parliament has no more inherent right to alter the federal structure than the ruler of a State. The long chapter of constitutional restrictions against discriminatory legislation, which, for instance, prohibits even reservation of coastal traffic to Indian shipping, is also expressly excepted from subsequent repeal. Had the federal part of the act ever come into operation, the second schedule would have created an effectual legal bar to the march of India's freedom.

It is in this background that the new project has to be viewed. For the first time in the history of Indo-British struggle, India obtains the right which Canada, Australia, South Africa and Eire had, to design her Constitutional structure on her own soil in accordance with her own will. If the proposals have laid the broad contours of the edifice, they are also laid within the framework of India's independence. India can now pattern her future on any model it chooses; responsible government on the lines of Westminster, Presidential Government as in the United States, or any other kind. If it swings towards the Dominion model, it is still open to it to adopt the King or his representative as the head of the State or elect a President by the voice of the nation, as under the present Constitution of Eire. It is important to note that no external limitations are imposed on the freedom of choice of the system of government within the federal fabric. In framing its future Constitution, India's interest can prevail.

The status of the Constituent Assembly and the treaty to be entered into with the United Kingdom provided for in the Plan have raised anxious doubts in the minds of many. The Constituent Assembly, it is said, has no sovereign authority to promulgate the Constitution it may ordain as the fundamental law of the land; nor has it the capacity to conclude the treaty. 'As a lawyer Sir Stafford Cripps knows, even if his colleagues do not,' says Sir Alfred Watson, MP, who was for long a distinguished editor of the *Statesman*, 'that Treaties are made between Sovereign States. The Indian Union Government cannot be bound by a document signed by a body having none of the powers of a Government.' As a proposition of abstract law this is no doubt correct. But few constitutional lawyers will fail to remember the Irish parallel. It was the British which, in 1921, in the first instance offered the revolutionary Sinn Fein a settlement in the form of a treaty to be ratified by the British and Irish Parliaments. The treaty that was finally concluded was signed by Lloyd George and Winston Churchill, among others, on behalf of His Majesty's government. When the treaty came for ratification before the House of Commons, the Unionist critics raised precisely the same protest [as pointed out by Watson]. Treaties, they said, could be made only between independent states; and it was not constitutionally possible for the ministers of the Crown to enter into treaties with the Crown subjects. Nevertheless, the process of settlement through treaty was defended as constitutional and finally given the imprimatur of Parliament by its enactment into a statute. On behalf of the Free State, the Treaty was signed not even by the Constituent Assembly but by the plenipotentiaries of the revolutionary Sinn Fein. The body that ratified the treaty was not the Irish Parliament established by the Government of Ireland Act of 1920, which was then its legal Constitution, but by the illegal 'Dail Eireann' sitting as a Constituent Assembly 'in this Provincial Parliament acknowledging that all lawful authority comes from God to the people . . . and in the exercise of undoubted right'. A Constituent Assembly ex-hypothesis is the creator, not the creature of a Constitution. It is invoked because of the inadequacy of the existing law to adjust itself to the growing needs of the community. While it does not function within the law, it ordains the fundamental law of the land, the law of all laws, the fountainhead and source from which other laws flow. Juridical concepts can seldom be carried to their logical length. In 1783, the United Kingdom concluded a treaty of peace with its rebel American colonies. Once a settlement by treaty is effected, the normal procedure of obtaining Parliamentary approval is not likely to be departed from by the Labour government. That will set at rest all doubts of all constitutional purists.

Clearly then, it is the substance of the proposals and not the form of their ultimate clothing that demands scrutiny. The keystone of the constitutional arch lies in the federal Union of the States and provinces. The disintegration of a sovereign India has been definitely stayed despite insistent separatist threats. Neither invasion after invasion nor internal strife and dynastic wars ever disrupted the fundamental historic unity of India. British rule served to emphasize its economic, strategic and administrative unity. Two world wars had demonstrated that Indian security lay in the disposition of her defences by one Central command. Every state document on constitutional reforms, from the Montford Report, has therefore, for its basic doctrine, the political thesis that a strong Centre is a manifest necessity. Obviously, no freedom is worth any trouble if it is just short-lived, to provide but an interregnum for a change of masters. But it is not merely the instinct for self-preservation that makes India's integrity indivisible. The transcendent forces which bind a nation in war and in peace, and animate the highest efforts, and the noblest sacrifices are not materialistic but spiritual. What inspired and sustained the long-drawn struggle for Indian independence was the mystic love and devotion to the country which Indian nationalism almost deified in the form of the common mother. The journey's end would have been void, the sacrifice and suffering sterile and the future forlorn, if the idol of nationalist dreams had crumbled into dust and ashes.

If there is any infirmity in the Constitution of the Centre, it is the restriction of the area of its authority to the three defined subjects. It is true that the provision for the raising of finance for its purposes might attract in its train taxable spheres of customs, excise and other sources of revenue. But no other federal Constitution in the Commonwealth has assigned so narrow a field of government to the Centre. Experience of the working of the administrative machinery in India, in other federal Constitutions should have discouraged such a course. But the Cabinet Mission, it is plain, was not entirely unfettered in its judgement. The conflict between the two great parties apparently drove the Mission to the view that it was better to have an attenuated Union than no Union at all. It is still open to Indian statesmanship to enlarge the sphere of the Centre by mutual agreement.

The federation that is proposed is a union of British India and Indian States. It may be recalled that in the Act of 1935, the relationship of the Crown to the Indian States was excluded from interference by the federal government by concentrating all powers of paramountcy into the hands of the Crown and the Crown's Representative. The Princes' willingness to enter into that federal Union was conditioned by the preservation of their sovereignty intact. They asked for the impossible, and continued as of old. The Cabinet Mission has made it clear that the grant of independence to India rendered the retention of the paramountcy of the Crown otiose. The States will no more have the protective arm of the Crown against the turbulence of their subjects or threats to their territorial integrity. Their future security therefore lies in the federal Union; nor could they have any objection to cede powers over the three federal subjects which, with the exception of domestic communications, they do not own or exercise at present. The States are invited to appoint a committee immediately to negotiate the terms of their entry into the Union with the Constituent Assembly. And finally, in hammering out the Union Constitution, they participate through their representatives in the Union Constituent Assembly, the number of such representatives being fixed on the same basis as of British India, which it may be recalled, is one to a million of population.

The rejection of the claim for sovereign Pakistan in the creation of one supreme All-India Federal Union appears to have given dissatisfaction to a section of the Muslim community. The factual reasons given by the Mission are incontrovertible. These apart, neither international law nor political theory knows any instance of the recognition of statehood for any community bound by neither territorial affinity nor a common nationality but only by identity of religion. Religion, it is clear, cannot be the touchstone of nationality. Nor is self-determination of any avail to found the claim for Pakistan. The principle of self-determination, it may be recalled, was first proclaimed by President Wilson in 1918 in his famous fourteen points for post-war settlement. But its universal application was soon found impossible of realization. Austria was restrained by treaty from uniting with Germany; nor was self-determination adhered to in the transfer of Austrian Tyrol to Germany, Kio Chow to Japan, German colonies to the mandatories and of millions of Germans to Poland and Czechoslovakia. The only time that doctrine came for scrutiny before an international tribunal was on a reference of the dispute between Finland and Sweden over the Aland island's plebiscite, which voted in favour of its union with Sweden. The commission of jurists then held that 'the right of free self-determination is not a rule of international law'. Self-determination, like liberty, cannot be so exercised as to impair or imperil the geographical, economic and military security of its neighbour, or prejudice the other's vital interests. If the Isle of Wight decided by a plebiscite to incorporate itself into Franco's Spain, no one will deny that the United Kingdom would have an undoubted right to intervene. The United States herself fought a bitter civil war in denial of the principle; and the Monroe Doctrine is a standing challenge to the freedom of self-determination to the South American Republics.

The Cabinet Mission has sought to appease Muslim sentiment by granting freedom of grouping to the provinces. Perhaps no part of the plan has given rise to greater controversy or misapprehension. Arthur Moore, the editor of the *Statesman*, appears to have stated in an interview:

> What the Mission's plan amounts to, and what the League has accepted is a blue print for a Federation of Federations. Group 'A' Provinces will federate in Hindustan, 'B' and 'C' in Pakistan, then Hindustan, Pakistan and Indian States will federate in Greater India. This is the model on which the whole government will eventually be built up.

Nothing could be further from the Cabinet Plan. Every federal system of government involves a division of powers between two parties, the federating unit and the federal Union. Para 15(3) of the constitutional plan states that 'all subjects other than the Union and all residuary powers should rest in the Provinces', and not in the groups of provinces. Even a cursory reading of the proposals would show that the formation of any group is speculative and cannot possibly be the nucleus of the all-India federal Union. For, the explanatory statement of the Cabinet Mission on 25 May 1946, that 'the interpretation put by the Congress resolution on paragraph 15 of the statement to the effect that the Provinces in the first instance make the choice whether or not to belong to the section in which they are placed does not accord with the Delegation's intentions' does not in any way compel a group Constitution or a group federation. All that it means is that a province must go into the sectional Constituent Assembly assigned to it for the framing of its own Constitution or a group federation. But Para 19 (v) of the original proposals stands. And it shows beyond doubt that 'These sections . . . shall also decide whether any Group constitution shall set up, and if so with what Provincial subjects the groups should deal.' What is mandatory is the entry into the section, not into the group. And even if the grouping is decided on, it does not follow that it should partake the texture of a federal Union. The grouping might still take the shape of a joint agency or a confederation. But if a federal Union is the form that the grouping takes with a legislature and an executive, there is still the choice to opt out after the first elections. The 'A' section provinces might refuse to group at all; and the 'C' sectional assembly might force Assam into a federal Union with Bengal. But Assam might still opt out after the first general election under the coming Constitution. Obviously, the Union Constituent Assembly, which should have stood dissolved long before that event, cannot enact a federal Union with so uncertain a unit as the Bengal-Assam federation. What the Cabinet Plan indicates in plain words, and in its scheme and context, is that the federal Union to be formed is of the individual provinces and Indian States with authority over the three specified subjects. Each province or State is the nucleus of the federal system. But the provinces in each section have also, if they so choose, the freedom to form groups, which may be in the nature of federations or small federations with authority over any assigned subjects. A province may cede to its group any of the subjects reserved to it by the Plan. With this the federation of India has no concern. It is an optional arrangement in regard to any agreed matters within the domestic jurisdiction of the provinces. There is no legal nexus between the small federations and the all-India Union.

The present Indian Constitution is familiar with common agencies devised for two or more provinces. There is a Joint Public Service Commission for Bihar and Orissa. There is a joint high court for Bengal, and Assam, Kerala, Karnataka, Andhra and Maharashtra are clamouring for separation and will soon form distinct provinces. If the formation of the groups shapes only in the creation of common agencies to deal with matters of common concern, the Plan will be economically sound. If, on the other hand, they should decide to enter into a small federal Union, it will then mean in the end three different governments, the general Union, the group Union, and the province operating on the same soil with three different sets of legislative, executive and judicial organs. There is no constitutional precedent to guide the Indian provinces to decide on the adoption of such a complex, and what must also be costly, governmental machinery. The demand of the Muslim League was confined to a federal Pakistan and a federal Hindustan, the two federal States acting in concert on matters of common concern through agencies created by mutual treaty. It envisaged only one federation for each province, two sovereign federations within India, and a confederation of the two federations at the top. The federal Union of the provinces and States renders the small federal Unions costly superfluities, which are more likely to prove millstones round the neck of the group units. The functions that the small federal Union will discharge the provinces can also discharge, with better efficiency and more simplicity. The group Union, it must be owned, is a fifth wheel to the constitutional coach.

By far the most important part of the new project is the offer of absolute freedom to India. She has now the choice of staying within the British Commonwealth, or of carving her own destiny free from all links. Indian nationalism has been insistent on India's complete, absolute independence. Yet, at the critical hour when India is at the crossroads, it is essential that reason and not sentiment should be the signpost for guidance. The statute of Westminster, it must be admitted, has formally freed all fetters from the Dominions. The statute of the Union Act, 1934, declares in its preamble that the

Union of South Africa is a sovereign independent State, and enacts that the Parliament of the Union shall be the sovereign legislative power over the Union. The King is, no doubt, the head of the State, but it is not the King in the right of the United Kingdom but the King in the right of South Africa, acting solely on the advice of the Union ministers. The new Constitution of the Irish Free State, which is still within the Commonwealth, proclaims in article 5 that Ireland is a sovereign, independent, democratic state, and has substituted an elected President in place of the King. Each Dominion which entered the second world war did so on its own declaration of war. Eire remained neutral. Every Dominion now is as free as any other independent State in the world; while it is subject to no external limitations whatever, it obtains the strength and security inherent in its membership of the British Commonwealth. Neither the atom bomb nor the UNO Charter can be safely said to eliminate war for all time. Even though the world is scarred and scorched by a conflagration that is just extinguished, the international horizon is hardly clear. Prudence demands that in a world of competing forces, India should so align herself as to breathe the air of freedom in peace, confidence and security.

But whether the decision is cast in favour of complete independence or Dominion status, the proposals, it must be recognized, seek to make India the master of her own fate. The Plan is undoubtedly a great constitutional project. It holds the promise of India's freedom. It rests now on Indian statesmanship to build the future on the framework that has been furnished on firm and enduring lines.

OUR FUNDAMENTAL RIGHTS[1]

(By M.K. Nambyar, LL.M (Lond.))

(Barrister-at-Law)

A new Constitution demands a new philosophy of life. Yet it is doubtful whether many of us, lawyers, legislators or judges, have fully wrenched ourselves from the fetters of the past and tuned ourselves to the freedom of the present. In an age of legislative supremacy, born of the doctrine of the omnipotence of Parliament, no citizen could claim any fundamental right. For the essence of a fundamental right lay in the paramountcy of the [citizen's] right over the legislature of the land. Nevertheless, though over a year has passed since the promulgation of the new Constitution, the civil servant, the administrator and the government still function apparently oblivious of the deep changes wrought in the mechanism of government. Legislative enactments are still passed; rules and orders made as if the old British regime still continued, without the slightest effort [on the part of lawyers, legislators and judges] to adjust themselves to the new order; and when such acts or orders end up before the high court with the issue of a writ rule nisi and a rule absolute, the offender throws up his hands in despair and blames fundamental rights as the source of all evils in the country.

Indeed, it is an interesting paradox that those who were loudest in their insistence on the inclusion of fundamental rights in the Constitution are now among their most bitter opponents. Power corrupts, but never so absolutely as to forswear the ideals of a lifetime.

The Constituent Assembly debates enshrine some of the most passionate speeches in the cause of the human rights to life, liberty and property, to freedom of speech and of association. But it is not very surprising that those who fought against tyranny and despotism and the curtailment of human rights should themselves, having been entrusted with the reins of power, find in the exigencies of the governance of the country excuses for the abandonment of the ideals which they had cherished and fought for. It is a remarkable fact that before the Constitution is two years old, the provisional Parliament, which is but another name for the old Constituent Assembly, should have thought it necessary to introduce the first amendment to the Constitution, striking at some of the basic fundamental rights enacted only a few months earlier. To those who are in the seat of power, fundamental rights have become fundamental impediments to the governance of the country. If the Constituent Assembly had delayed the passage of the Constitution until 1951, it is indeed doubtful whether any fundamental rights chapter would have stood in the Constitution at all. Perhaps there is little to choose between government and government. Whether the government is by the many or by an individual, its commands must be obeyed. Its will must be the law of the land. If it is thwarted in its objectives, it liquidates the obstruction with the means at its command.

The conflict between State control and individual freedom has been one of the perennial problems of political organization. To the State, self-preservation is the supreme social end. But a State is an abstraction. Its directive will is therefore the will of its controlling authority, whether called a monarchical despot, a fascist dictator or a democratic cabinet. But such is the illusion of power that those enthroned in the seat of authority are apt to identify their own self-preservation as the preservation of the State, and therefore as the supreme social good. The old doctrine that the King is the State and the State is the King still persists with modern substitutions. Opposition to authority therefore becomes opposition to the State. Where the sovereign authority in a State is supreme, paramount and uncontrolled, the will of the sovereign is the law of the land, whether the sovereignty rests in a personal monarch or in an impersonal Parliament. Power unrestricted is power absolute; and it does not affect the nature of the power in the least whether such power is exercised by one or by many. In such a system of government, a citizen has no rights but what the State may grant him. But since the State could always take away such rights at its will and pleasure, such rights become dependent on the bounty of the State and can endure only so long as the State permits. The State thus becomes the arbiter of both the existence and the extent of the citizen's rights. Against such a State, a citizen can have no fundamental rights.

Of the three organs of the State, the most potent has been the legislature. Where the legislature is sovereign, its enactments are unquestioned and unquestionable. But the concept of law has undergone a change. We no longer think of law along with Bacon and Bracton as of divine origin. Law in the modern State has no moral content. Its authority now rests neither in its divine origin nor in its moral appeal, but merely on the strength of the organized force of the State. Whether an act keeps one to the right of the road or to its left, whether it enacts a rule of conduct with respect to transfer of property or murder, the act is law, and its compulsion rests not in its inherent content but in the competence of the legislative body from which it originates. But the technique of law-making has not stopped merely with the framing of rules of conduct. A legislature may enact laws depriving a person of his life, liberty or property. When the British Parliament enacted in 1401 the statute 'De Heretico comburendo', confirming the right of the church to have heretics burnt by the common hangman, Parliament was enacting a law of the same efficacy as, say, the Statute of Mortmain or any other enactment on the Statute Book. When again, in 1530, the Parliament passed an act directing that the Bishop of Rochester's cook be boiled to death, it was placing on the Statute Book an enactment on the same par as any other statute that it had passed. In 1641, the Earl of Stafford was beheaded by an act of Parliament. The powers of a legislature which is uncontrolled are, therefore, vast and unlimited. It holds in the hollow of its hands the life, liberty and property of the citizens. It matters little, therefore, whether such a law-making authority goes by the name of the Shah of Persia or of Parliament.

All these instances might look irreconcilable with the elements of constitutional law that we have been familiar with. Most of us have learned that the leading characteristic of the British Constitution, as expounded by Dicey in his classical treatise, is the rule of law. According to Dicey,

> . . . the Rule of law means in the first place absolute supremacy or predominance of regular law as opposed to the influence of arbitrary power and excludes the existence of arbitrariness, or prerogative or even of wide discretionary authority on the part of the Government. Englishmen are governed by the law and by the law alone. A man may thus be punished for a breach of law, but he can be punished for nothing else.

But the major premise—that the rule of law excludes the exercise of arbitrary powers—vanishes when the law itself is arbitrary in conception and discretionary in content. Dicey did not live to hear the pronouncement of the House of Lords in *Rex v. Halliday*[2] or *Liversidge v. Anderson*.[3] If in England a person could be incarcerated on the mere satisfaction of a Secretary of State without any trial or remedy by judicial review, it is a travesty to extol the rule of law as an antithesis to arbitrary action. Between detention in a concentration camp at Buchenwald on the orders of Hitler or his minions and detention at Wormwoods on the mandate of a Home Secretary, the difference is one of form and not of substance. And the law that sanctifies either detention is not less arbitrary than the other because one is the decree of a dictator and the other a product of a Parliament passed after three solemn readings. But it is difficult to understand how the rule of law can be the peculiarity only of the British Constitution. In every organized system of government where the sovereign power rests in a monarchical despot or in a multitudinous Parliament, the will of the sovereign authority is the law of the land. What matters is not the form in which the sovereign will is expressed, whether it is expressed in the form of a statute entered on the rolls of the Statute Book, or in the form of a ukase, oral or written. The laws or ordinances promulgated by a dictator or a monarch have the same legal efficacy and validity as the law enacted by a Parliament. The rule of law, therefore, obtained both in parliamentary Britain and also in Nazi Germany. It may be that a dictator or a monarch may change the laws at any time; but so too may a Parliament. If a parliamentary enactment later in time is inconsistent with an earlier act, it is well-known that the later act prevails. The doctrine of the rule of law does not depend upon the elaborate way in which an enactment comes into being or the number of readings it is subjected to, but purely on the sovereign authority, the expression of whose will is binding on the land.

But what is more important to notice is that the rule of law expresses only a half-truth. It is no doubt true that we are governed by the law. But the law is equally governed by us. Law in the modern State is what we make, and unmake. Therefore, we rule the law no less than we are ruled by the law. So long as a law is enforced, we are ruled by the law. But we have also the right to change, abridge or abrogate a law. Law is therefore neither immutable nor unchanging, neither fixed nor crystallized, neither absolute nor permanent. It owes its life and origin to the will of its maker and can exist only so long as it is permitted to continue. In this analysis, the doctrine of rule of law does not operate against legislative oppression. Its only function and purpose is to safeguard the citizen against executive excesses. For so long as a law obtains, the executive in an organized State is bound by the law, and the person and property of a subject may be interfered with only in accordance with the law. To that extent the rule of law has been one of the cornerstones of British jurisprudence; and not merely of British jurisprudence but of every organized society that is entitled to statehood in the modern community of nations. Without the rule of law, there can be no organized community—in fact, no organized institution of any type whatever. But if fundamental rights must be fundamental, they are rights against the State and all its organs and instrumentalities; and no right is fundamental unless the legislature of the State is bound thereby and may not transgress these rights except at its own peril.

Clearly then, what secures a citizen against the State is not the doctrine of the rule of law but the mechanism of the law-making authority, the method of its working and the restraints on its movements. Different countries have different political Constitutions, and the process of history records the impact of individual liberty on the supreme authority of the State. In England, the Magna Carta, the Petition of Rights and the Bill of Rights are landmarks in the struggle between the King personifying the supreme authority of the State and the people. To the Magna Carta we owe the recognition that there is a law above all laws which no King may disrespect. When article 39 of the Magna Carta proclaimed that 'No free man shall be captured or imprisoned or disseized or outlawed or exiled or in any way destroyed; nor will we against him or send against him except by the lawful judgment of his peers and by the law of the land,' it embodied the concept of the 'law of the land' as something more than the edicts of the supreme authority promulgated from time to time, something permanent, something constant, something beyond the reach of Kings and Parliaments. When the great constitutional conflict between the King and Parliament finally ended in the triumph of the sovereignty of the Parliament over the sovereignty of the King, it became no longer necessary to secure the subject against the tyranny of the Crown. But against Parliament the subject had no fundamental rights. Whatever Parliament enacts, he is bound to obey. In England, Parliament is free; the courts are bound; for no court may impugn an act of Parliament as ultra vires or invalid, whether it conflicts with a previous act of Parliament or the law of nature, or of reason, however arbitrary, tyrannical or discriminatory the act may be. It would, however, be not in accord with truth to stop with the formal law of the British Constitution and disregard its working. Possibly no country in the world enjoys as great freedom as a British citizen does, and that freedom, though subject entirely to the will of Parliament, has always been assured and continued by various statutory enactments, which, though liable to alteration, are nevertheless enactments which one may feel fairly certain will never be abrogated except in times of grave danger. Take for instance the Englishman's right to personal liberty. During the reign of Charles I, when a subject was imprisoned by order of the King, the return to a habeas corpus writ used to be made that the person was held '*Per Speciale Mandatum Regis*'—that is to say, by the special command of the King. Such a return was a perfectly valid answer to the courts, just as at present in India, if a return states that the prisoner is held as per the satisfaction of the detaining authority under our preventive detention acts, the courts cannot question the legality of the satisfaction. The Parliament in England, therefore, enacted the Habeas Corpus Act of 1679 by which such returns were held to be invalid and the King's Bench and every judge of His Majesty were laid under a legal duty to inquire into the legality of detention. If any judge refused to hear a habeas corpus application, he was liable to a fine under a provision which does not appear to have been copied by any other legislature in the world. A second commitment on the same cause was punishable, though it is interesting to observe that in India at present, even a release by court does not apparently afford sufficient immunity against a second re-arrest on the same cause. The habeas corpus acts have been very zealously enforced by the courts, and it is indeed noteworthy that if at the commencement of the day's work in court a counsel rises and states that he has an application concerning the liberty of a subject, a judge in England immediately puts aside all the rest of his cases, however urgent and important they may be, and hears the habeas corpus application forthwith. It serves little purpose to have a law on the Statute Book unless it is applied and enforced in the spirit in which it is made.

The habeas corpus acts may, of course, be suspended or repealed by Parliament; for Parliament is supreme. But as against parliamentary excesses, there is a strong and virile public opinion, which no party in power will dare disregard. Education and tradition have moulded the Englishman into both a law-abiding and also liberty-loving citizen. To whatever party he may belong, there are certain fundamentals on which everyone is united. Generally speaking, those who hold the reins of the government for the time being are not so blinded by power as to forget all restraints and toleration. For instance, the reform of the House of Lords has been a perennial issue in the last one century. Nevertheless, though in the last two decades there have been occasions when the party in power, whether Conservative or Labour, had overwhelming majorities, no party would think of initiating legislation for its complete abolition or elevation of the House of Lords into a co-equal chamber. In England, public opinion is the strongest bulwark against parliamentary tyranny. The formal law of the Constitution recognizes no fundamental rights. But nevertheless, the fundamental rights in England are as real and effective as in the United States.

In sharp contrast to the difference between theory and practice in regard to fundamental rights in the British Constitution lies the treatment accorded to such rights in the Continental Constitutions of France, Belgium and Switzerland. These Constitutions proclaim the freedom of conscience, the liberty of the person, the freedom of speech and of the press, and indeed several other fundamental declarations. But while these solemn declarations are intended as injunctions to their Parliaments, the Constitutions themselves hold no safeguard against their infringement. If, therefore, the legislatures of these countries exceed their competence or violate these constitutional provisions, the citizen has no remedy except to wait for the next elections and change the party in power and obtain their abrogation, though in Switzerland there is the revisionary process by referendum. The individual citizen has no right to go to a court of law and no remedy by judicial redress. These Continental declarations are no doubt part of the organic law, but they are what Salmond would call 'imperfect rights'. They are not justiciable in a court of law, for the courts have no jurisdiction to declare an act invalid. As in England, the courts in these countries are bound though their Parliaments and are not free in constitutional theory. In effect, therefore, these fundamental declarations are largely copy-book maxims in the organic law of the country. They have the same sanctity as, for instance, the solemn declarations in part IV of our Constitution. A right is no right unless it is capable of enforcement. Nor is it fundamental if the legislature may transgress the same with impunity.

While, therefore, fundamental rights in the continental Constitutions are largely illusory in their import, it is in the American Constitution that they find concrete reality and acceptance. It would hardly be practicable in a short compass, nor would it be necessary to state in detail the rights which have been enshrined in the text of the American Constitution. They have for their conscious aim and purpose the erection of guarantees of life, liberty and property against arbitrary deprivation by law. They are intended as a protection against tyranny by any of the organs of the State—the legislature, the executive or the judiciary. Though in the formal law of the Constitution no provision is found that any law enacted by the Congress inconsistent with the fundamental rights would be void, judicial interpretation from very early times made it clear that any law in conflict with any of the clauses in the supreme law would be a nullity and would have no legal validity. But in the working of the Constitution, the most interesting feature has been the way in which the courts have construed the phrase 'due process of law'. The fifth and fourteenth amendments commanded that no person shall be deprived of life, liberty or property without 'due process of law'.

What did 'law' mean in the context? Did it mean an enacted law by the Congress or the state legislature? Or did it mean law in the general sense? *Jus,* as distinguished from *Lex,* the normal and the constant law, the natural law to which all laws, national and international, paid homage? If it meant an enacted law, in the sense that no person shall be deprived of life, liberty or property except by a law enacted by the Congress or by the state legislature, it followed that all that the legislature had to do to transgress the provisions of the fifth and fourteenth amendments was to enact a law for the purpose. It could deprive a person of life, liberty and property if it enacted a law for depriving him of life, liberty or property, however arbitrary the law may be in content or in operation. Such a construction would defeat the very basis of a fundamental right. For a fundamental right would necessarily involve the conception of an organic right, a right uncontrolled by the legislature or by any other organ of the State. A right is fundamental because it is part of the fundamental law and liable to no infringement by the State. If, therefore, law in 'due process of law' was intended to mean only an enacted law, the entire structure of the fundamental rights fell to the ground. The provisions became otiose. It was between these competing claims that the Supreme Court of America in its early days evolved the great doctrine of 'due process of law' in American constitutional jurisprudence. Was 'due process of law' equivalent to 'the law of the land', as found in the thirty-ninth chapter of the Magna Charta? Had it any technical meaning? In Hurtado's case,[4] Justice Mathews, in delivering the opinion of the court, traced the history of the Magna Carta and stated:

> In this country written constitutions were deemed essential to protect the rights and liberties of the people against the encroachments of power delegated to their Governments, and the provisions of Magna Charta were incorporated into bills of rights. They were limitations upon all the powers of Government, legislative as well as executive and judicial.

It necessarily happened, therefore, that as these broad and general maxims of liberty arid justice held in our system a different place and performed a different function from their position and office in English constitutional history and law, they would receive and justify a corresponding and more comprehensive interpretation. Applied in England only as guards against executive usurpation and tyranny, here they have become bulwarks also against arbitrary legislation but, in that application, as it would be incongruous to measure and restrict them by the ancient customary English law, they must be held to guaranty not particular forms of procedure, but the very substance of individual rights to life, liberty and property. But it is not to be supposed that these legislative powers are absolute and despotic, and that the Amendment prescribing due process of law is too vague and indefinite to operate as a practical restraint. It is not every Act, legislative in form, that is law. Law is something more than mere will exerted as an act of power. It must be not a special rule for a particular person or a particular case, but, in the language of Mr. Webster, in his familiar definition, the general law, a law which hears before it condemns, which proceeds upon inquiry, and renders judgment only after trial, 'so that every citizen shall hold his life, liberty, property and immunities under the protection of the general rules which govern *society*', and thus excluding, as not due process of law, Acts of attainment, Bills of pains and penalties, Acts of confiscation, Acts reversing judgments and Acts directly transferring one man's estate to another, legislative judgments and decrees, and other similar special, partial and arbitrary exertions of power under the forms of legislation. Arbitrary power, enforcing its edicts to the injury of the persons and property of its subjects, is not law, whether manifested as the decree of a personal monarch or of an impersonal multitude. And the limitations imposed by our constitutional law upon the action of the Governments, both state and national, are essential to the preservation of public and private rights, notwithstanding the representative character of our political institutions. The enforcement of these limitations by judicial process is the device of self-governing communities to protect the rights of individuals and minorities, as well against the power of a numbers, as against the violence of public agents transcending the limits of lawful authority, even when acting in the name and wielding the force of the Government.

But it was not to be supposed that 'due process of law' conferred absolute liberty to the individual. That should have of course created chaos and anarchy. All these freedoms were subject to the limitations imposed in the interest of the welfare of the general public. The power to restrain individual liberty for the common social good was implicit in every organized government, and the Supreme Court soon evolved what is known in America as the doctrine of 'police power', for the purpose of regulating the freedom of life, liberty and property. Whether any Act passed by the Congress or by a State infringed the constitutional guarantees was therefore liable to judicial review, the criterion being whether in its procedural or substantive aspect it was reasonable in form and in substance, and not arbitrary in its application. Fundamental rights in the American Constitution, therefore, were not imperfect but perfect rights justiciable in a court of law. The Supreme Court reconciled the conflict between individual liberty and State control by making reasonableness of the law as the yardstick of its sustainability.

The Indian leaders who gathered at New Delhi in 1947 for the purpose of Constitution-making were familiar with the Constitutions of different countries and the attempts made to ensure individual liberty in the context of social needs. They had enjoyed neither free speech nor a free press, neither liberty of person nor of property. Most of them had been scarred and scorched in the bitter struggle for freedom. Many had undergone protracted imprisonments for long periods, either by way of preventive or punitive detention for violation of what in the language of the Congress Resolutions used to be called lawless laws. They had various alternatives to choose from: parliamentary sovereignty of the Westminster model, which recognized no fundamental rights; the continental types, which made fundamental rights mere pious resolutions; and the American Constitution, which made fundamental rights inviolable, with the Supreme Court as their ultimate arbiter. After considerable thought and anxious care, they drafted the Constitution on the framework of the American model.

Systems and governments born of revolution, violent or non-violent, have always borne the indelible impress of the tyranny of the past in their efforts to secure the freedom of the future. In the first flush of freedom, the framers of the Indian Constitution drew their inspiration from the struggle of the American people and combined within its framework both the justiciable rights of the American Constitution as also the fundamental declarations of the Continental Constitutions. Part III therefore incorporated the category of justiciable freedoms, and Part IV the nonjusticiable declarations of the Continental and Irish organic law. Part III opened in Article 12 with a definition of the 'State', including therein not merely the executive but also the legislatures of both the State and of the Union. Article 13 rendered void all laws inconsistent with the fundamental rights guaranteed under Part III. Then followed the enunciation of substantive freedoms, the most important of which fall to be briefly considered.

Article 14 is partly an Irish and partly an American import. It postulates equality before the law and equal protection of the laws. Equal protection pledges the protection of equal laws. It prohibits arbitrary discrimination. But since all men, things, conditions and circumstances are not equal, equal protection does not forbid a reasonable classification having regard to the purpose the enactment has in view. If, for instance, compulsory acquisition of property is authorized under a land acquisition act, the standard of compensation cannot vary with the caste of the property owner or the colour of his complexion. Article 14 holds a major, all-pervasive fundamental right, the potentialities of which are being slowly recognized. A law directed against even an individual or corporation may not offend the equal-protection clause if the singling out is not based on arbitrary but reasonable grounds. But the power should not be capable of discriminatory application. The observations of Justice Mathews in the 'laundry case', *Yick Wo v. Hopkins*,[5] have become classic:

> When we consider the nature and the theory of our institutions of government, the principles upon which they are supposed to rest, and review the history of their development, we are constrained to conclude that they do not mean to leave room for the play and action of purely personal and arbitrary power. Sovereignty itself is, of course, not subject to law, for it is the author and source of law; but in our system, while sovereign powers are delegated to the agencies of Government, sovereignty itself remains with the people, by whom and for whom all government exists and acts. And the law is the definition and limitation of power. It is, indeed, quite true, that there must always be lodged somewhere, and in some person or body, the authority of final decision; and, in many cases of mere administration the responsibility is purely political, no appeal lying except to the ultimate tribunal of the public judgment, exercised either in the pressure of opinion or by means of the suffrage. But the fundamental rights to life, liberty and the pursuit of happiness, considered as individual possessions, are secured by those maxims of constitutional law which are the monuments showing the victorious progress of the race in securing to men the blessings of civilisation under the reign of just and equal laws, so that, in the famous language of the Massachusetts Bill of Rights, the Government of the Commonwealth 'may be a government of laws and not of men.' For, the very idea that one man may be compelled to hold his life, or the means of living, or any material right essential to the enjoyment of life, at the mere will of another, seems to be intolerable in any country where freedom prevails, as being the essence of slavery itself . . . Though

the law itself be fair on its face and impartial in appearance, yet, if it is applied and administered by public authority with an evil eye and an equal hand, so as practically to make unjust and illegal discriminations between persons in similar circumstances, material to their rights, the denial of equal justice is still within the prohibition of the Constitution.

The *Yick Wo* judgment is of frequent application is cases arising under Article 14 of the Indian Constitution.

The next article of importance is Article 19, which combines in its fold the seven freedoms—of speech and expression, of assembly and association of movement and residence, of property and of occupation. Save in regard to freedom of speech and expression, wherein legislation respecting libel, contempt of court, or any matter offending decency and morality was authorized, all the rest of the freedoms were subject to laws imposing reasonable restrictions thereon in the interests of public order or of the general public. The framers of the Constitution have thus integrated the police power of America into the absolute freedoms which they would otherwise have become. Whether a particular restriction is reasonable or not is entirely for the courts to decide, the Supreme Court having unambiguously laid down this principle right from the time its jurisdiction was invoked in the first case involving constitutional construction. Secondly, the reasonableness of the restriction has to be judged both from the substantive and procedural part of the law; as stated by Chief Justice Kania in Dr Khare's case,[6] so that if the reasonableness of the law cannot be sustained from either angle the law cannot be upheld.

The provision regarding freedom of speech stood in a different category altogether, the Constitution originally embodying the traditional concept of the liberty of the press free from all pre-restraints and adopting the law as it stood in America. But the recent amendment to the Constitution has made a tremendous change with retrospective effect. The freedom of speech and expression is 'made subject to reasonable restrictions that may be imposed by law in the interests of the security of the State, friendly relations with foreign states, public order, decency, or morality or in relation to contempt of Court, defamation or incitement to an offence'. The indefiniteness of this vague verbiage would no doubt give legal validity to the re-enactment of the lawless laws of the old regime; but in sad contrast, one turns to the concept of free speech in America as expounded by American judges. Here is what Justice Brandeis states in *Whitney v. California*:[7]

> Those who won our independence believed that the final end of the State was to make men free to develop their faculties; and that in its government the deliberative forces should prevail over the arbitrary. They valued liberty both as an end and as a means. They believed liberty to be the secret of happiness and courage to be the secret of liberty. They believed that freedom to think as you will and to speak as you think are means indispensable to the discovery and spread of political truth; that without free speech and assembly discussion would be futile; that with them, discussion affords ordinarily adequate protection against the dissemination of noxious doctrines; that the greatest menace to freedom is an inert people; that public discussion is a political duty; and that this should be a fundamental principle of the American government. They recognised the risks to which all human institutions are subject. But they knew that order cannot be secured merely through fear of punishment for its infraction; that it is hazardous to discourage thought, hope and imagination; that fear breeds repression; that repression breeds hate; that hate menaces stable government; that the path of safety lies in the opportunity to discuss freely supposed grievances and proposed remedies; and that the fitting remedy for evil counsels is good ones. Believing in the power of reason as applied through public discussion, they eschewed silence coerced by law—the argument of force in its worst form. Recognizing the occasional tyrannies

of governing majorities, they amended the Constitution so that free speech and assembly should be guaranteed.

These are immortal words that deserve to be inscribed in letters of gold on the walls of our Parliament. Only they who are animated by such sentiments can realize the great imponderables of free speech and of a free Constitution.

Freedom of conscience and of religion is secured by article 25, and freedom to manage religious affairs by article 26. In a country like India, where religious observances govern life from birth to death, from the cradle to the grave, freedom of religious practices unfettered would cover far too large an area than in any other country. Secular activities are therefore dissociated by the Constitution from religious freedom, and the practice and profession of religion is made expressly subject to public order, morality and health. While the bounds of this freedom may be fairly susceptible to easy delimitation, controversy is likely to rage over the freedom of management of religious affairs and of the administration of religious institutions and endowments in accordance with law. Independent India has proclaimed in the great Preamble to the Constitution that India is constituted into a Sovereign Democratic Republic to secure, among other things, liberty of thought, expression, belief, faith and worship. India is now a secular State and recognizes no State religion. Nor may any taxes be levied for the promotion or maintenance of any particular religion. The civil jurisprudence of every civilized State contains principles of legal control over breach of trust or other kindred matters with regard to every kind of trust, public or private, religious or charitable. But when something more is attempted or a particular religion is singled out for governmental control, questions are likely to arise as to the ambit of the rights secured by the Constitution. It is well-known that Regulation VII of 1817 authorized governmental superintendence over all religious endowments, Hindu and Mohammedan, and that as a result of agitation, Act XXIII of

1863 was passed withdrawing such control altogether. It was only after the introduction of diarchy that religious neutrality was departed from and the Hindu Religious Endowments Act of 1925 was enacted. From that time right up-to-date, one act after another has been passed throwing a network of State control over Hindu religious institutions, slowly dragging all the temples and mutts into the fold of governmental management. The high watermark of State control has been reached under the latest act, the Madras Act XIX of 1951, which formally subjects the administration of all Hindu religious endowments to the superintendence and control of a commissioner appointed by the government, but concentrates all authority in the hands of the party in power by empowering the government to call for and examine the records of any commissioner or any of his subordinates, or of any area committee or even of any trustee in respect of any proceeding other than those in respect of which a suit or appeal to a court is provided by the act and cancel or modify such orders. It is rather difficult to reconcile the provisions of the new act with the theory of a secular State. But it is interesting to notice that a novel provision has been introduced in the act that nothing contained therein shall affect any right under Article 26, clauses (a) to (c) of the Constitution. If therefore, immunity is sought from judicial invalidation, all that the framers of future enactments in India have to do is to insert a provision stating that nothing in this act shall be deemed to contravene any section of the Constitution.

By far the more important rights relating to deprivation of life, liberty and property are dealt with by Article 21 and Article 31 (I). Article 21 in its original draft embodied the American 'due process of law' with regard to the deprivation of life and liberty, while by a separate article, article 31 (I), no person could be deprived of property save by authority of law. There were no provisions at all with regard to preventive detention. It may be said without exaggeration that had the Indian Constitution stood so drafted, it would have incorporated probably the best features of the leading Constitutions in the world. There may have been imperfections in its phrasing here and there, but there can be very little doubt that in three of its notable provisions, it excelled every other Constitution in the world: firstly, in erecting the fundamental rights against exercise of arbitrary power by both the executive and the legislature; secondly, in expressly invalidating laws infringing those fundamental rights; and thirdly, in guaranteeing the enforcement of these rights directly by the Supreme Court at the instance of any aggrieved person.

But as months passed and the process of Constitution-making lengthened, changes developed. The 'due process of law' in the draft of Article 21 was converted into 'procedure established by law'. What exactly were the implications of the change that the framers had in view were not very clear, except that 'due process of law' was not wanted in the Indian Constitution. But neither Article 12 defining the State nor article 13, which rendered laws infringing the fundamental rights void, were interfered with. In course of time, new provisions were added to Part III, which are now numbered as Articles 22 (4) to 22 (7), introducing preventive detention in the chapter of fundamental rights. That again was unique in the organic law of any country in the world. Preventive detention *eo nominee* came within the category of fundamental rights of the Indian citizen.

It was obvious that the shades of the past were growing dim. What exactly was the distinction sought to be made in eliminating 'due process of law' and substituting in its stead 'procedure established by law' in relation to deprivation of life and personal liberty? Did the word 'law' in the context connote law in the due-process clause, law in the abstract or law in the concrete, *Jus* or *lex,* the general law or the enacted law, the natural law or the statute law? If law therein meant enacted law, what was the scope of the fundamental right guaranteed under Article 21 or under Article 31 (I)? British jurisprudence had introduced the rule of law in India as a safeguard against executive interference with the liberty of person or of property. There was not the slightest doubt that declaration of a fundamental right against executive excesses was therefore absolutely superfluous, for it was part of the jurisprudence of India that no government or official could take away the life, liberty or property of a person unless he could rely on statutory sanction. If Article 21 bore only this limited construction, what was its import as a guarantee against legislative arbitrariness? The State, as defined in Article 12, included the legislature as well.

Nor was it easy to correlate Article 13 with the content of Article 21. If a law abridging or abrogating the right under Article 21 was void—that is to say, if the Constitution postulated in terms that an enacted law infringing procedure established by law may be void—then surely the law under Article 21 could not mean the changing enacted law, but the constant and the normal law.

The first impact of these alternatives on the Constitution came within a few weeks of its promulgation before a division bench of the High Court of Madras, consisting of Govinda Menon and Krishnaswami Naidu, JJ., in a habeas corpus application in Re. *Venkataraman*. Justice Govinda Menon, after examining the provisions of the Magna Carta, the fifth and fourteenth amendments to the American Constitution and American precedents, adopted the view that any legislative enactment that is utterly repugnant to one's sense of natural justice would be an act that would infringe the provisions of Article 21. It followed that by implication the word 'law' in 'procedure established by law' did not mean enacted law, but the general law, within the meaning of 'due process of law'. Unfortunately, that judgment has not yet been reported. But very soon the matter came up for consideration before the Supreme Court in *A. K. Gopalan's* case.[8] The competing interpretations were exhaustively analysed. In construing the expression 'procedure established by law', four out of the six learned judges who constituted the bench held that 'procedure established by law' meant 'procedure prescribed by the law of a State', that is to say, a law which had a statutory origin. They repelled the view that the word 'law' in Article 21 had been used in the sense of general law connoting the principles of natural justice outside the realm of positive law. Law in that article was equivalent to State-made law. Justice Patanjali Sastri, while adopting this conclusion, struck an entirely a new note of his own. In the view of the learned judge, the interpretation suggested by the State—that the expression '"procedure established by law" meant nothing more than law prescribed by any law made by a competent legislature—was hardly acceptable, for to accept that construction would be to stultify Article 13 (2) and indeed the very conception of the fundamental right.' What then was the solution? Justice Patanjali Sastry found a via media between the two extreme positions contended for on either side, by stressing the word 'established'. According to the learned judge,

> Certain basic principles emerge as the constant factors common to all those procedures, and they form the core of the procedure established by law. I realise that even on this view, the life and liberty of the individual will not be immune from legislative interference, for a competent Legislature may change the procedure so as to whittle down the protection if so minded. But, in the view I have indicated, it must not be a change *ad hoc* for any special purpose or occasion, but a change in the general law of procedure embodied in the Code. So long as such a change is not effected, the protection under Article 21 would be available.

Justice Mukherjea recognized that if law is taken to mean a State-made law, then Article 21 would not be a restriction on legislation at all. No question of passing any law abridging the right conferred by this Article could possibly arise and Article 13 (2) of the Constitution would have no operation so far as this provision is concerned.

Nevertheless, the learned judge came to the conclusion that the word 'law' in Article 21 has been used in the sense of State-made law and that Article 21 is apparently a check on the exercise of executive power. Article 31(I) was also referred to incidentally for the purpose of clarification of the word 'law', and the same conclusion arrived at. Therefore, in regard to deprivation of life, liberty and property, the fundamental right granted by the Constitution, according to the learned judges who formed the majority, was the right which extended only to the requirement of an enacted law. If, therefore, Parliament or a state legislature passed an act depriving a person of his life, liberty or property, no citizen could impugn its validity, however arbitrary or unjust the act might be.

The question, however, had been raised in the course of the arguments as to *whether* an Act in terms of 22 Henry VIII, Chapter 9, ordering that the Bishop of Rochester's cook be boiled to death, would be valid under the Indian Constitution. Such an act certainly amounted to deprivation of the life of the unfortunate cook and the procedure established by law was the procedure of boiling [the guilty] to death. Justice Das, one of the majority judges, answered the question in these words:

> Our Constitution is a compromise between Parliamentary supremacy of England and the supremacy of the Supreme Court of the United States. Subject to the limitations I have mentioned which are certainly justiciable, our Constitution has accepted the supremacy of the legislative authority and, that being so we must be prepared to face occasional vagaries of that body and to put up with enactments of the nature of the atrocious English statute to

which learned counsel for the petitioner has repeatedly referred, namely, that the Bishop of Rochester's cook be boiled to death. If Parliament may take away life by providing for hanging by the neck, logically there can be no objection if it provides for a sentence of death by shooting by a firing squad or by guillotine or in the electric chair or even by boiling in oil. A procedure laid down by the Legislature may offend against the Court's sense of justice and fair play and a sentence provided by the Legislature may outrage the Court's notions of penology, but that is a wholly irrelevant consideration. The Court may construe and interpret the Constitution and ascertain its true meaning but once that is done the Court cannot question its wisdom or policy. The Constitution is supreme. The Court must take the Constitution as it finds it even if it does not accord with its preconceived notions of what an ideal Constitution should be. Our protection against legislative tyranny, if any, lies in ultimate analysis in a free and intelligent public opinion which must eventually assert itself.

If the word 'law' in Article 21 meant a State-made law, the thesis of Justice Das that any enactment in the nature of the Henry VIII Act just mentioned would be valid under the Indian Constitution necessarily followed. But in such a view, the Constitution stands self-condemned. With regard to the major rights against arbitrary deprivation of life, liberty and property, our Constitution holds no protection against legislative tyranny. All that is required is to procure the passing of an act, and the basest wrong may be perpetrated.

But then, as pointed out by Justice Bronson in *Taylor v. Porter*,[9] the words 'by the law of the land', (which is the same as 'due process of law') as used in the Constitution, do not mean a statute passed for the purpose of working the wrong. That construction would render the restriction absolutely nugatory and turn this part of the Constitution into mere nonsense. People would be made to say to the two Houses: 'You shall be vested with the legislative power of the State, but no one shall be disfranchised or deprived of any of the rights or privileges of a citizen unless you pass a statute for that purpose. In other words, you shall not do the wrong, unless you choose to do it.' And this is exactly the position now under the Indian Constitution.

Nor does the doctrine of the supremacy of the Indian Parliament rest on unassailable grounds. A federation, in the well-known language of Dicey, is 'an indestructible Union of indestructible States'; and the federal compact embodies the division of powers between the units and the Union. The legislative organs of the State must therefore necessarily be bound by the instrument of the Union. The supremacy of the Constitution follows. So too the subordination of the legislatures to the Constitution. The ambit of the legislative authority may vary for different Constitutions; but the status of the legislature in every federal Constitution must be identical. Within the bounds of its freedom it is no doubt free from a doctrine that has been applied to all subordinate legislatures. But the core of the problem lies in its powers of amendment, as pointed out by Lord Birkenhead in *McCowley* v. *King*.[10] Can the legislature amend the Constitution in the same mode and by the same process as it can enact an ordinary piece of legislation? In that case the legislature is uncontrolled. Or does the Constitution prescribe a particular procedure for the purpose of amending the Constitution? In that case the legislature is controlled and not uncontrolled. In the former case the doctrine of ultra vires would have no application at all; for every enactment inconsistent with the organic law would pro tanto amount to an amendment to the Constitution and would be valid. In the latter case, the doctrine of ultra vires would necessarily apply; for every act in conflict with the Constitution transgresses the bounds of its authority and is void. If the legislature is uncontrolled, the legislature is supreme. If the legislature is controlled, the legislature is the slave of the Constitution and can never be supreme. Article 368 prescribes a special procedure for constitutional amendments in India; and the terms of the federal compact cannot be altered or nullified by the unilateral act of the legislative organ. The observations of the learned judge in regard to the supremacy of the Indian Parliament, with great respect, call for reconsideration.

To a large extent, the interpretation of the majority view of the Supreme Court or Article 21 was influenced by the deletion of 'due process of law 'in the original draft and the substitution of 'procedure established by law'. While it is clear that the framers of the Constitution did not wish to import the entire due process of law of the American make, what exactly did they intend to connote by 'procedure established by law'? A reference to the Constituent Assembly debates does not elucidate either the content of the fundamental right secured by the new formula, nor even the scope of the alteration effected in Article 21. Dr Ambedkar understood the substitution one way; Sir Alladi Krishnaswami Iyer a different way, and the speeches of others indicate that they took it only as a verbal change restricting the due process to its procedural content. If the amendment was intended to abrogate the fundamental right of due process altogether and reduce it to an eyewash, as it is now found to be, it should have been more intelligible and less farcical to delete Article 21 and Article 31 (I) altogether rather than retain them in a form which renders them impotent.

It is not without significance that the change came towards the end of the Constituent Assembly, when the party in power had gathered a little more experience of both governmental difficulties and governmental authority. But not less sinister were the accompanying amendments introduced as clauses of preventive detention in the chapter on fundamental rights.

Detention without trial has been an unavoidable necessity in the stress of war. But detention without trial in times of peace is reminiscent of the Spanish Inquisition and Louis

XIV, the Bastille, and the Concentration Camp, Buchenwald and Siberia. In no civilized country in the world does arbitrary detention obtain as the normal feature of everyday life. And the history of Fascism, Nazism and communism has necessitated the setting up of a committee of the UN to frame a World Charter of Human Rights binding on every State. No amount of fine phrasing can disguise the fact that preventive detention without trial is utterly repugnant to the universal conscience of civilized mankind. And Article 22 has enshrined in the Indian Constitution preventive detention as a fundamental right of a citizen, a normal and constant right above other rights. Till a few months back it was thought that Article 22 provided safeguards against indefinite detention. But the recent amendment to the Preventive Detention Act, the validity of which has been upheld by the Supreme Court, has dispelled such illusions. If Parliament enacts suitable amendments to the existing preventive detention law, detention can be legally extended to any length of time.

It has already been mentioned that Article 32 grants a guaranteed right of petitioning the Supreme Court for speedy redress by certiorari, mandamus and by other orders. The technicalities of the ancient writs obtaining in England have been swept away by widening the ambit of such jurisdiction by authorizing the Supreme Court to issue any appropriate orders or directions. But while access to the Supreme Court is likely to prove difficult and expensive [to the citizen], the framers of the Constitution have rendered these remedies far more practicable by empowering every high court to issue such writs both for the enforcement of fundamental rights and also for other purposes. But the cornerstone of fundamental rights rests on the independence of judgement of those who are entrusted with their enforcement. While there are provisions in the Constitution to secure the independence of both the judges of the Supreme Court and of the high court, akin to those in the Act of Settlement in

England, there is one clause in the Indian Constitution that gives grave room for disquiet, and that is the power vested in the Union government to transfer any of the high court judges to any state. While in a vast country like India, the barriers of provincialism should no doubt be destroyed, and the best legal talent should be made available to any part of India, it has also to be borne in mind that the power of transfer may be capable of exercise 'with an evil eye and an unequal hand'. In a stage of transition, some judgments are likely to prove unpalatable to the executive; and transfer then should not prove an insidious instrument for harassing an inconvenient judge, or conditioning him into the proper frame of mind. One should never forget that the real bulwark of our fundamental rights is a strong and independent judiciary, which should discharge its duties without fear or favour. What is our freedom worth if our judges are not free?

Such in brief are the main contours of the fundamental rights incorporated in the Constitution of India. That these rights have not grown quite popular with the executive admits of no dispute. Whether their existence would be permitted to be continued in the Constitution has become a matter of grave concern. It is noteworthy that the first amendment to the Constitution had for its conscious aim and purpose the devitalization of some of the fundamental rights even before the ink in which the Constitution was inscribed was hardly dry. By forcing the first amendment through, precedent has been laid for further amendments. Future governments confronted with the obstacle of fundamental rights may not hesitate very much to adopt the same device found by the first free government in India. It is true that there are countries like Great Britain where there are no fundamental rights. But conditions in England are different from those in India. In England, centuries of tradition and history have thrown a halo round individual liberty, creating thereby a guarantee against its infringement far stronger than the fundamental rights of the written

Constitutions of the Continent. India has just emerged from slavery. Nor have we developed a virile and intelligent public opinion to deter executive inroads into the area of our freedom. After all, let it be remembered that fundamental freedoms are intended to secure nothing more than equality, impartiality and fair play. They are shields against governmental tyranny, not swords against the just exercise of governmental authority.

A Constitution is not an end in itself. It is only a means to an end. It is what it is intended to be—a mechanism of government designed to secure national prosperity and national greatness. We live in an interdependent age of highly competing forces, and no country can withstand the impact of world events without the corporate efforts of its citizens. Whether in peace or in war, the greatest asset of a nation is the loyalty and the character of its people. The striking force of a State is assessed not merely by its armaments and equipments but in terms of the initiative, integrity, fearlessness and readiness of self-sacrifice of its nationals. If independent India must survive, India must nurture a strong and virile race having minds without fear and heads held high. It is only in the penumbra of fundamental freedoms that a people can grow free.

Notes

Introduction

1 These were the courts established in rural or peripheral areas beyond the main city or town.

Chapter 1: Transcending the *Tharuvaad:* M.K. Nambyar's Formative Years

1 This English version appears in the article 'Malayalam Literature through the Ages' by Dr K.M. George in the *Souvenir of the World Conference on Malayalam, Kerala Culture and Development*, p. 35. (See A. Sreedhara Menon, *Social and Cultural History of Kerala* [Delhi: Sterling Publishers, 1979], p. 2.)

2 L.A. Krishna Iyer, *Social History of Kerala, Vol. II. The Dravidians* (New Delhi: Book Centre Publications, 1970), p. 46.

3 M. Gangadhara Menon, *Malabar Rebellion: 1921–1922* (Allahabad: Vohra Publishers and Distributors, 1989), p. 39.

4 F. Fawcett, *Nayars of Malabar* (New Delhi: Asian Educational Services, 1985, 1901).

5 Philip Baldeus, *A True and Exact Description of the Most Celebrated East-India Coasts of Malabar and Coromandel and Also of the Isle of Ceylon* (Amsterdam, 1671).

6 A. Sreedhara Menon, *Social and Cultural History of Kerala* (Delhi: Sterling Publishers, 1979), pp. 288–290.

7 Rohith S. and N. Amutha Kumari, 'The Origin of Nairs', *History Research Journal*, pp. 2096–97. See also A. Sreedhara Menon,

Social and Cultural History of Kerala (Delhi: Sterling Publishers, 1979), p. 67.

8   Ibid.

9   L.A. Krishna Iyer, *Social History of Kerala, Vol. II. The Dravidians*, pp. 38–39.

10   Ibid., p. 56.

11   All that follows about the family—its wealth, the lifestyle and the various anecdotes—is largely taken from the autobiography published by him, as well as the historical sketch written by T.V. Krishnan.

12   K. Madhavan, *On the Banks of the Tejaswini—An Autobiography* (New Delhi: National Book Trust of India, 2011), pp. 5–6.

13   M. Gangadhara Menon, *Malabar Rebellion: 1921–1922* (Allahabad: Vohra Publishers and Distributors), pp. 3–8.

14   Ibid., p. 3.

15   Ibid., pp. 10–12.

16   M. Gangadhara Menon, *Malabar Rebellion: 1921–1922* (Allahabad: Vohra Publishers and Distributors, 1989), p. 41.

Chapter 2: Touch of Fate: From the Mofussil to the Madras High Court

1   Denis Fernandes, 'Using the Past: *Mangalore Magazine* and the History of Kanara', *Proceedings of the Indian History Congress*, Vol. 66 (2005–06), pp. 918–25, https://www.jstor.org/stable/44145905.

2   *Mahatma Gandhi's First Visit to Mangalore* (Udupi: Gandhian Study Centre, Mahatma Gandhi Memorial College).

3   Ibid.

4   Dilip M. Menon, *Caste, Nationalism and Communism in South India: Malabar: 1900–1948* (Cambridge: Cambridge University Press, 1994), p. 2.

5   Historians have stated that when the British first arrived in the Malabar they favoured the existing agrarian structures and wholeheartedly supported the landlords, even at time

appointing them to important posts. See Dilip M. Menon, *Caste, Nationalism and Communism in South India: Malabar:* 1900–1948 (Cambridge: Cambridge University Press, 1994), p. 2.

6 Denis Fernandes, 'Using the Past: *Mangalore Magazine* and the History of Kanara', *Proceedings of the Indian History Congress*, Vol. 66 (2005–06), pp. 918–25, https://www.jstor.org/stable/44145905.

7 Dilip Menon, *Caste, Nationalism and Communism in South India: Malabar: 1900–1948* (Cambridge: Cambridge University Press, 1994), p. 13.

8 'M.K. Nambyar: The Great Constitutionalist', speech by M.N. Krishnamani, Senior Advocate.

9 An erstwhile hereditary proprietary right held by certain families in Kerala.

10 M. Gangadhara Menon, *Malabar Rebellion: 1921–1922* (Allahabad: Vohra Publishers and Distributors, 1989), pp. 39, 41.

Chapter 3: Taking the High Road: From Kanara to Kilpauk

1 Dilip Menon, *Caste, Nationalism and Communism in South India: Malabar: 1900–1948* (Cambridge: Cambridge University Press, 1994), pp. 94–95.

2 Subramaniam Chandra, 'Political Process and Governance in Tamil Nadu', 24 February 2016.

3 '125-Year-Old Home of a 155-Year-Old Court', *Madras Musings*, Vol. 27, No. 8, 1–15 August 2017, https://www.madrasmusings.com/vol-27-no-8/125-year-old-home-of-a-155-year-old-court/.

4 'V.L. Ethiraj: Unrivalled in Court Craft', *Indian Express*, 11 August 1990.

5 Soli Sorabjee, 'From Gopalan to Golaknath and Beyond: A Tribute to M.K. Nambyar', *Indian Journal of Constitutional Law*, Vol.1, Issue 1, 2007, p. 22.

Chapter 4: The First Constitutional Case: *A.K. Gopalan*

1   M.K. Nambyar, 'The Contours of the Constitution', unpublished article.

2   A.K. Gopalan, *In the Cause of the People: Reminiscences* (Madras: Orient Longman, 1973), p. 5.

3   Ibid., p. 94.

4   Ibid., p. 118.

5   Ibid., p. 167.

6   Ibid., p. 172.

7   B. Sen, *Six Decades of Law, Politics and Diplomacy: Some Reminiscences and Reflections* (New Delhi: Universal Law Publishing, 2016 [reprint]), p. 57.

8   Inder Malhotra, 'Present at the Creation', *Supreme But Not Infallible: Essays in Honour of the Supreme Court*, ed. B.N. Kirpal (New Delhi: Oxford University Press, 2000), pp. 474–75.

9   Motilal C. Setalvad, *My Life: Law and Other Things* (New Delhi: Universal Law Publishing, 2015 [reprint]), pp. 154–59.

10 *Murray's Lessee v. Hoboken Land & Improvement Co.* 1959 US 282 [1856].

11 *Dartmouth College v. Woodward* 17 US 481(1819), See also *Records and Briefs of the United States Supreme Court* (Washington D.C.: Supreme Court of the United States, 1832), p. 77.

12 M.K. Nambyar, 'Life, Liberty and Property', unpublished article.

13 J.B. Dadachanji, 'Landmarks', *Supreme But Not Infallible: Essays in Honour of the Supreme Court,* ed. B.N. Kirpal, et. al (New Delhi: Oxford University Press, 2000), p. 471.

14 Inder Malhotra, 'Present at the Creation', *Supreme But Not Infallible: Essays in Honour of the Supreme Court*, ed. B.N. Kirpal (New Delhi: Oxford University Press, 2000), pp. 474–75.

15 M.K. Nambyar, 'Life, Liberty and Property', unpublished article.

16 Inder Malhotra, 'Present at the Creation', *Supreme But Not Infallible: Essays in Honour of the Supreme Court*, ed. B.N. Kirpal (New Delhi: Oxford University Press, 2000), pp. 474–75.

17 Ibid., p. 476.

18 Ibid.
19 Ibid.
20 M.K. Nambyar, 'Life, Liberty and Property', unpublished article.

Chapter 5: The Aftermath of *A.K. Gopalan* and Life in the Madras High Court

1   Kolady Govindan Kutty, 'Memorable Events'. This article was published in Malayalam in *Desabhimani*, further details unknown.
2   *A.K. Gopalan*, AIR 1953 Mad 41; (1952) 2 MLJ 690.
3   Ibid.

Chapter 6: Piercing the Dark Shadows of Preventive Detention: *S. Krishnan v. The State of Madras*

1   Granville Austin, *Working a Democratic Constitution* (Oxford: Oxford University Press, 2014 [thirteenth impression]), p. 60.
2   Ibid.
3   S. Mohan Kumaramangalam, AIR 1951 Mad 583.
4   S. Mohan Kumaramangalam, AIR 1951 Mad 583.
5   Ibid.
6   *Machindar Shivji v. The King*, A.I.R. (37) 1950 F.C. 129, as cited in S. Mohan Kumaramangalam, AIR 1951 Mad 583.
7   David Bayley, 'The Indian Experience with Preventive Detention', *Pacific Affairs*, Vol. 35, No. 2 (Summer, 1962), pp. 99–115.
8   Granville Austin, *Working a Democratic Constitution* (Oxford: Oxford University Press, 2014 [thirteenth impression]), p. 60.
9   Ibid.
10 M.K. Nambyar, 'Our Fundamental Rights', *Madras Law Journal*, Vol. 41, 1951, p. 41.
11 Ibid., p. 53.
12 *S. Krishnan v. The State of Madras*, AIR 1951 SC 301, para 63.
13 Ibid., para 62.

Chapter 7: The Right to Property and Parliamentary Powers to Abridge the Fundamental Rights: The First, Fourth and Seventeenth Constitutional Amendments

1   Jeremy Waldron, *The Right to Private Property* (Oxford: Clarendon Press, 1988), p. 16.

2   Theodor Bergmann, *Agrarian Reform in India: With Special Reference to Kerala, Karnataka, Andhra Pradesh and West Bengal* (West Germany: Agricole Publishing Academy, 1984), p. 1.

3   Today, the right to private property is recognized in the legal regimes of most nations. Often described as a 'bundle of rights', legal philosophers have posited that the right to property refers to a number of distinct rights that are enforceable against others, for example, the right to possess, the right to use, the immunity from expropriation, etc. The term 'right to property' in its *constitutional* sense however, has historically come to be understood as implying that the holder of private property has a right against its appropriation by the State, unless a suitable compensation is paid, and the appropriation is motivated by a wider public purpose intended for the common good of society.

4   There is no doubt that this system was highly iniquitous, and for a sense of scale, consider the words of K.N. Panikkar, who stated that 'The major portion of janmam lands was concentrated in the hands of a few families, notably, the Zamurin of Calicut, the Raja of Nilambur, Kavalappara Nair, Kottakal Kizhakke Kovilakam, the Raja of Kolengode and Poomalli Nambudiri. Out of a total cultivated area of 1,229,216.88 acres in 1920-21 6,28,921.30 acres were held by 32 janmis' as calculated from the Malabar Tenancy Committee Report, 1929. See Rekha Bandhopadhyay, 'Land System in India: A Historical Review', *Economic and Political Weekly*, Vol. 28, No. 52, 25 December 1993, pp. A149–A155.

5   'As far as landholders in this area are concerned, their present state is extremely deplorable', he wrote. 'In 1931, the prices began to fall.

The reactions were immediately felt. The landholders waited on the District Collector in deputation and submitted a memorial.' 'It is an open secret,' he said, 'that some of the wealthiest among the ryots (not to speak of the middle classes) who would be ashamed to borrow a rupee, have had to seek the assistance of Mangalore Banks for loans after exhausting the village money-lenders. The position is acute. If that was the position in 1931, the position in 1939 may well be imagined. Since then, their indebtedness has increased and is increasing. The landholder is hardly able to meet the heavy assessment that he has unfortunately to bear in this part of the district . . . The reasons for this unhappy state of affairs are not far to seek . . . When the ancient Kinds exacted their dues they confined themselves to a fixed share of the gross produce . . . But the settlement under British rule proceeded on entirely different lines. Modern conditions made an import in kind an impossible task . . . The outturns of an experimental acre were first converted into money value at a fixed commutation rate and deductions were made for vicissitudes of season and cultivation expenses. If therefore the actual value realized by the ryots should fall below the commutation values any one year, the results would be disastrous . . .' Evidence of M.K. Nambyar to the Malabar Tenancy Committee, 1939.

6   Granville Austin, *Cornerstone of a Nation* (Oxford: Oxford University Press, 2002 [fifth impression]), pp. 87–101.

7   Granville Austin, *Working a Democratic Constitution* (Oxford: Oxford University Press, 2014 [thirteenth impression]), p. 69.

8   Ibid.

9   Ibid.

10   Ibid.

11   Ibid., pp. 69–94.

12   Ibid.

13   Ibid.

14   Burt Neuborne, 'Constitutional Court Profile', *International Journal of Constitutional Law*, 2003, p. 487.

15 M.K. Nambyar, 'Seventeenth Amendment of the Constitution', Inaugural Address delivered on 6 August 1963 at Bangalore at the Conference of Southern States on the Seventeenth Amendment of the Constitution, *Madras Law Journal*, 1963, p. 17.

16 M.K. Nambyar, 'Right to Property', unpublished article.

17 M.K. Nambyar, 'Seventeenth Amendment of the Constitution', Inaugural Address delivered on 6 August 1963 at Bangalore at the Conference of Southern States on the Seventeenth Amendment of the Constitution, *Madras Law Journal*, Vol. 17, 1963, p. 19.

18 Ibid.

19 AIR 1959 SC 519.

20 Namita Wahi, 'Property', *The Oxford Handbook of the Indian Constitution*, ed. Sujit Choudhry et al. (Oxford: Oxford University Press, 2016), p. 943.

21 Benjamin Robert Siegel, *Hungry Nation: Food, Famine, and the Making of Modern India* (Cambridge: Cambridge University Press, 2018), p. 167.

22 *Karimbil Kunhikoman v. The State of Kerala*, 1962 Supp (1) SCR 289.

23 Ibid.

24 Ibid.

25 *Karimbil Kunhikoman v. The State of Kerala* 1962 Supp (1) SCR 289.

26 M.K. Nambyar, 'Seventeenth Amendment of the Constitution', Inaugural Address delivered on 6 August 1963 at Bangalore at the Conference of Southern States on the Seventeenth Amendment of the Constitution, *Madras Law Journal*, 1963, p. 21.

27 *Karimbil Kunhikoman v. The State of Kerala* AIR 1962 SC 723.

28 M.K. Nambyar, 'Seventeenth Amendment of the Constitution', Inaugural Address delivered on 6 August 1963 at Bangalore at the Conference of Southern States on the Seventeenth Amendment of the Constitution, *Madras Law Journal*, 1963.

29 M.K. Nambyar, 'Seventeenth Amendment of the Constitution', Inaugural Address delivered on 6 August 1963 at Bangalore at the

Conference of Southern States on the Seventeenth Amendment of the Constitution, *Madras Law Journal*, 1963, p. 20.

30 M.K. Nambyar, 'Constitutional Provisions and Social Justice', *Journal of Indian Law,* (1967), Vol. 1, p. 101.

31 Ibid.

32 M.K. Nambyar,'Constitutional Provisions and Social Justice', *Journal of Indian Law Institute,* (1967) Vol. 1, pp. 105–06.

33 Ibid., p. 106.

34 M.K. Nambyar, 'The Contours of the Constitution', unpublished article, p. 12.

35 Ibid., pp. 13–14.

36 M.K. Nambyar, 'Life, Liberty and Property', unpublished article.

37 Fali S. Nariman, *Before Memory Fades* (Delhi: Thomson Press, 2010), p. 321.

38 AIR 1965 SC 845.

39 *Sajjan Singh v. The State of Rajasthan* AIR 1965 SC 845, para 27.

40 Ibid., para 46.

Chapter 8: *I.C. Golak Nath v. The State of Punjab:* Laying the Foundations of the Basic Structure

1 R. Sudarshan, '"Stateness" and Democracy in India's Constitution', *India's Living Constitution*, ed. Zoya Hasan et al. (New Delhi: Permanent Black, 2002, 2004; London: Anthem Press, 2005).

2 Ibid.

3 Granville Austin, *Working a Democratic Constitution* (Oxford: Oxford University Press, 2014 [thirteenth impression]), pp. 69, 196.

4 Fali S. Nariman, *Before Memory Fades* (Delhi: Thomson Press, 2010), p. 321.

5 Ibid., p. 347.

6 *I.C. Golak Nath v. The State of Punjab* (1967) 2 SCR 762, para 54.

7 *Kesavananda Bharati v. The State of Kerala* (1973) 4 SCC 227, para 1431, 1433.

Chapter 9: The March of the Law: Nambyar, the Constitutional 'Colossus'

1   (1959) *Supp* 1 SCR 319.
2   1959 SCR 1440.
3   Ibid.
4   1962 SCC Online Mad 40.
5   *Sri Lakshmindra Theertha Swamiar of Sri Shirur Mutt & Anr. v. The Commissioner*, Hindu Religious Endowments, Madras AIR 1952 Mad 613.
6   1954 SCR 1005.
7   1951 SCC OnLine Mad 383.
8   *Sri Venkatramana Devaru & Anr. v. The State of Mysore* 1954 SCR 895.
9   *Sri Venkatramana Devaru & Anr. v. The State of Mysore*, 1954 SCR 895, para 29.
10 *Madras Sourashtra Sabha v. The Commissioner*, Hindu Religious and Charitable Endowments, Appeal No. 645/1963, 84 L.W. 86 (1970).
11 AIR 1959 SC 648.
12 (1963) 2 SCR 747.
13 M.K. Nambyar, 'Life, Liberty and Property', unpublished article.
14 Ibid.
15 AIR 1951 Mad 1015.
16 *V.G. Row v. The State of Madras* AIR 1951 Mad 147.
17 AIR 1951 Mad 1015.
18 *A.K. Gopalan v. The State of Madras* AIR 1950 SC, Opinion of Justice Das, p. 288.
19 Justice Viswanatha Sastry however dissented and agreed with Nambyar on the scope of the court's power.
20 AIR 1951 Mad 70.
21 As the provision stood in 1950.
22 *W.N. Srinivasa Bhatt v. The State of Madras* AIR 1951 Mad 70, judgment of Justice Basheer Ahmed Sayeed.
23 AIR 1954 Mad 901.

24 K.K. Venugopal, AIR 1954 Mad 901, para 20.
25 Ibid.
26 (1972) 2 SCC 788.
27 M.P. Jain, 'Article 19(1)(a): Freedom of the Press: Bennett Coleman & Co. v. Union of India', *Journal of the Indian Law Institute*, Vol. 15, No. 1, January–March 1973, p. 162. Available at https://www.jstor.org/stable/43950191.
28 (1978) 1 SCC 248.

Epilogue

1 Niren De, Attorney General for India, Speech delivered at Full Court Reference in memory of Sh. M.K. Nambyar, January 1976.
2 Chief Justice A.N. Ray, speech delivered at Full Court Reference in memory of Sh. M.K. Nambyar, January 1976.
3 M.N. Krishnamani, 'M.K. Nambyar—The Great Constitutionalist', unpublished article.

Appendix: Our Fundamental Rights

1 Paper read at the Madras State Lawyers' Conference held at Calicut on 13 October 1951.
2 (1917) A.C. 260.
3 (1942) A.C. 206.
4 110 U.S. 516, 531.
5 (1865) 118 U.S. 356 : 30 Law Ed. 220.
6 (1950) S.C.J 328.
7 274 U.S. 357, 375.
8 (1950) 2 M.L.J 42 : 1950 S.C.R. 88 : 1950 S.C.J. 174 (SC).
9 4 Hill 140, 145.
10 1920 A.C. 681.

Scan QR code to access the
Penguin Random House India website